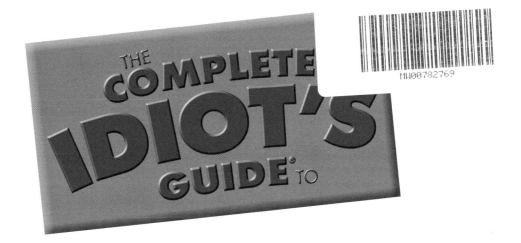

THE COMPLETE IDIOT'S GUIDE® TO

Supercharged
Kama Sutra
Illustrated

by Al Link & Pala Copeland

ALPHA

A member of Penguin Group (USA) Inc.

Publisher:
Marie Butler-Knight

Editorial Director:
Mike Sanders

Managing Editor:
Billy Fields

Senior Acquisitions Editor:
Paul Dinas

Senior Development Editor:
Phil Kitchel

Production Editor:
Megan Douglass

Copy Editor:
Jan Zoya

Cover/Book Designer:
William Thomas

Proofreader:
Mary Hunt

Photographer:
Eric Levin

Model Consultant:
Bob Shell

Director of Marketing:
Dawn Werk

ALPHA BOOKS

Published by the Penguin Group

Penguin Group (USA) Inc., 375 Hudson Street, New York, New York 10014, U.S.A.

Penguin Group (Canada), 10 Alcorn Avenue, Toronto, Ontario, Canada M4V 3B2
(a division of Pearson Penguin Canada Inc.)

Penguin Books Ltd, 80 Strand, London WC2R 0RL, England

Penguin Ireland, 25 St Stephen's Green, Dublin 2, Ireland
(a division of Penguin Books Ltd)

Penguin Group (Australia), 250 Camberwell Road, Camberwell, Victoria 3124, Australia
(a division of Pearson Australia Group Pty Ltd)

Penguin Books India Pvt Ltd, 11 Community Centre, Panchsheel Park, New Delhi—110 017, India

Penguin Group (NZ), cnr Airborne and Rosedale Roads, Albany, Auckland 1310, New Zealand
(a division of Pearson New Zealand Ltd)

Penguin Books (South Africa) (Pty) Ltd, 24 Sturdee Avenue, Rosebank, Johannesburg 2196,
South Africa

Penguin Books Ltd, Registered Offices: 80 Strand, London WC2R 0RL, England

International Standard Book Number: 978-1-59257574-9
Library of Congress Catalog Card Number: 2006930731

09   08   8   7   6   5   4

Interpretation of the printing code: The rightmost number of the first series of numbers is the year of the book's printing; the rightmost number of the second series of numbers is the number of the book's printing. For example, a printing code of 07-1 shows that the first printing occurred in 2007.

Printed in the United States of America

Note: This publication contains the opinions and ideas of its authors. It is intended to provide helpful and informative material on the subject matter covered. It is sold with the understanding that the authors and publisher are not engaged in rendering professional services in the book. If the reader requires personal assistance or advice, a competent professional should be consulted.

The authors and publisher specifically disclaim any responsibility for any liability, loss, or risk, personal or otherwise, which is incurred as a consequence, directly or indirectly, of the use and application of any of the contents of this book.

Most Alpha books are available at special quantity discounts for bulk purchases for sales promotions, premiums, fund-raising, or educational use. Special books, or book excerpts, can also be created to fit specific needs.

For details, write: Special Markets, Alpha Books, 375 Hudson Street, New York, NY 10014.

Contents

Introduction

The *Kama Sutra* has been inspiring lovers for more than 1,600 years. Although your authors have only been around for a minute fraction of that time, our readers, our clients, and the Discovery Channel all say we teach people how to have the best sex of their lives. Bring us together and you're bound to get some very powerful lessons in love.

The *Kama Sutra* taught that lovemaking is an art and a science—something that everyone should study in order to have a complete and rewarding life. You have the capacity to make its ideas and practices your own. We'll guide you through the nuances of these ancient sex techniques from joyful beginning to ecstatic end.

As you read, you'll find that this book isn't about good sex: it's about great sex, *supercharged sex*—the best of the best. With it, you'll learn the finesse required to become a master lover, a superlative sexual partner. If that sounds a bit daunting, take a big breath and relax. All that's really required is an enthusiasm for adventure and a willingness to spend time exploring.

The satisfaction you'll create together in the bedroom will spill over into the rest of your lives. Couples who are very pleased with their sexual connection are much more likely to be very pleased with their entire relationship. Wonderful sex boosts your physical and emotional well-being. It puts a spring in your step, a song in your heart, and sets your spirit soaring. Dare to imagine how enriched you'll be when you learn to make your sex supercharged.

How To Use This Book

There's more than one way to work with this guide. You can read it through, learn some of the techniques, and introduce them the next time you make love. You can go through it together in a nonsexual setting and try out some of the poses—with your clothes on. It's a lot of fun, and can ease some of the awkwardness that might arise when you're introducing something new. Or you might imitate ancient Oriental lovers and use it as a pillow book, a guide that you refer to for inspiration during the course of your loveplay. The full-color photos will give you a very clear picture of what to do.

However you decide to bring these techniques into your love life, remember that sex is playful as well as profound. An open mind, a willing heart, and a sense of humor will all help you transform ordinary sex into sizzling sex.

How This Book Is Organized

This guide is presented in 4 parts, with a total of 13 chapters. They lead you on a rousing exploration of erotic *Kama Sutra* techniques for supercharging your sex life.

Part I, "Red-Hot Sex—Yes!" introduces the ancient love text *Kama Sutra* and explores its relevance for modern lovers. Consider the *Kama Sutra* in its historical, cultural, and spiritual context. Learn about the author, Vatsyayana, as well as where, when, and why he wrote. Understand his views on the importance of harmony between lovers, in terms of genital size, emotional temperament, and sexual desire. There's a difference between supercharged sex and regular, friction sex; learn how you can make the leap from ordinary to extraordinary.

Part II, "Come on Baby, Light My Fire" teases you through all the passionate play leading up to sexual intercourse. Consider Vatsyayana's advice about setting the scene for love, and creating a sacred space for your sexual encounter. Explore his artful approach to embraces, caresses, kisses, sighs, and moans. Understand the difference between violence and fierceness, and learn how to scratch, bite, and slap your way to red-hot arousal. Open up to the ancient secrets of "going down," including fellatio (oral sex for men) and cunnilingus (oral sex for women).

Part III, "In the Heart of the Fire" details the juicy intercourse positions described in the *Kama Sutra*, and illustrates them with color photographs. We point out which postures are advanced and which are easy. Discover the best positions for building intimacy and emotional heart connection, stimulating the clitoris and G-spot, getting and maintaining erections for as long as you both want, and fueling erotic excitement and deep penetration. Learn about going fast and staying still, and discover the peaks and valleys of orgasm. Understand that there's much more to thrusting than your basic in and out. Find ways to combine those masterful moves with skillful caresses for intercourse that's truly over the top.

Part IV, "In the Afterglow" helps you understand why it's so important to pay attention to what happens when intercourse is over. Learn about sensual nutrition, how to please, appreciate, and adore each other with your words, your eyes, and your bodies. Nourish your senses with sexy food and drink. Learn how to maintain, and re-excite, your physical and emotional connection after the dance of love. Explore the mystery of multiple orgasms for women and men.

In addition to a glossary of terms, there are also these five appendixes.

Appendix B, "Tools and Toys," looks at ancient and modern sex toys and aphrodisiacs for spicing up your love life, adding variety, stimulating your libido, getting and keeping rock-hard erections, and experiencing orgasm in new ways.

In **Appendix C, "Tantric Sex Practices: Reuniting Heaven and Earth,"** we help you learn that sexuality and spirituality can go together, that sexuality can be a spiritual experience. Find out how Tantric sex and the *Kama Sutra* are related to each other.

Learn the ancient secret methods and practices of Tantric sex masters.

Appendix D, "The *Ananga Ranga*," introduces India's next best love guide. Find out how it compares with the *Kama Sutra*. Pick up a few more steamy sex poses.

Appendix E, "The *Perfumed Garden*," considers this famous Arabian love manual in light of its Indian predecessors. And, for your very special pleasure, offers even more sex positions.

Appendix F, "Recommended Reading and Resources," presents you with more resources so that you can expand your exciting journey toward supercharged sex.

Saucy Sidebars

These boxes add interesting asides, more information, and helpful direction for your supercharged sex exploration.

Al's Outlook & Pala's Perspective

We've been dancing with love and sex for quite some time. Here you'll get a man's and a woman's point of view, based on our personal experience.

Love Bites

Discover interesting information, tips, and hints, plus *Kama Sutra* oddities and other sex-related fun.

Pillow Talk

Sometimes things need a little more explanation, so these boxes add definitions of important or unusual words and terms.

Stop in the Name of Love

These are words of warning, caution, and critique about do's and don'ts in the world of supercharged sex.

A Note on the Translations

We've used three English language translations of the *Kama Sutra* in preparing this guide—by Richard Burton, Indra Sinha, and Alain Daniélou. When we quote from the text, we most often use the Burton translation, of which there are many versions, so we simply refer to the section of the book and the chapter where the quote came from, like this (II-1), which means Part Two, Chapter 1. When we quote the other versions, we give author name, section, chapter, and page number, like this: (Daniélou II-1, p.99).

Acknowledgments

We've had such a great time working together on this book—it's stimulated us in more ways than one! So we'd like to thank a few people who've helped make it possible: Paul Dinas, our enthusiastic editor; Eric Levin, who took the fabulous photos; model lovers Candace Nirvana and Aaron Bruns; and Sage Vivant, who suggested us for the project—visit her website: customeroticasource.com.

We're privileged to have a wonderful family and terrific friends. They're always supportive of our work. They offer suggestions, give us lots of hugs and help, and leave us alone when we need time to write. Here's to all of you with love, appreciation, and gratitude. We'd also like to give a special word of support for our musical children and their hard-working bands, Hamper, in Paris, France, and The Watters Brothers Rebellion, in Ottawa, Canada. They make amazing music.

Trademarks

All terms mentioned in this book that are known to be or are suspected of being trademarks or service marks have been appropriately capitalized. Alpha Books and Penguin Group (USA) Inc. cannot attest to the accuracy of this information. Use of a term in this book should not be regarded as affecting the validity of any trademark or service mark.

PART ONE

Red Hot Sex—Yes!

When you think about the *Kama Sutra*, what do you picture? Have you ever wondered how that ancient erotic book could influence your sex life? Are you intrigued by the possibility of adding depth and breadth to sex, so that it becomes more than a few moments of pleasure and a release of tension? Do you dare to dream about elevating your sexual expression to the level of an art?

In this first part, we take a look at the *Kama Sutra*, exploring its world and its approach to sex. You'll see that sex is one of the most powerful life forces, and that you've already got everything you need to tap into it. By following the *Kama Sutra*'s advice you can open your mind and your heart, and alter your entire experience. Learn that the ancient ways of love can guide you to a sex life that's always new.

What's It All About, Vatsyayana?

In This Chapter

- Where, when, and why the *Kama Sutra* was written
- About the author: Vatsyayana
- Society and relationships at the time
- How the *Kama Sutra* fits into the tradition of Indian sacred literature
- How the *Kama Sutra* came to the West

The *Kama Sutra*. It's a name that conjures up images of exotic lovemaking, of acrobatic ecstasy in ancient foreign lands. But it's much more than that. The *Kama Sutra* is a timeless manual of love, a commentary on and a guide to relationships between men and women in the bedroom and in the world. Covering a range of topics from the specifically social to the explicitly sexual, it records and advises on the many ways to create harmony between the sexes. It offers practical suggestions on how to manifest the delights of romance and sensual pleasure in everyday life.

The Origins, Intent, and Structure of the Kama Sutra

A Hindu scholar named Vatsyayana compiled the *Kama Sutra* sometime during the fourth century C.E. It was not his original work, but rather a collection and distillation of treatises on love that originated in the early passages of Indian history. The first writings were said to have been made by the bull-god Nandi, who recorded what he heard as he stood guard outside the bedchamber of the god and goddess Shiva and Parvati. For 1,000 years they remained locked in passionate embrace, with Nandi eagerly absorbing every pearl of lovers' wisdom and then passing the message on to the waiting eyes and ears of humanity.

Pillow Talk

In simplest translation, **Kama** means love in Sanskrit, the ancient Indian language Vatsyayana wrote in, and **sutra** means aphorism or maxim, a brief statement of a general rule. We can interpret **Kama sutra** as *rules of love*. **Shastras** are scriptural and/or scientific texts. **Kama shastra** can be translated as the *science of love*.

Nandi's *Kama Shastra* was a colossal work of more than 1,000 chapters. Over the course of many years it was reduced to 500 chapters, then further condensed to 150 and divided into 7 sections on specific topics like amorous advances, the choice of a wife, and occult practices. Centuries passed and other sages further split the great work, concentrating on only one section each, until by Vatsyayana's time the overall concept was in danger of being lost. While the 500-chapter version was still extant, it was much too unwieldy for general reference, and so Vatsyayana took it upon himself to create a rendition from all these sources—one that would be accessible to everyone. He called it the *Kama Sutra*.

The Four Aims of Life

Why did Vatsyayana place such importance on creating a book of love? Because Kama was considered to be one of the four great aims of Hindu life. When pursued diligently, Dharma, Artha, and Kama would lead ultimately to the fourth, Moksha, or liberation from this worldly plane and the cycle of death and rebirth. These are all complex concepts, and each has a number of meanings depending on the context in which it appears.

- **Dharma** can mean truth, spiritual truth, religious practice, virtue, morality, and duty. Dharma is relevant to every action. From the point of view of ethics or virtue, how and why you do something may be more important than what you do. Dharma is a life-code, the way of good living.

- **Artha** generally refers to the material world of possessions, property, money, and commerce; for example, earning an income, acquiring wealth, and increasing one's standard of living.

- **Kama** means love, but also generally relates to the body and the senses, affection, romance, sex, emotional relationships, and the power of desire. It confirms the importance of appreciating and exploring the great gifts of sensory pleasure and the erotic impulse, so it includes the world of the arts as well.

Vatsyayana was careful to stress that Kama should never be separated from the other aims of life, nor pursued obsessively or selfishly. Although Dharma carried the most weight, Artha and Kama were considered close seconds. It was of the utmost importance to maintain a balance of all these aspects of living and to pursue them with different degrees of emphasis depending on various factors such as *caste*, gender, age, stage in life, geographical location, and profession. To lead a true, rich, and full life, all elements must be present, because awakening to spiritual freedom is much easier to do when your physical body is well cared for, stimulated, and satisfied, and when your mind is constructively occupied and your conscience is clear. As Vatsyayana said, "A man practicing Dharma, Artha, and Kama enjoys happiness both in this world and in the world to come." (I-2)

Pillow Talk

In Hindu society, a **caste** is a strict social division that a person is born into.

The Kama Sutra at a Glance

In his compilation, Vatsyayana maintained the structure of 7 parts, which he further subdivided into 36 chapters containing a total of 1,250 verses.

Part One, "The Vatsyayana Sutra," with five chapters, is a general introduction to the work. It deals with society and social concepts and presents information about the three aims of life. It also contains instructions for furnishing and decorating the home and the bedchamber, directives for bathing and caring for the body and hair, massage, preparing and eating food and drinks, dressing and wearing jewelry, and participating in games and festivals. There are descriptions of various types of men and women and discussion of lovemaking among different castes. Lovemaking with other men's wives and homosexuality are other topics briefly covered.

Part Two, "Of Sexual Union," with 10 chapters, discusses the significance of a lovers' match in genital size, sexual temperament, and capacity. Vatsyayana gave helpful hints on what to do when partners aren't evenly matched and detailed the many variations of loveplay prior to intercourse—what you might think of as foreplay—including separate chapters for embraces, caresses, kisses, bites, scratches, sighs, and blows. Fellatio is thoroughly described, cunnilingus and anal sex briefly mentioned.

Chapter 2 in this section, "Of the Embrace," classifies how and when lovers touch each other. There's a chapter dealing with afterplay (how lovers should conduct themselves after intercourse), for "the signs of affection must be continued before and after." (Daniélou II-10, p.197) Chapter 6 presents descriptions of sexual-intercourse positions.

Part Three, "About the Acquisition of a Wife," comprised of five chapters, presents detailed instructions for finding a spouse. At the time the *Kama Sutra* was written, arranged marriages were the norm. But Vatsyayana advised that, even within the structure of contracted marriage, it's best to marry someone you love, because "prosperity is gained only by marrying that girl to whom one becomes attached." (III-1)

Part Four, "About a Wife," has two chapters and outlines the duties and privileges of a woman, whether she is the only wife or one of several. Although when the *Kama Sutra* was written it was acceptable for men to have more than one wife, generally only well-off men had more than one. The wealthier and more prominent a man was, the more wives he could afford to keep.

Love Bites

"On the Various Ways of Lying Down," the chapter about intercourse, is what the *Kama Sutra*'s most famous for. Yet it only contains 52 verses, or less than 5 percent of the book's total.

Part Five, "About the Wives of Other Men," presents six chapters filled with techniques by which men can seduce other men's wives. While Vatsyayana stopped short of recommending infidelity, he pointed out that "moral objections do not resist the mounting of passion." (Daniélou V-1, p.317) This is an example of a topic Vatsyayana incorporated to make his work an all-inclusive instruction manual, taking into account that moral values differ widely from country to country. And, of course, the whole concept of fidelity was perceived differently in a culture in which men could have more than one wife as well as one or more mistresses. Infidelity was apparently socially acceptable (even a symbol of status) for men, but not for women.

Part Six, "About Courtesans," in six chapters, provides detailed instructions for the behavior of prostitutes. Courtesans were highly regarded professionals in ancient India, as in many other parts of the world at that time. They were intelligent, attractive, astute, gracious, and sexually adept. Becoming a courtesan was an accepted way for a woman to earn an income of her own.

Love Bites

The entire Courtesan section was originally written by the poet Dattaka at the request of the courtesans in the city of Pataliputra (now Patna). It was a working girl's guide, a sort of "Happy Hooker's Handbook."

Part Seven, "About the Means of Attracting Others to Yourself," presents two chapters dealing with aphrodisiacs, sex toys, magical spells, and charms to increase sexual attractiveness and performance. Included are techniques for enhancing beauty, permanently enlarging the penis, getting erections, and bewitching your lover.

This *Complete Idiot's Guide* draws primarily from Part Two. We interpret for you the matters of sexual technique that Vatsyayana described so thoroughly. But the whole work is of great value, and, although sections like the guidance for courtesans may seem irrelevant for most of us today, it provides gems of understanding for the interaction of the sexes. Vatsyayana presented ideas and concepts that are amusing and entertaining, but also provide ample material for anyone interested in social science and the study of human development. He catalogued and categorized not only specific sexual and romantic practices, but also identified the personal natures and peculiar preferences of citizens from various regions of the country.

Vatsyayana's intention was to include detailed descriptions and instructions on all aspects of sexuality, not restricting his coverage to only those aspects widely acknowledged as morally acceptable. His opinion was that moral standards in society constantly evolve and change, so to be scientifically valid he had to include even those practices that he personally rejected. Taking this position is probably why his treatise has withstood the test of time so well, retaining its popularity and credibility 16 centuries after it was written.

Stop in the Name of Love

Although his predecessor Suvarnanabha suggested practicing different intercourse postures in water, Vatsyayana considered it "improper, because it is prohibited by the religious law." (II-6)

Vatsyayana wanted to create a document relevant to the whole world, and he succeeded admirably. He was confident that, based on knowledge of local custom and an awareness of their own moral sensibilities, readers would assume self-responsibility in adopting or rejecting the topics he presented. If you want to read the complete *Kama Sutra*, refer to Appendix F, where you'll find a list of English language editions to choose from.

The Role of Commentators

As in all sutra texts, each *Kama Sutra* verse is a short, succinct abstract of its subject. Because short verses are more easily and accurately memorized, they're well suited to a culture relying on the oral transmission of information, as India was at the time. The difficulty with writing in verse is that because verses are so abbreviated, they can often be extremely vague and subject to a great deal of interpretation (or misinterpretation). Therefore, for those studying the *Kama Sutra*, each verse was expanded on by a teacher, who helped make the brief ideas more understandable.

While the *Kama Sutra* was primarily directed at men, women were encouraged to study it as well, even though they were prohibited from the more formal schooling men received. Before marriage, young women could be instructed by trusted married women, such as older sisters, aunts, or servants. After marriage, they could continue to learn the ways of the *Kama Sutra* "with the consent of their husbands." (I-3)

In later centuries, written commentaries were added as a study aid for the *Kama Sutra*. The two most well-respected commentaries are the *Jayamangla,* by Yashodhara (written sometime between 1100 and 1200 C.E.), and the modern Hindi commentary by Devadutta Shastri (1964). Both contain elaborate explanations of the original verses. As part of their clarification, they refer to important works that were written both before and after the *Kama Sutra*. While you read through this guide, we'll act as your translators and commentators, interpreting this age-old wisdom so that you can apply it in your life.

The Life and Times of Vatsyayana

We can only make an informed guess on the date of Vatsyayana's life. He lived between the first and sixth centuries C.E.; most authorities agree that he lived and wrote sometime around 350 C.E., more than 1,600 years ago.

Hardly anything is known about Vatsyayana's personal life. Some believe his complete name was Mallanaga Vatsyayana (Vatsyayana being his family name). The wisdom and maturity revealed in his writing indicate an older rather than a younger man. According to Vatsyayana's comments about himself in the *Kama Sutra*, he wrote it "after reading the texts of ancient authors, and following the ways of enjoyment mentioned in them." (VII-2) This suggests that in his earlier years he had explored the art of love and sensual pleasure, and then chose to share this knowledge when he was an older man, retired from active life. In his own words, he wrote at a time when he was "wholly engaged in the contemplation of the Deity." (VII-2)

Life During the Gupta Empire

To understand some of the ideas presented in the *Kama Sutra*, it's helpful to know a little of what life was like at the time. It's widely believed that Vatsyayana wrote during the reign of the emperor Samudragupta, one of the greatest of the Gupta kings, whose rule spanned more than 200 years—from 320 C.E. until the mid-sixth century. At its height the empire embraced almost all of northern India. Trade was widespread, not only throughout the kingdom itself, but also as far east as China and Japan and west to Rome. It was a time of great prosperity; the already-rich grew richer and the upper classes thrived. They embraced the pleasures life gave them, particularly in the cities, where they enjoyed music, dancing, plays, art, and beautiful buildings and gardens.

It was the "golden age" of Indian history, a time of unprecedented excellence in the culture, when philosophy, science, art, and architecture flourished. The Gupta emperors extended their patronage to art, science, education, and medicine, providing charitable hospitals for the citizens. Great strides were made in the world of medicine, astronomy, and mathematics—including a major step in the development of the modern decimal system. One of India's most renowned dramatists, Kalidasa, lived during those years.

Love Bites

Although Hinduism was the main religion during the Gupta's reign, there was great freedom of worship and tolerance for other religious paths.

The *Kama Sutra* was addressed primarily to affluent, educated, culturally sophisticated, male citizens. Many would have been merchants or civil servants owning land and living in the larger cities. They enjoyed a refined, upper-class lifestyle, with time for leisure, and they shared an appreciation for all forms of artistic expression. Lovemaking itself was elevated to the status of an art, with its requisite knowledge and skill considered mandatory for anyone seeking social recognition in this elite group.

Women of the time enjoyed a fair degree of freedom and respect. From the Jayamangla commentary: "Being the source of virtue, woman is the best means of reaching heaven. Man's efforts to be virtuous are impossible outside conjugal virtue …. There is no doubt but that women are the source of happiness." (Daniélou I-2, p.43)

On the other hand, at the time the *Kama Sutra* was written, women were secondary to men and subject to their authority. For the most part, life for women depended on the main males in their lives—fathers, husbands, and adult sons. While married women wielded a certain amount of power in family life, they were not active in business, politics, or other professions. Women were mainly caretakers of the home, mothers of children, and sexual partners for their husbands.

Exceptions to this were professional courtesans, who held a place of status and prestige in Indian society. Highly educated and exceptional in beauty and elegance, they often became famous poets or artists. Sons of affluent townsmen would spend time with courtesans to complete their own education, particularly their erotic education. Throughout Indian society in this period, there was an open celebration of healthy sexuality in a wide variety of expressions.

The Caste System

A major part of the Hindu social system revolved around the role of castes. Originally there were four castes, or varnas, each of which was also divided into sub-castes, or jatis. Castes were hierarchically ordered in terms of purity or advancement of a soul along the path to ultimate enlightenment. The highest caste was that of Brahmin, the priests, religious officials, and learned class, who were the spiritual guides and intellectual leaders of the community. Vatsyayana was probably a Brahmin. Next in line were the Kshatriya, the warriors and rulers, including the Gupta emperors themselves, whose job it was to defend and govern.

The role of those in the Vaishya caste, comprised of merchants, craftsmen, and farmers, was to succeed in business, or to make beautiful and useful objects, or to raise wholesome and healthful livestock and crops. The lowest caste was Shudra—the servants, laborers, and peasants, who served the three castes above them. Within each of these groups there was also a wide range of social distinctions, from highest to lowest.

Finally, added to this original fourfold group was another, a noncaste, the lowest of the low, now known as Dalits, also called the Untouchables, because to do so was ritually polluting to the upper castes. These people were relegated to the most menial jobs.

People were born into a particular caste based on their intrinsic nature and their behavior in previous lifetimes. That's why it was important to practice the three aims of life so carefully, particularly Dharma. If you assiduously followed the way of life expected of you within your group, you had a much better chance of moving up the caste ladder next time around. If you didn't, there was great likelihood you'd come back further down the line.

You got your caste status when you were born and there was no moving across that line during your lifetime. You couldn't work your way up or down—however, through some major social misbehavior, you could be excommunicated from your caste and become an "outcaste."

Because of the perceived relative purity or impurity of each caste, restrictions were placed on people's behavior regarding activity within the caste and in connection to people outside it. Marriage, for instance, was only supposed to be possible to someone within your caste. Even touching someone outside your group, especially those of the untouchable class, could have dire consequences. That's why in the *Kama Sutra*, Vatsyayana specifically listed which women it was allowable for citizens to amorously pursue and the ways to do it. It definitely wasn't all right to make advances to a woman of a higher caste. It was sometimes okay to have sex with women of lower castes, but only for pleasure or advancement in business or social life, not for producing children.

The Four Stages of Life

To bring even more structure and stability, in addition to the four aims and the four castes, were the four stages of life. In the proper order of things, most men would have the opportunity to pass through these stages: student, householder, retirement, and ascetic. As a student, from early puberty to about the age of 20, a young man was taught the sacred texts and the traditions and obligations of his caste. Perhaps he would go away for several years to study with a special teacher, or guru, at which time he would learn the ways of the *Kama Sutra*, including the 64 arts that would help bring him social respect and admiration from the ladies. The carnal pleasures, the specific ways of pleasing a woman, were to be learned in theory only, for a student was expected to be celibate. (Chapter 3 of this book will tell you more about the 64 arts.)

When he finished his studies, it was time for a young man to enter the next phase, that of the householder. He would marry, have children, and establish a home and family life. Households could be quite large, with several generations, servants, and retainers. During these years, it was a man's duty to increase his wealth, support his community, and explore fully the sensual side of life. He would refer to, and put into practice, the many teachings of the *Kama Sutra*. It was his religious and societal duty to bring his wife sexual pleasure and to create more children.

When his children were grown, a man could move into the phase of retirement. His adult son would take over the responsibility for the family. He could let go of the many social duties and turn his focus to the meaning of life and the cycle of birth and death. He could remain in the household and stay active in society, or he could leave and take up a more secluded, even hermit-like, lifestyle.

Love Bites

Most likely Vatsyayana was in the retirement stage of life when he wrote the *Kama Sutra*.

The fourth stage was optional and could be entered into at any time. This was the ascetic or sannyasin, the wanderer who gave up worldly goods and responsibilities in search of enlightenment. Sannyasins lived as simple traveling holy men, renouncing all aspects of the world in order to reach the fourth aim, Moksha.

Marriage Practices

During the time of the *Kama Sutra* most marriages were arranged for the bride and groom by their parents. Because marriage was such a holy affair, a way that a man could follow the aims of life and please his ancestors by carrying on the family line, a great deal of consideration went into finding the appropriate match. However, just because others were involved in the selection didn't mean that the marriageable couple had no say in the matter. Vatsyayana gave detailed instructions on how a man should go about finding a suitable wife and the

various people and practices he could enlist to help him in his quest.

Young women, "dressed and decorated in a becoming manner," (III-1) were urged to attend social events where they could meet and attract suitable prospects. When they found one they were attracted to, they were to show their love by a specific set of "outward signs and actions." (III-3) Not everyone chose to obey the standard of arranged marriage, so there was also a type of marriage based solely on love and personal choice—the Gandharva. Although considered quite unorthodox, it was still a respected practice, because "it brings forth happiness, [and] causes less trouble in its performance than the other forms of marriage." (III-5)

Generally, men were considered ready for matrimony after they finished their studies. Because the main role of women was to get married and produce children, they were ready for marriage as soon as they reached puberty. Vatsyayana stated that a woman should be at least three years younger than a man, but often they would be much younger than that. In fact, girls were frequently married before puberty. They would stay with their parents until after they began menstruating and then would be sent to their husbands.

Love Bites

Young marriage continues to be a feature of modern Indian life, even though it is illegal. According to a 2005 National Family Health survey, 56 percent of girls in rural India are married before they turn 18, the legal age of consent.

Ancient Manuals of Sexual and Spiritual Instruction

The *Kama Sutra* does not stand alone in India's history of great spiritual and sexual writings. It's part of a long tradition of guidance on how life should be lived in all its aspects.

Predecessors of the Kama Sutra

The spiritual predecessors of the *Kama Sutra* were the *Vedas*, *Upanishads*, and *Tantras*. The *Vedas*, meaning knowledge or wisdom in Sanskrit, are the primary texts of Hinduism. They're thought to be among the most ancient religious texts in existence, even though historians can't agree at all on their dates. Arguments range from 6000 B.C.E. to 1500 B.C.E. Believed to be direct transmissions from the Creator, the *Vedas* are a collection of hymns and rituals beseeching 33 gods for favors and for deliverance from hardship and evil. In the earliest *Vedas*, gods were personifications of nature's elemental forces, such as fire and water. Later they became more abstract concepts such as freedom and liberation. *Kama*, the god of love, desire, and pleasure, first appeared in the *Artharva Veda*, the last of the *Vedas*. A few hymns refer to a supreme Creator, a god of gods, who brought the world into existence. Goddesses played a relatively minor role. There's little in the *Vedas* about sex.

Love Bites

The Indian traditional system of medicine, called Ayurveda, has its roots in the *Artharva Veda*. Ayurveda means "knowledge of longevity."

By the end of the Vedic period when the *Upanishads* appeared, between 800 and 400 B.C.E., all existence was believed to come out of and return to a universal, nondual Oneness. At the same time, the caste system became fully entrenched in Indian society. Reincarnation was widely accepted and the concept of *karma* was introduced. The principle of Dharma became the universal guide for life. For the first time, it was understood that if you followed your Dharma, you'd make good karma and you could move up in the caste system. The *Upanishads* also told people that everyone, regardless of caste or karma, had a soul that could awaken to the realization that it is God. The idea that there was a normal and appropriate time of life for religious study and awakening the spirit, for attaining liberation, made its appearance. This emphasis on Dharma, Kama, and the realization of Moksha were guiding principles in Vatsyayana's writing of the *Kama Sutra*.

Pillow Talk

Karma means action or activity in Sanskrit. It's the causal connection between all past and future actions—your activity in this life directly affects your next life.

There are some sexual references in the *Upanishads*. For example, the oldest of the *Upanishads*, the *Brihadaranyaka*, says:

> *Woman is the sacrificial fire,*
> *the lips of her yoni the fuel,*
> *the hairs around them the smoke,*
> *and the vagina itself the flame.*

> *The act of penetration is the lightning,*
> *the feelings of pleasure are the sparks.*
> *in this fire the gods offer up semen-seed,*
> *and from this offering man is born.*

Pillow Talk

Yoni is the Sanskrit term for female genitals. **Lingam** is the word for penis.

The important, explicitly sexual, predecessors to the *Kama Sutra* include the ancient oral versions of the *Tantra Shastras* and, of course, Nandi's work the *Kama Shastra* and all its following variations. See Appendix C for a discussion of the *Tantras*.

Later Manuals of Love

Written between 1100 and 1200 C.E., the *Ratirahasya*, or *Secrets of Love,* by the poet Kukkoka contains about 800 verses divided into 10 chapters. When the work was translated from Sanskrit into various other Indian languages, the author's name was shortened to Koka, and his work became popularly known as *Koka Shastra*.

After the *Kama Sutra*, perhaps the next-best-known Indian manual of lovemaking is the *Ananga Ranga*, or *The Stage of the Bodiless One* (also called *Kamaledhiplava*, or *A Boat in the Ocean of Love*), written sometime between 1500 and 1600. The *Koka Shastra* and the *Ananga Ranga* are more or less re-workings of the *Kama Sutra*, with little of its insight or originality. See Appendix D for an exploration of this work.

English Translations of the Kama Sutra

The three significant, and most popular, translations from the original Sanskrit of Vatsyayana's *Kama Sutra* are by Sir Richard F. Burton and F. F. Arbuthnot (1883), Indra Sinha (1980), and Alain Daniélou (1994). Although the *Kama Sutra* had been a major force in Indian culture for well over 1,500 years, nothing was known of it in the West until the nineteenth century. We can thank Sir Burton for first introducing it to the western world. His many years spent in the East and his fascination with all things Oriental, particularly anything related to sex, inspired him to publish such exotic works as the *Kama Sutra*, the *Ananga Ranga*, the *Perfumed Garden*, and the *1001 Arabian Nights*. Because Victorian England was so prudish, he couldn't present them publicly, but had to publish them as scholarly works for subscribers only through his Kama Shastra Society.

Burton produced his translation with the assistance of a scholar named Indraji, who gathered manuscript copies of parts of the original from Sanskrit libraries in three different Indian cities. He left some of the translation in verse form, while other parts he set out as prose paragraphs. Portions of later commentaries are also mixed in with the original *Kama Sutra* text. His edition wasn't illustrated. Dozens of editions of the Burton translation have been published over the last 100 years, each with a short forward or introduction by another author. Many are lavishly illustrated with color photographs or line drawings, particularly of sexual-intercourse positions.

Indra Sinha's more poetic translation is illustrated with photographs of Indian temple sculpture and exotic miniature paintings dating from the sixteenth century onward. He reworked the *Kama Sutra* verses and the commentaries into five-line stanzas to try

to capture Vatsyayana's mood for modern Western readers. He also incorporated contents from other erotic texts, particularly those that included more intercourse positions, like the *Ananga Ranga*, the *Ratiratnapradipika*, and the *Smaradipika*.

Love Bites

Richard Francis Burton was one of the most colorful characters of the nineteenth century. As well as a translator of sexy texts, he was an army officer, an adventurer, a poet, an undercover agent, and an explorer.

Alain Daniélou's translation is unabridged and retains the original numbering for all verses. It includes the two commentaries by Yashodhara and Devadutta Shastri and presents a clear separation between the verses of the *Kama Sutra* and the commentary text. It's the best source of the three for academic research. This translation isn't illustrated.

It's a testament to the brilliance and clarity of the original *Kama Sutra* that these three quite different translations are all immensely enjoyable and valuable in their own right.

The Least You Need to Know

- The *Kama Sutra* was written in India by Vatsyayana about 350 C.E.
- It's a manual about all aspects of relationship between men and women, including explicit sexuality.
- The pursuit of love and sensual pleasure was considered one of the aims of life in Vatsyayana's time.
- The *Kama Sutra* is part of a long tradition of spiritual and sexual writings in India.
- Sir Francis Burton published the first English language translation in 1883.

That Was Then, This Is Now

2

In This Chapter

* How you can benefit from Vatsyayana's approach to sex
* How sexual intelligence and emotional intelligence can supercharge your sex life
* Sexual learning is a lifelong process
* The many ways lovers can match, and what to do if they don't
* How your hormones affect your sex drive

The people the *Kama Sutra* was written for were taught that consciously living a life of sensual pleasure was part of their path to spiritual liberation. How does that compare to modern life, where pleasure, particularly sexual pleasure, is often portrayed as a distraction, an escape, or even a sin? If you follow Vatsyayana's lead, you'll come to understand that, contrary to our current social conditioning, supercharged sex is part of a healthy and, yes, *moral* lifestyle.

Vatsyayana not only explained why sex was essentially good, he also described how to make it better through study and practice. Because it takes two to tango, he emphasized the importance of physically and emotionally matched partners. And, for those who are mismatched in some way, he provided instructions for bringing just about everything into harmonious alignment. Although he wrote so long ago, you'll find much of his advice astoundingly relevant for today's lovers.

Sex Is Good

According to the *Kama Sutra,* sex is very good indeed. It's essential for survival of the human race, and necessary for health and happiness, at least in certain stages of your life: "pleasures being as necessary for existence and well-being of the body as food, are consequently equally required." (I-2) As part of Kama, life's third aim, pleasure, sex, and love can help a soul reach spiritual liberation. Vatsyayana taught that you don't have to deny the body or escape from the world to achieve ultimate enlightenment; rather you should be fully present and live life to the utmost.

Love Bites

One British study revealed that the risk of having a fatal heart attack was cut in half for men who had sex at least twice a week.

It's about participating with all of you—body, mind, heart, and soul—because "Kama is the enjoyment of appropriate objects by the five senses … assisted by the mind, together with the soul." (I-2) Supported by these beliefs, sexuality in Vatsyayana's time was a natural, virtuous, integral part of everyday life. It wasn't just a pleasant pastime and a means of procreation; it was an art and a science well worth studying by everyone.

Love Bites

Good sex makes your whole system happy. Endorphins, your body's natural mood enhancers, increase by 200 percent during lovemaking.

Attitude Is Everything

Modern Westerners can benefit greatly by adopting Vatsyayana's approach. Even though sex has a high profile in our culture, underneath the bravado, sex is somehow morally questionable. We like it—a lot—but a part of us is ashamed that we do. The innocent appreciation and easy acceptance of sex that characterized the lifestyle of Vatsyayana's contemporaries has never been evident in our society. Our shame would amaze those ancient people.

Where did it come from, this love-hate relationship we have with our sexuality? It goes back a long way, to many sources. For instance, during the sixth and fifth centuries B.C.E., Classical Greek idealists such as Heraclitus popularized the concept *soma semá*, suggesting that the body is a tomb or prison from which the soul must escape to realize spiritual salvation. This concept, shared by Pythagoreanism, Orphism, and mystery religions, directly influenced early Christianity, particularly through St. Paul and St. Clement. Such a line of thought eventually led to the conclusion that the body is bad and dirty, sinful even. Thus the pleasures associated with the body, particularly really fabulous pleasures like sex, became sinful, too.

Pillow Talk

Soma means *body* in ancient Greek. **Semá** can be translated as *tomb.*

The idea that sex is bad has tragic consequences for many, as they try to reconcile their natural desire for sexual experiences with the message that sex is bad. If sex and the body are bad, then they must be bad for wanting it. People learn to hate their bodies and mistreat or neglect them, and life-threatening illnesses, both mental and physical, can result. If they guiltily try to suppress their inherent human eroticism, bizarre and violent tendencies, like sexual abuse, can emerge.

Stop in the Name of Love

In the 1940s, Freudian psychoanalyst Wilhelm Reich caused great controversy with his theory that repressing sexual emotion causes cancer. Whether you believe him or not, it's time to stop giving yourself any messages that make you feel ashamed of your sexual desires.

Our culture's sexual attitudes have evolved considerably over the past century, with wider acceptance of all things sexual; but, even for the majority of people who are relatively comfortable with their sexuality, there's still a niggling unease about the propriety of it all. For women in particular, sex remains a two-pronged sword. "Good" girls still aren't supposed to want it. Now, however, women are encouraged to occasionally allow their "bad" girls out to play. Once, twice, several times a week, the erotic side of our nature is given some freedom, and then put back in its place as respectability reasserts itself. And so we compartmentalize our sexuality, separating our sensual selves from our roles as business people, community volunteers, parents, and churchgoers. As a consequence, sex either gets way too much attention or way too little. We deny it to ourselves; then we obsess over it. We've yet to find the acceptance and balance between sex and the rest of life that Vatsyayana knew. But we're searching for it.

Love Bites

In a poll conducted by popular sex educator Sue Johanson of *Talk Sex with Sue,* over 60 percent of respondents felt that "American culture suppresses the fundamental right of human beings to have a fulfilling sex life by restricting information."

Supercharged Sex—Yes!

The first step in creating supercharged sex is to fully embrace the goodness of sex and pleasure, to understand that the body is a sacred temple, and your five senses are gateways that enable you to experience that pleasure. Embracing sex in this way, saying yes to sex, doesn't mean you'll become promiscuous. You won't automatically have sex with anyone, at any time. On the contrary, rather than alternately starving yourself then letting your appetite run wild, you'll take full responsibility for your sexuality, ensuring that all your actions are in alignment with your values, your code of morality and ethics, your Dharma. You'll be cognizant of the dangers of sexually transmitted diseases and act appropriately. You'll be accountable for how your actions affect other people, including most obviously your lover(s).

The next step is to understand that supercharged sex requires study. As Vatsyayana acknowledged, even "brute creation" knows how to have instinctual sex, but great sex, virtuous sex, illuminating sex is particular to humanity because of our intellect. "Sexual intercourse being a thing dependent on man and woman requires the application of proper means by them, and those means are to be learnt from the *Kama Shastra.*" (I-2) You, of course, already know that—after all, you bought this guide for that very purpose!

Supercharging Your Sex Life

Basically all adults today understand the rudiments of basic friction sex—rubbing bodies together in order to experience pleasure, relieve sexual tension, and, hopefully, reach orgasm. In fact the goal of friction sex is to get to orgasm, usually as quickly as possible. But supercharged sex is much, much more. It includes not only your body, but also your mind and your heart—in other words your entire being, not just your genitals. If you want to graduate from ordinary friction sex to supercharged sex, you need two things: sexual intelligence and emotional intelligence.

Sexual Intelligence

Sexual intelligence refers to your level of sexual knowledge and degree of sexual skill. Both significantly affect the quality of your lovemaking experience. There may be some natural lovers who learn all they need to know from personal experimentation, but most people aren't born with an exceptional aptitude for sexual mastery. It's much easier to learn from someone who already knows how.

In Vatsyayana's day, "sexual behavior [was] to be learned with the aid of the *Kama Sutra* and the counsel of worthy men, experts in the arts of pleasure." (Daniélou I-2, p.30) Boys, girls, men, and women were all encouraged to study the ways of Kama, including both explicitly sexual pleasure and the general principles of eroticism underlying all life. That important information was to be passed on, either from an official teacher or from a trusted family member. No education, formal or informal, was considered complete without it.

Unlike in Vatsyayana's time, formal sex education for adolescents today is usually confined to reproductive processes and sexual diseases, without much examination of the erotic nature of life and the role of desire and emotion in sexual expression. Informal learning comes partly from family, but mostly through media, peers, and uninformed personal exploration, all of which can lead to a rather skewed view of sex. But as adults, we're fortunate to have access to a wide range of learning tools and teachers, so we can correct misinformation and broaden our experience into a richly vital sexuality.

Books, videos, the Internet, seminars, and counselors offer practical advice on this most sought-after of subjects. Refer to Appendix F for a selection of resources. If, or when, you're a parent, one of the best things you can do for your children is to share with them the wisdom that sexuality, when accompanied by mature self-awareness and responsibility, is one of the most beautiful things life has to offer. Don't you wish your parents had?

Love Bites

More than 350,000 people from 41 countries took part in Durex™ condom company's 2004 global survey of sexual attitudes and behavior. Almost half of the participants (47 percent) believed that parents should teach their kids about sex; only 27 percent chose school.

Sexual intelligence also means that you know learning is a lifelong process, especially where sexuality is concerned. Adopting a beginner's mind as you go

helps you see all things with new eyes. You won't be afraid to admit you don't know something or that you're curious to experiment. And, as your body and your desires change through life, your sexuality will change and grow with you. You'll be able to enjoy a rich sexual life for many, many years. You won't be part of that self-limiting group who "believe that a couple has no need to learn erotic arts, and that nature will teach them everything. Those who believe that, on reaching middle age, become unhappy and desperate." (Daniélou II-3, p.122)

Love Bites

According to Sanskrit scholar and author Indra Sinha, it's commonly accepted in India that the *Kama Sutra* suggests carrying on an active sex life until at least the age of 70.

Emotional Intelligence

Emotional intelligence means being real, open, honest, and present with your partner. It means freely sharing what you're feeling and listening to and honoring your lover's feelings. It doesn't mean you have to be in a committed relationship with your sexual partner, or even in love with each other. But you do need to have the capacity for commitment and an openness to intense emotional connection.

"He who knows how to make himself beloved by women, as well as to increase their honor and create confidence in them, this man becomes an object of their love." (III-2) Although Vatsyayana directed this comment to men, it's equally applicable to women. They, too, must engage their sexual partners with respect, sincerity, and a willingness to go beyond their emotional boundaries. "For a man as for a woman, the total gift of self is a source of wonderful happiness and luck. Sexual intercourse is not merely a pleasure of the senses: more important is the sacrifice of oneself, the gift of self." (Daniélou, II-3 p.122)

A primary challenge of emotional intelligence is to open your heart, letting your love out and letting love in. Opening your heart means that you dare to risk being emotionally transparent and vulnerable with your lover. You allow yourself to feel everything, both good and bad, and you share those feelings in an appropriate way with each other. You work to reopen your heart every time it closes—over and over. You take the risk that you might be hurt again. We say again, because almost all of us have experienced the pain of a broken heart. Opening your heart repeatedly takes uncommon courage and is one of the defining characteristics of high emotional intelligence.

Love Bites

An ABC News *"Primetime Live"* survey revealed that only 15 percent of women feel it's all right to have sex without an emotional relationship, whereas 35 percent of men think that "just doing it for the sex" is quite okay.

Vatsyayana described many types of satisfying sexual adventures, but to him the best were based in a love relationship. Sex as an expression of love gains a remarkable power, nourishing your partner with a kind of *sensual nutrition* that's available from no other source. Often it's this added dimension of love that helps you make the jump from ordinary friction sex to supercharged sex. And if there's a commitment to each other as well, it can be an even smoother transition. A committed relationship offers you a cocoon of security. You're free to abandon yourself in complete surrender to your lover, holding nothing back. Your lovemaking can go from wild and wonderful to quiet, calm, and mystical. Each and every moment of it supercharged.

Pillow Talk

Sensual nutrition refers to the life-enhancing and health-promoting properties of sensual stimulation, particularly physical touching, hugging, and kissing.

Supercharged Sex According to Vatsyayana

For many people, sex just means intercourse. From this perspective, foreplay is what precedes real sex, and when intercourse is over, that's the end of sex.

Everything after intercourse is something else—cuddling, maybe, but not sex. Such a limited concept of sex leads to short, fast encounters that can leave both partners unsatisfied. Of course "quickies" are dandy—they can slake your thirst for each other between bouts of longer loving, and add spice and spontaneity to your love life. Just make sure they aren't your entire sexual bill of fare.

Vatsyayana categorized most quickies as the kind of sex men had with servant girls of lower castes—a simple satisfying of sexual hunger that he ranked fairly low on the scale of sensual pleasure. Supercharged sex usually takes a while and includes much more than intercourse. During those satisfying encounters you'll build a fire of passion and connection that will sustain you, so your quickies will be supercharged, too.

Love Bites

Research by a pair of economists suggests that sex is more important than money for happiness. Their study of 16,000 American adults showed that increasing intercourse from once per month to once per week brought the same amount of happiness as an extra $50,000.

Probably the single-most important factor in transforming sex into supercharged sex is spending quality time together as lovers. No matter how much time you spend together for all the other responsibilities in your lives (socializing, working, parenting), being together during those activities is not the same as being together as lovers. When you're lovers, your complete attention is on each other.

We recommend that you and your partner schedule a weekly lovers' time. Disconnect from the world and spend at least 2, 4, 6, or more hours paying attention only to each other. In Part II, we give you very specific instruction, based on Vatsyayana's expertise, about what to do during those hours.

Al's Outlook

Everyone has the same 24 hours. You know what really matters to people by how they spend their time. Are you feeding your relationship by spending time together as lovers?

The Importance of Intention

Intention is a simple but powerful key to unlock the magic of supercharged sex. What do you want to create in your sexual encounter? Are you just looking for a quick release of tension and a modicum of pleasure? Then that's what you'll likely get. On the other hand, if your intention is to find ecstasy together, and an exquisite body, mind, and heart connection, then your experience will be more in alignment with your desire.

It's important to know that voicing an intention is not the same as setting a goal. Intention refers to your approach to the situation, how you act in it, and what you're open to, not what you expect to get out of it. It's a subtle but very important difference, because supercharged sex is sex without goals. According to the *Kama Sutra*, "The achievement of a goal is therefore distinct from eroticism." (Daniélou I-2, p. 29)

People want to be good lovers and they want satisfying sex. It's normal. But beware of performance anxiety. A performance implies an outcome you wish to reach, which in lovemaking is usually orgasm. The anxiety created when you believe you have to get to orgasm can be deadly. If he's feeling performance pressure, a man might lose his erection or ejaculate prematurely. A woman under that same stress may find it impossible to have an orgasm at all.

The opposite of goal orientation in lovemaking is *pleasure orientation*. With a pleasure orientation, you're relaxed, and completely absorbed in the moment. Each touch, kiss, caress, breath, contact of the eyes, is complete and perfect in and of itself. You're not trying to get someplace specific. You're content and fulfilled right where you are, giving and receiving pleasure, whether it's for a few intensely passionate minutes or several smoldering hours. Then your excitement, your connection, and your energy naturally build to orgasmic union. Ironically, when you let go of the goal of orgasm, you get lots more of them.

A Match Made in Heaven

For Vatsyayana, creating the kind of totally fulfilling sex we call supercharged required a match, a harmonious balance between lovers on many levels—in their bodies, their libido, and their emotional compatibility. Obviously, exact matches would be the easiest couplings to make work, but Vatsyayana also gave advice for lovers who are mismatched, particularly regarding genital size.

Physical Matches

Vatsyayana, the social scientist, loved to classify just about everything, so it's no surprise that he did the same with male and female genitals. He divided them into three categories based on size and gave each category a name. Depending on his penis length, a man would be …

- **Hare:** Small, less than 5 inches when fully erect (12.5 cm)
- **Bull:** Medium, under 7 inches when fully erect (18 cm)
- **Horse:** Large, up to 10 inches (or more) when fully erect (25 cm)

According to the depth of her vagina, a woman would be …

- **Deer:** Small, 5 inches deep or less (12.5 cm)
- **Mare:** Medium, up to 7 inches deep (18 cm)
- **Elephant:** Large, more than 7 inches deep (18 cm +)

Size matters, but not necessarily in the way you might think. Some men today have become obsessed with the size of their penis, believing that they are too small. Vatsyayana didn't care so much about whether you're big or small, but rather that when you got together you'd fit in all the right places and all the right ways. Genital size itself isn't really important; it's how things measure up between lovers. The best *congress* happens in what Vatsyayana called equal unions, Hare and Deer, Bull and Mare, and Horse and Elephant. However, six penis/vagina combinations make unequal unions. If a man's penis is one size smaller than his partner's vagina, Vatsyayana named such intercourse *low congress*. If it's two sizes smaller, *lowest congress*. If his penis is one size larger, it's called *high congress*. Two sizes larger is *highest congress*.

Pillow Talk

Translators of the *Kama Sutra* mostly use the terms **congress** and coition to mean sexual intercourse, in which either the penis or a penis substitute—a dildo for instance—penetrates the vagina. Sometimes congress and coition refer to oral sex as well.

High congress is better than low, because even if a man is considerably larger than a woman, with proper caution and technique they can pleasure each other quite nicely. Of all the possible matches, Vatsyayana was most concerned for lovers in lowest congress because neither partner was likely to get much satisfaction. He suggested that in such a situation, a man might want to use a penis extender. See Appendix B for some of Vatsyayana's selections and their modern counterparts. Also, in our chapters on intercourse, you'll find particular positions that the *Kama Sutra* suggests for evening out size differences.

Stop in the Name of Love

No matter how much you'd like to make your lingam longer, we don't recommend this method of Vatsyayana's: "First rub your penis with wasp stings and massage it with sweet oil. When it swells, let it dangle for ten nights through a hole in your bed." (Daniélou VII-1, p.182)

Women don't usually fret about the depth of their vaginas, but men can become quite preoccupied with their penis length. Mostly they worry that it's too small. But the vast majority of men aren't as small as they assume they are. One reason men think they're undersized is that the penis looks smaller when you look down at it than it does if you see it from the side or front. Another factor is that some men's penises shrink more when flaccid. These penises usually tend to increase more

dramatically when erect than one that's relatively large in its flaccid state. You might want to look at your erect penis from a side view in the mirror to get a true sense of your size. Or, if you want your precise dimensions, ask your darling to measure you during your next playtime. For most accurate results, measure along the topside of your penis from your pubic bone to the tip.

Love Bites

Surprise, surprise—most studies report that the majority of men are medium-size bulls, with an average erect penis length of 6 inches.

While women generally agree with Vatsyayana that if there's got to be a difference, bigger is better, mostly they want a man who comfortably fills them up. The best size for your penis is the size that's truly right for her. Remember, too, that just as important as the might of your member is the skill with which you wield it. Chapter 7 gives you advice on thrusting moves that will make her quake.

Sexual Temperament and Libido

To complete his charts of possible permutations in the chemistry of love, Vatsyayana further categorized men and women in terms of desire for sex and how much time they required to reach sexual satisfaction. He noted three possibilities for strength of carnal desire—small, middling, and intense. Likewise, duration of activity was classified as short, moderate, and long.

Love Bites

As a general rule for duration of lovemaking, Vatsyayana advised stretching it out, because, "if a man be long-timed the female loves him the more, but if he be short-timed, she is dissatisfied with him." (II-1)

In a fantasy world, we'd all meet someone whose body fit ours completely, whose force of passion aligned with ours, and who came at the same instant we did. But reality presents us with different scenarios, and as Vatsyayana said, "there being thus nine kinds of union with regard to dimensions, force of passion, and time, respectively, by making combinations of them, innumerable kinds of union would be produced." (II-1) He counseled lovers to pay very close attention and to use all their skills and "such means as they may think suitable for the occasion." (II-1)

Follow his advice and use your powers of observation as a love scientist to become aware of your partner's needs and wants. Employ your skill as a love artist to create scenarios that will satisfy you both—no matter what differences there may be between you. Consider, for instance, a common issue many couples face: one desires sex more often than the other. This doesn't have to become a problem. Combine your sexual intelligence and your emotional intelligence to move beyond "my way" (sex now) or "your way" (no sex now) to a new way (sensual play). When one of you is not in the mood for sex, but the other is, try a new stance and shift from purely sexual to affectionately sensual. Bring pleasure to your lover and yourself with sensual—not overtly sexual—touching, kissing, or massage, in a loving, playful, and undemanding way. By simply choosing to respond affectionately and sensually and acting accordingly, many times a partner with low desire will get turned on and want to have sex, especially if you're not putting on the pressure.

Emotional Intimacy and Sexual Intimacy

Besides general differences within the sexes, there's a big difference between them that needs careful consideration. It's the difference between emotional intimacy and sexual intimacy. Women seem to crave emotional intimacy during sex more than men do. While they sometimes want full-on, go-for-it sex, often they want some affectionate attention to open their hearts before they'll open their legs. As Vatsyayana said, "Women being of a tender nature, want tender beginnings." (III-2) Men, on the other hand, find sexual intimacy the easier path. They not only don't need emotional intimacy for physically satisfying sex, but they frequently shy away from it.

It's interesting, though, that when the sex is really good, the warmth in their genitals spreads to their hearts and emotional connection follows.

Love Bites

In a *Redbook* magazine survey of 3,000 married couples, when asked what they wanted more of during sex, 57 percent of the women replied: romance.

One explanation for these apparent differences concerns the polarity of male and female *chakras*. In Eastern spirituality and medicine, you don't just have a physical body, you have an energy body as well. Chakras are specific centers of energy along that body. In most systems there are seven chakra centers that align with certain locations on your physical body. They also relate to particular internal organs and to various emotional and mental states.

Two important chakras for our discussion are the root chakra, at the genitals, from the pubic bone back to the tailbone, and the heart chakra, in the center of the chest. In men, the root chakra, of which the penis is part, is positively charged. Their heart centers carry a negative charge. For women, the opposite is true. Their hearts have a positive charge and their vaginas a negative one. When you consider that energy flows from positive to negative, it makes perfect sense why a woman wants some adoration before the penetration. As her heart warms with love, that energy spills over and streams down to liven up her vagina, making it juicy and welcoming.

Pillow Talk

Chakra means circle or wheel in Sanskrit. Chakras are pictured as spinning vortexes aligned along the spinal column. Energy passes through them, front and back, up and down.

Raging Hormones

Generally women and men engage in foreplay—sexual activities before intercourse—with very different motivations. Knowing how each perceives foreplay can help you navigate the currents of men wanting sex first and women wanting sex second.

Men may engage in the sensual activities of foreplay because they think they have to in order to get to what they really want—sexual intercourse. Women engage in foreplay because, well, they love foreplay. They love to be kissed, caressed, and cuddled. Besides being immensely enjoyable, it helps them feel safe, appreciated, loved, and adored. And, it awakens powerful feelings of attraction and desire for their man. Men can train themselves to be fully present and derive great pleasure from these amorous activities, rather than just going through the motions so they can get to the "good stuff." A woman knows where your attention really is. If it's right there in the experience of that kiss, she'll open to you like a flower in the sun. If it's not, she can shrivel up and fade away.

Pala's Perspective

In our work as sexuality teachers, we often receive requests from men for advice on how to make their women get turned on quicker and come faster. We ask, are you sure you want to deny yourself more pleasure by going faster? Slow down! The journey's the thing, not just the destination.

We emphasize that being present in foreplay, relaxing and enjoying every touch, is a learned process for most men, because their body's natural inclination is to go for the gold. You can blame it on that raging masculine hormone—testosterone. Testosterone is aggressive and action oriented. It fuels the drive for sex in both men and women, although men have 20 to 40 times more of it. Testosterone craves newness and variety. It's contrary, because even though it wants to be alone and shies away from commitment, at the same time it wants to claim possession. Testosterone governs the urge for orgasm. It's a big reason why men want sex first.

Estrogen is testosterone's feminine companion. It's receptive, but not passive. It's willing and available for sexual fun, but doesn't like to take the initiative. It seeks connection and comfort and responds to testosterone's pursuit with a breathy, "Possess me, I belong to you." Women have lots of it, men very little. In women, estrogen increases with intercourse and drops off in times of abstinence, which helps explain why the more good sex women get, the readier they are for even more.

Vatsyayana had no knowledge of testosterone and estrogen, or that they were responsible for much of men's and women's sexual responses, but he was very aware of the "difference in the consciousness of pleasure." As he observed, "Man's nature has always been to crow, 'I am making love!' while she coos, 'This man is making love with me!'" (Sinha II-1, p. 44)

Testosterone and estrogen aren't the only hormones affecting our sexual appetites—there are a whole host of them. A man, however, is primarily ruled by testosterone, whereas a woman falls under the sway of multi-part hormonal mixtures. In her more than 30 years of sex research, Dr. Theresa L. Crenshaw found that because of complex chemical blends, a woman's sex drive has many faces, while a man's generally just has one. For most of his life he's perpetually switched on—in active mode. A woman, however, depending on the hormonal cocktail her body's producing, can be sexually aggressive, receptive, seductive, or resistant. Allowing for the cultural differences between our times—women now are encouraged to take more sexual initiative—Crenshaw's divisions of a woman's sexual mood bear remarkable similarity to those described in the *Kama Sutra* so long ago. It says, "the state of mind of girls who can be possessed is of three kinds: accessible, cooperating, hostile." (Daniélou II-8, p. 173)

Hormone levels fluctuate regularly, throughout your day and over the course of your life. As they change, so, too, does your desire for sex. Women, for instance, experience regular shifts in hormones on a monthly basis during their reproductive years. After menopause, hormone production usually slows down. A man in his teens and early 20s has so much testosterone, it's a wonder he can think of anything other than getting off. By the time he reaches his 60s, he has less testosterone and more estrogen, so he's happy to cuddle a lot more on his way to the Big O.

Love Bites

Under normal conditions a man's testosterone levels are higher in the morning and lower at night. They can fluctuate as much as 50 percent over the course of the day.

While they play a big role in your sexual life, hormones aren't the only factor. You aren't, after all, just your body—experience, intention, circumstance, and your partner all make their contribution, too. So, if you follow Vatsyayana's advice and become a skillful lover, you'll enjoy a lifetime of sexual pleasure no matter what your age. "Desire, which springs from nature, and which is increased by art, and from which all danger is taken away by wisdom, becomes firm and secure." (V-1)

The Least You Need to Know

* To create supercharged sex, embrace the positive goodness of sex and pleasure.

* Sexual knowledge and skill are learned over a lifetime.

* Being emotionally open and real with your lover are essential for great sex.

* Vatsyayana taught that the size of your genitals isn't what's important; it's that you match with your partner.

* Part of the difference in men's and women's sexual temperament is due to relative amounts of testosterone and estrogen.

PART TWO

Come on Baby, Light My Fire

What's your attitude about foreplay? Is it only a map to move you from point A to point B on your way to the good stuff? Even the term we use, foreplay, implies that it's just a lead up to what's really important. But even though it's all about arousal, you can learn to savor every second of this intimate contact.

Exploring Vatsyayana's explicit practices will awaken every part of your body to pleasure. You'll begin to understand that there's no rush. You'll be thoroughly engaged from the first looks of lust to the sweet sighs of surrender. When you've developed an artistry of love, each kiss, each touch, each nibble offers its own moment of magic. Hone your skills with lessons about lips, teeth, nails, fingers, and toes. They'll light your fire so bright it won't ever die down.

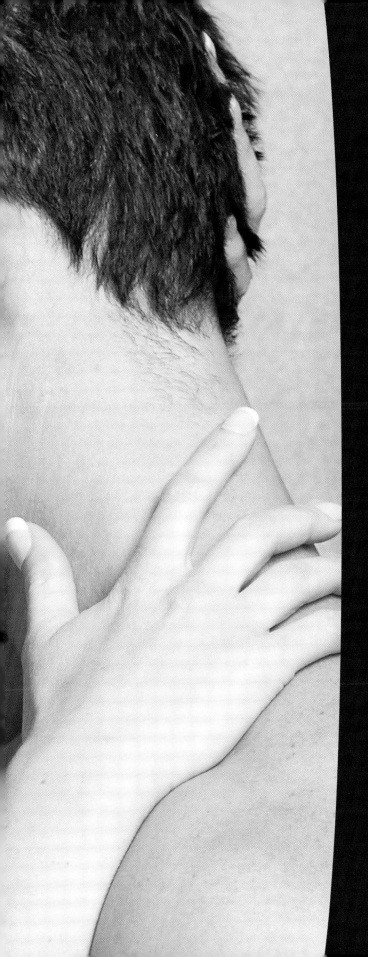

In the Mood for Love

3

In This Chapter

- ❧ The three A's of spectacular sex
- ❧ How the 64 arts can help you be a better lover
- ❧ How to create a sensual space for lovemaking
- ❧ Ways to awaken your senses
- ❧ Vatsyayana's suggestions for preludes to sex

Supercharged sex is a triple-A event—it's about attitude, ambience, and action. First you prepare yourself mentally for the most amazing sex of your life. Then you set the scene for seduction. Finally, you take the steps that make it all happen. In case you're wondering exactly what to do, Vatsyayana gave very specific advice on all three aspects.

Attitude

You've probably heard it said that your mind is your biggest erogenous zone. Well, supercharged sex isn't all in your head, but it sure starts there. As the *Kama Sutra* says, "attraction and enjoyment are mental phenomena." (Daniélou II-1, p.103)

What makes men and women attractive to each other isn't just what's on the outside; it's what's inside, too. That's why Vatsyayana stressed the need for knowledge, not only of erotic technique, but also of the arts and sciences associated with Kama.

The 64 Arts

Both women and men were encouraged by Vatsyayana to learn the love arts and learn them well, because "even the bare knowledge of them gives attractiveness to a woman." As for men, well, "a man who is versed in these arts, who is loquacious and acquainted with the arts of gallantry, gains very soon the hearts of women." (I-3)

Love Bites

The *Kama Sutra* says there are 64 love arts and also 64 particular lovemaking practices.

While some of the arts Vatsyayana listed—like the art of cock fighting, or of accumulating water in cisterns—aren't relevant in our culture today, the general idea behind them still is. They're all subjects that help make a person entertaining, capable, and confident, in large public gatherings or in a romantic rendezvous. They include developing your physical prowess, your ability with words, your artistic sensibilities, your mental capacity, and your social skills—in short, becoming a well-rounded, interesting, and creative person.

A modern version of Vatsyayana's list of love arts and sciences would include the following:

* **Music:** singing, dancing, playing an instrument
* **Art:** drawing, painting, photography, pottery, making stained glass, sculpting
* **Games:** card games, word games, brain teasers, gambling skills

* **Physical activity:** martial arts, team and solo sports
* **Language skills:** both oral and written; poetry, story writing and telling, speaking more than one language
* **Decorative talents:** both for the body and for the space around you
* **Culinary competence:** cooking, mixing drinks, knowing wines
* **Gardening:** indoor and outdoor, growing herbs, arranging flowers

If you want to become a superior lover, become a superior person. Broaden your mind and you'll expand your pleasure in the bedroom, because, as Vatsyayana well knew, supercharged sex isn't just about technique. It's about how two lovers interact in all ways. Exciting your minds excites your bodies. Stimulate your imagination and your other senses will awaken. You may end up in bed doing titillating things to each other, but you've got to want to get there first.

Harmony

In Vatsyayana's eyes, harmony was at the core of really good lovemaking—that matching of minds as well as bodies. For passion to reach its peak, he considered it essential that lovers be in total sync with each other. "For erotic success the peculiarities of both parties must be known before commencing to embrace." (Daniélou II-1, p.89)

Stop in the Name of Love

The ancients believed that obligatory or disharmonious sex could be damaging to your health.

As usual, he placed most responsibility on a man for reading his lady's moods, responding to them, and then leading her to that place of sensual abandon. A man was to pay very careful attention to his lover's emotional state, otherwise "neither he nor the woman will experience true satisfaction." (Daniélou II-2, p.111) That advice is still as good as gold, but women, who nowadays take more direct initiative in romantic interludes, need to be alert to their men's state of mind as well.

Love Bites

In his erotic manual, *Nagarasarvasva*, the sage Padmashri lists 16 states of mind that women can pass through during the preliminaries leading up to lovemaking. Men were counseled to watch for all of them.

Pay attention to each other's needs and you'll both get exactly what you want. Although it's important to let your lover know what you like, drop your self-absorption and tune in to your partner's desires. It sounds simple, but it works. Very generally speaking, in romantic relationships men want respect and sexual satisfaction and women want adoration and affection. Keep those basic needs in mind when you hook up with your beloved and you'll be well on your way to sweet harmony.

Time for Love

Synchronizing lovers' moods doesn't usually happen instantly. That's why supreme sex is never rushed, except of course, for your supercharged quickies when you're both already hot to trot. Vatsyayana instructed his gentlemen to spend lots of time on the pleasantries of seduction so that a natural symmetry would occur. We suggest you follow his advice—we do.

We set aside several hours, once per week, to be lovers. It's an unhurried time, when we disconnect from the world and focus only on each other. Disconnecting from the world means your cell phones are turned off and your regular phone is on silent answering mode. Your doors are locked and you're not available for interruptions.

For highest quality sex, set a lovers' date together and don't let anything interfere with your rendezvous. By putting the date in your planners, you'll be able to schedule other things around it. If you try to fit each other into the time left over from your busy lives, there won't be any. It's like saving money. If you only save when you have money left over, you'll never save a cent. Pay yourself first! Schedule time together each week to feed your relationship and supercharge your sex life.

Ambience

Okay, so you've decided to get together for some uninterrupted super loving. What's next? Well, even though you can have good sex almost anywhere when you're already up for it, carefully setting the scene is a major mood enhancer. Passion can be piqued by any of your senses—sight, hearing, taste, touch, and smell—as well as by your mind, so appeal to each and every one of them as you create your sensual space.

It's not all that difficult to transform your bedroom for a special love fest. Vatsyayana spelled out very clearly the décor and accoutrements that should be in the skilled lover's room for awakening all your senses. With a little preparation beforehand, you can follow many of the suggestions we make here in a matter of minutes.

Furnishings

It's fun to make love all over the place—on chairs, tables, countertops, the floor—but most people usually like to do it, or at least end up, in bed. In Vatsyayana's day, "pleasure rooms" had a couple of beds, couches, and stools. Today, double, queen, or king beds all give you a goodly amount of room to roll around from pose to pose. But most beds are made with sleep as their first priority and so, unfortunately, mattresses can be too soft to support really creative lovemaking. When you buy a mattress, get one that is as firm as you can handle for both sleep and sex. You can also keep a separate mattress to put directly on the floor for a firmer surface.

Bedframes with posts or headboards are handy for tying your lover to or for grabbing onto when you need a little help with balance. Canopy beds, especially with draperies all around, create a sensuous haven. Buy the best sheets you can afford, of natural fabrics like cotton, which breathe with your skin. The *Kama Sutra's* lovers' bed was "agreeable to the sight, covered with a clean white cloth …

having garlands and bunches of flowers upon it, and a canopy above." (I-4)

Other furnishings to consider for your love nest are:

- A thick soft rug, either wall-to-wall carpet or a large area rug—for playful, on-the-ground tussling.

- An upholstered, straight-backed chair without arms—perfect for more vertical versions of amorous adventures.

- Bedside stands with drawers to hold your lotions, potions, and toys.

- Mirrors, so that you can see how magnificent you are together. Some people are flamboyant about it and put mirrors on their ceilings or cover a whole wall. Others are more modest and install mirrors on the backs of closet doors that can be opened when they want a peek, or purchase portable stand-up mirrors that can be moved about and placed just so for the right view.

  If you're thinking, "Oh my God, no way, I'll look ridiculous," push your boundaries a bit and you'll be amazed at how truly beautiful you become when you're in the throes of lusty loving.

- Exotic or erotic art—paintings, drawings, prints, sculpture. In Vatsyayana's time, walls were painted with beautiful frescoes.

- Pillows, hard and soft, large and small, for head and neck, hips and butt. Standard *Kama Sutra* bedroom décor included large cushions, small, solid pillows, and firm, round bolsters for sensual beauty and comfortable support during lovemaking.

- For the highly adventurous, a love swing. Swings were standard additions to high-class Indian households, and many miniature erotic paintings show lovers sailing through the air and into each other.

Love Bites

Besides pillows, try mix-and-match stackable forms like Liberator® Shapes (www.liberator.com). Made with industrial-strength urethane centers and machine-washable covers, they help make your usual positions better and fantasy positions possible.

In just a few minutes you can transform your everyday bedroom into a sensual *seraglio* with pieces of beautiful cloth. You can find amazing selections on the remnant tables at fabric shops. Drape colorful fabric over hard-edged objects, stuff you just don't want to see, and extra pieces of furniture, especially the television if you must have one in the room. Bring in plants or fresh cut flowers to add beauty, color, and fragrance.

Pillow Talk

A **seraglio** is a sultan's palace. It's also a word for a Turkish harem, a place associated with mystery, intrigue, and sexual adventure.

Color

When you're thinking of redecorating your bedroom, either by painting or papering the walls or by changing curtains, blinds, and bed linens, consider colors that are stimulating to your sex life as well as to a restful slumber.

Certain colors have physical and psychological effects. For instance, red stimulates your sympathetic nervous system, heightening your senses and increasing blood circulation. Red, a color associated with passion, arouses you—burn red candles, put a red cloth over your light or a red bulb in your lamp, place red pillows around the room, scatter red rose petals on your white sheets.

Blue, one of the most popular colors, is calming. It's a great color for meditation and for sleeping, but it won't excite you for hot sex. So if your bedroom is blue, like lots of people's, jazz it up with some hotter colors—reds, oranges, golds—when you want some wide-awake action.

Orange, and its wide palette from salmon to gold, is associated with emotions. These colors create warmth. Golden orange is the color of vitality and is the color associated with your belly chakra. This energy center, about two finger widths below your navel, is your place of power and sexuality. Decorating your room in golden and earthy tones will both soothe and sensualize you.

Stop in the Name of Love

Get that TV out of your bedroom! Couples with bedroom television sets have lots less sex than those without them.

Lighting

Making love in complete darkness, going by sound and feel alone, can be fun occasionally, like when you wake in the dead of night longing for each other. But for supercharged sessions, use at least a little light. Light works wonders for romance. Varieties of lighting create different moods and change how you see and experience. For dramatic effect, place colored lights on the floor to shine up the walls. For mystery, put a soft light behind a sheer, lacy fabric or behind a plant. During your lovers' time, change regular white lightbulbs to rose-colored bulbs. Your skin will look fabulous. Softer, more diffuse, and dimmer lighting is much more flattering than stark, bright light.

Moonlight is magical. On a full moon night, open your curtains and make love by its glow alone. If you're fortunate enough to have a fireplace, make love by its flickering light. Fire combines the security of warmth and light with just a hint of danger. You can get similar effects with candles. Lots of people like to dine by candlelight; bring that same vision to your bedroom as you feast on each other.

Love Bites

Watching firelight can bring on alpha and theta brain states. Alpha brain waves are associated with relaxation, visualization, and creativity. Theta brain waves evoke deep trance states, sexual ecstasy, and shamanic visions.

Music

In Vatsyayana's day there were no CD or MP3 players to instantly pipe in whatever tune turns you on. But music was nevertheless a powerful part of preparation for love. In their bedrooms, gentlemen were encouraged to have a "*lute* hanging from a peg made of the tooth of an elephant." (I-4) Lovers would sing and play music together, because "singing and music are encitements to love. Music reaches the center of female sexuality." (Daniélou II-10, p.211)

Pillow Talk

A **lute** is a stringed musical instrument. One of the oldest Indian types, and likely a kind Vatsyayana referred to, is the simple one-stringed lute (*ekatantri vina* in Sanskrit), made of a gourd penetrated by a stick of bamboo.

Now you're fortunate enough to be able to compel the fullness of a symphony, or the stirring notes of flamenco guitar, or the lyric renderings of solo love songs, at the mere flick of a switch. Some lovers prefer recordings of nature's sounds—ocean waves, summer rain, morning birdsong, wind in the trees. Select music that will run the range of emotion—from relaxing and soothing, to wildly passionate, to sensually soaring. Make sure it's handy when you're ready to rock. And if you're talented, or just plain daring, nothing melts a heart faster than a love song sung just for your beloved.

Scent

Smell is the sense most intensely connected with emotional experiences. It's basic and primitive, controlled by your limbic brain, the simple ancient brain that governs your most primary feelings, such as love, hate, fear, fury, and sexual desire. Just one whiff of the right, or wrong, aroma can turn you on or off.

Although women's sense of smell is keener, men react more to smell as a sexual lure. A woman's natural scent is heaven to her lover's nose. Her aroma changes as she goes through various stages of sexual excitement, pushing his desire higher. When selecting perfumes and lotions to wear for your lover, choose scents that complement your natural body's aroma, not ones that disguise or eliminate it. Decorate your lovers' space with scents as well. Incense, flowers, scented oils, spritzes of perfume, all soothe and intrigue. During the time Vatsyayana wrote the *Kama Sutra*, women used saffron, musk, amber, and sandalwood. They are "all substances whose smell blends with that of the woman and encourages sexual excitation." (Daniélou II-10, p.211)

Stop in the Name of Love

For truly lusty loving, wash your body to make sure it's fresh and clean—but don't use deodorant, either for armpits or genitals. You'll be eliminating a major source of sensual stimulation.

Al's Outlook

One of my favorite erotic turn-ons is to smell Pala's intimate places as she gets more and more sexually aroused during lovemaking. If you haven't done so, sniff your lady all over, with particular attention to the armpits and vulva. I love Pala's *Chanel* perfume, but her natural musk is incomparable.

In addition to a body's natural perfumes or a room's artificial ones, your nose picks up other signals as well—those subconscious seducers, pheromones. Pheromones are chemicals produced by the apocrine glands in your armpits and genitals. They're mating messages that send out a subliminal invitation for sex. Although human pheromones aren't quite as strong as those in other animals, they're powerful enough to create a chemistry that attracts you to someone. As in so many other things, men's and women's pheromones are quite different, designed to tempt each other. Pheromones don't have an actual scent, but sensors in the nasal cavity pick them up. Follow your nose to "scentsual" bliss.

Love Bites

You can now purchase perfumes and colognes containing artificially created pheromones to boost your own allure. There are versions for both men and women.

Wardrobe

"In the sexual life sight is a weapon of primary importance." (Daniélou II-10, p.211) Particular munitions in Vatsyayana's armory of amour were clothing, jewels, and makeup. He firmly believed in elegance of attire for enhancing sex appeal. Women and men alike adorned themselves lavishly for their lovers, in public and in private. The well-dressed man of the *Kama Sutra* wore fine silk and cotton clothes, makeup on eyes and lips, layers of jewelry on ankles, hands, arms, neck, and ears, and garlands of flowers. He also dyed his hair.

Follow their example and dress for love success. Whether you're starting your lovers' time with an evening on the town, or confining your tryst to be exclusively one on one, clothe yourself with your beloved's eyes in mind. If you're at home you can choose a selection of apparel to put on and take off over the course of your night together. You needn't just start with one outfit then end up naked. Different clothes set different moods and enable you to bring out distinct aspects of your personality. You can switch from virginal to voracious, from mysterious to masterful, simply by changing what you're wearing. Learn this special love art: how to gracefully take each other's clothes off—especially with one hand.

Love Bites

Redbook's couples survey revealed that men are more turned on by a woman in sexy lingerie (61 percent) than by one who's naked (39 percent).

Partially dressed is an extremely sexy look on both women and men. The possibilities are inspiring: an oversized dress shirt on him or her, g-strings on him or her, stay-up stockings and elbow-length gloves for her, silk pajama bottoms for him, a see-through cotton dress for her. Let your imagination go. And take this tip from India's ancient beauties: although they removed their clothing for loving, they left their many body ornaments on—earrings, necklaces, bracelets on arms and ankles, rings on fingers and toes.

Action

Now, your intention is established and the scene is set. Do you dive headlong into heavy sex action? No. To create that all-important harmony, take time to connect with each other in nonsexual, but stimulating, sensual, and sexy ways. Make a ceremony of every moment you're together. You're creating a courtship that will culminate in sex so astounding you'll thank your lucky stars that you've got a body.

Pala's Perspective

One of the most common complaints I hear from women is what some of them call "the bull's eye syndrome." That's when their sweeties are already fondling their breasts and yoni, while they're still thinking about whether they want to have sex at all.

Before you start any intensely sexual activity, Vatsyayana advised, you should wait until "the woman is overcome with love and desire." (II-10) He suggested intimate and ribald conversation, games, singing, dancing, making music, eating, and drinking as means to make the heart grow fonder and the body get hotter. We wholeheartedly agree and offer you these ideas that you can make your own.

Love Talk

Beautifully choreographed verbal intercourse can dance you smoothly toward virtuoso sexual intercourse. Charm your lover with words and ideas, and speak your innermost feelings, for the *Kama Sutra* advises that, "though a man loves a girl ever so much, he never succeeds in winning her without a great deal of talking." (III-4)

Lovers' talk is not only minds and mouths, but also a language of the whole body: lips with enchanting smiles speak words of seduction, sparkling eyes add exclamation and excitement, expressive hands punctuate a point with promises of tender touch. Flirtatious, playful, and captivating, that's the type of pre-sex talk Vatsyayana recommended—"an amusing conversation on various subjects," including suggestive topics "not to be mentioned generally in society." (II-10)

Add invitation to your conversation. Break down your lover's barriers by requesting permission to embark on a lovemaking adventure together. Hold hands, gaze into each other's eyes, and speak words from your heart, asking your partner to be your lover.

Sexual desire is such a powerful, even overwhelming, force that often lovers perceive the whole event much too seriously. This is a time to remember that sex is one of the absolutely best forms of adult play. Let yourself enjoy the sheer fun of wanting each other—it's quite all right to be a fool for love. Declaring your love or desire doesn't mean you have to be sedate or grave. Laughter and lust go hand in hand to the true lover's bed.

Eat, Drink, and Be Merry

Sex and food have a lot in common:

* Both are absolutely essential for survival—food for the individual, sex for the human race.
* Both powerfully affect our moods, attitudes, and lifestyles.
* Both are associated with pleasure, shame, and guilt.
* Both can create complete enjoyment or utter discomfort.
* Both can involve all of the five senses.
* Both can be indulged in with the mouth.
* Both can become addictions.
* Both have been considered sinful in Western culture—think back to Genesis and the Adam and Eve story. Eve tempts Adam with the apple. He bites. They suddenly become aware of sex. They're thrown out of the Garden.
* Both eating and lovemaking can be performed ritually and ceremonially.
* Both have a fast food and gourmet variety.

Vatsyayana counseled lovers to ply each other with food and drink before and after lovemaking. In Chapter 12 we give you lots of details about sexy edibles and potables. But here are some basics to consider when you're planning what you'll ingest during long love bouts:

- **Keep it light.** Heavy food, and too much of it, will make you sleepy at best and physically uncomfortable at worst. Wine can enhance both the taste of food and your appreciation of it. Alcohol can loosen your libido, but too much of it makes you foolish, not fetching. Know what your line is and walk it.

- **Appeal to all your senses.** Choose foods that smell appetizing, have interesting textures, taste fabulous, and make you munch with delight. Then present them beautifully, to feed your eyes as well as your tummy.

- **Prepare as much as you can beforehand.** While grilling together can be incredibly steamy, if you've got three hours for loving, you don't want to spend half that time cooking.

- **Be mischievous and audacious with your food.** The way you eat can be enticingly erotic. Seductively peel and suck on a banana. Sensuously slurp an oyster. Lasciviously lick an ice cream cone. Put one end of an asparagus rod in each of your mouths and munch your way to the middle. Use your hands and fingers, a lot. Let yourself be messy—you can always lick your partner clean.

Pala's Perspective

I love it when my darling fills his mouth with warm brandy then kisses me and sends that fiery liquid down my throat. Try it some time—yum, yum.

Blessed Bathing

You can, of course, shower and shave separately, as part of your individual preparations for your hours of romance. But bathing can be much more than a body scrub; it can be a sensual ceremony to elicit passion and playfulness, especially if you do it together. Include a ritual wash early on in your lovemaking. You'll be rinsing away more than physical dirt. You're symbolically cleansing each other of all life's cares, sending that psychic grime down the drain.

Love Bites

Ritual bathing, particularly in the sacred rivers of India, such as the Ganges, is an important part of Hindu practice.

Create an inviting ambience in the bathroom with candles—try scented ones—flowers, and music, just like you've done in your bedroom. Experiment with bubbles, gels, oils, and salts. If it's big enough for two, get in the tub or shower together. If it's not, reach in and serve your mate. Wash each other's hair. Scrub each other's backs. Tenderly clean every inch of your beloved. Dry each other when your bath is complete. Convey respect, as well as desire, in your touch. Combine daring, trust, vulnerability, and power by allowing your lover to shave you, before, during, or after your bath.

Al's Outlook

Letting my lady shave me is at once the most tender and terrifying of acts. What a turn-on!

Shake Your Booty

In ancient India, dancing, music, and theater were more than just entertainment, they were also ways to teach the four aims of life. Courtesans were often exceptional dancers who could arouse and instruct their lovers with their rhythmic displays. Dancing can set modern lovers' internal music flowing, too. Moving your bodies in rhythm together prepares them for that other, more intimate, close encounter. Whether it's fast or slow, the immediacy of the connection is what's important.

In the privacy of your home, you don't need to know the latest dance fad in order to trip the light fantastic with your darling. Put on some romantic music, take your beloved into your arms, and sway. Or turn up the beat, wiggle your hips, and shuffle your feet. Hip swiveling in particular helps you keep a loose *sacrum*, which is important if you want to make the most of sexual intercourse.

Pillow Talk

Your triangle-shaped **sacrum**, fashioned from five fused bones, lies at the base of your spine, just above your tailbone. It connects to your pelvic bones, forming strong joints for good thrusting.

Try one of our favorite dance moves—something we call yin/yang dancing. Put on some slow, romantic music. Melt into each other's arms and begin dancing sensually together. One partner will lead. The other will follow. Partway through the song, the first partner surrenders the lead and the other takes over. Volley back and forth this way through a number of tunes. It's challenging and lighthearted and sexy. And, it's a stand-up form of the give and take talented lovers bring into their bed.

Take matters a step further and give your partner the scintillating surprise of a striptease. Wear clothes that are easy to remove, with buttons or zippers up the front for instance. (Practice in front of a mirror beforehand if you want.) It won't be the perfection of your performance that will thrill your sweetie. It's your daring and caring, and the sight of your body being revealed inch by wriggling inch. While people most often think of women stripping for their guys—just because men are so visually oriented—ladies love it when their lads do the honors, too. So unbuckle, men, it's time for peel and play!

Stop in the Name of Love

Don't hold yourself back from one of life's purest pleasures out of fear that you don't really know how to dance and will look silly. Remember, being uptight and being a great lover are mutually exclusive.

Pictures and Poems

Inspire your mutual desire with images. Look at picture books together—volumes of erotic photographs or collections of exotic drawings, paintings, and sculpture. Pose for each other in particularly appealing stances you find and in various stages of undress. Be especially brave—capture your

impression forever as a Kodak moment. If you like to watch other people, check out short, steamy sections of adult movies.

Vatsyayana attached great importance to the sense of hearing. The sound of a lover's voice has the power to mesmerize, so read aloud to each other. Love poems, both ancient and modern, may motivate you to pen your own. That will definitely elevate your standing on the love roster. Entertain your ears with selections from collections of erotica. Better yet, write your own fantasies and read them aloud to your inamorata. Maybe even go on to act them out together.

The Least You Need to Know

- Supercharged sex involves your mind as well as your body.
- Vatsyayana suggested that to be a great lover you need to know the arts and sciences associated with love as well as the physical techniques.
- Stimulating your senses will awaken your desire for lovemaking.
- Changing your bedroom with light, color, aroma, and music will heighten your sexual experience.
- Engage in sensual, playful, intimate activities before you proceed to explicit sex.

Hug Me, Hold Me, Kiss Me, Lick Me

In This Chapter

- ❧ Vatsyayana's loving embraces
- ❧ The many ways of kissing
- ❧ Special kisses for specific body parts
- ❧ Some unusual erogenous zones
- ❧ How to arouse your lover with massage

Before intercourse, the *Kama Sutra* tells us, Kama, the god of love, "must be invoked, and installed in every part of the body." (Daniélou II-2, p.118) With his usual dedication to detail and his knowledge of the amorous differences between men and women, Vatsyayana provided a selection of desire implanters drawn from the 64 love practices. He offered pointers on the most potent ways to touch and kiss each other, so that Kama would live in you both forever.

Sweet, Embraceable You

When you picture an embrace, you most likely visualize a couple hugging, but any loving physical connection between two people can be an embrace: clasping hands as you walk down the street, twining feet as you sit watching the sunset, linking arms as you drink a romantic toast. It's the contact that counts, and your intention behind it.

Loving touch, especially lots of hugging, snuggling, and sexual activity, releases the relaxing hormone oxytocin into your system. Sometimes referred to as the bonding hormone, oxytocin makes both of you feel very intimate and leaves you wanting to touch, cuddle, and have sex again. Linked to both emotional and physical closeness, it provides a really good incentive to up your embrace quotient!

Love Bites

Because high oxytocin levels in women correspond to lower blood pressure, frequent daily hugging also has big health benefits for females.

Vatsyayana presented 12 specific types of embrace for your skin to savor. The first four are casual and flirtatious, with the promise of much more in their brief touch. The second group are all business—they're focused, intense, and full of longing. The final four refine the art of embracing, illustrating how you can cleave to your lover with particular body parts.

The Flirtatious Four

The purpose of these welcoming caresses is seduction. They signal open interest and a readiness to take things further. Their brevity is the spark that kindles your fire. They make you want to get hotter, but there's no hurry. You bask in the lazy spread of heat. Enjoy these embraces early in your extended loving or *any* time you're near each other. They'll keep your temperature high.

The Rubbing Embrace

The Touching Embrace is a casual, almost accidental, brushing of one lover against the other. It's a light, luring touch that's inviting, but not in the least insistent. Through it you say, "I'm interested, are you?" This approach can be most intriguing to a woman. It can gently steer her thoughts to the possibility of sex with you—not because you want it, but because she'd like it.

With the Piercing Embrace, a woman bends forward and provocatively stabs her lover with her breasts. She's boldly and freely offering them to you, giving you permission to touch them. You hold them for a moment in your happy hands. When she employs the Piercing Embrace, the decision to share her treasures is hers. She feels safe, an equal and respected partner in your love play.

Pala's Perspective

We women don't usually enjoy it when our men amble by and begin to play with our breasts without warning, even if you think it means you love us and find us really beautiful. When we feel appreciated and sexy, we'll share them with you.

The Rubbing Embrace engages both partners in a slow, deliberate rubbing of their bodies together. You're standing up, moving about the room, or maybe walking side by side. Like cats you curl and wriggle against one another—front to front, side to side, front to back. Don't be surprised if you purr.

The Pressing Embrace shows more urgency. It's an eager, amorous attack by one or the other. You back your lover against a wall or into a corner and press your body in tight. There's no grabbing or fumbling—it's a straightforward, momentary, whole body engagement: chest to chest, belly to belly, groin to groin, and thigh to thigh.

Amorous Advances

These next four embraces add a heap of fuel to your smoldering fire. Their intention is clear and direct, "I want to be a whole lot closer to you." Every bit of you is involved in these clinches.

The first two, both standing embraces, are initiated by a woman. They're a signal that all your adoring attention has awakened her excitement and now she's willing to act on it.

In the Twining of a Creeper (*Jataveshtitaka*), you drape your arms around him and cling to him as "a creeper twines round a tree." (II-2) With loving looks, pouty lips, and soft sighs of yearning, you bend his head down for an explosive kiss.

Twining of a Creeper

The Climbing of a Tree (*Vrikshadhirudhaka*) makes it known that your ardor's on the rise. You want to be as close to him as you can and still stay on your feet. Lightly placing one foot over his, you wrap your other leg around him, as if he were a tree you could climb to reach its ripe fruit. With arms around his shoulders, you pull yourself up, asking for a kiss. Your "slight sounds of singing and cooing" (II-2) cajole him to give you what you want.

Climbing of a Tree

The next two embraces increase your heat at least another 20 degrees. Inflamed with desire, you move from standing up to sitting (Mixture of Milk and Water) and lying down (Sesame Seed with Rice). You melt into each other with tender abandon—arms, legs, torsos, and pelvises so closely encased that you become one fiery, sexual celebrant.

These embraces can be intensely passionate precursors to intercourse or, as Vatsyayana suggested, they can actually "take place at the time of sexual union." (II-2) We've decided to follow his advice and have included detailed descriptions of them as intercourse positions in Chapter 8.

Suvarnanabha's Clasping Body Bits

Vatsyayana also described four artful embraces suggested by the sage Suvarnanabha. They're focused on connecting specific, erotic parts of your bodies. *Acupressure points* for sexual arousal or emotional connection are activated with each of these embraces.

Pressing on these points increases circulation, and it's not just your blood that flows more freely. Your body's electrical energy zooms through its now-unblocked circuits with ease. One more benefit of pressure on these points is that endorphins flood into your system, bringing with them a natural euphoria.

Pillow Talk

There are 365 **acupressure points** all over your body, spots that collect tension—both physical and energetic tension. When pressed firmly for a minute or more, the tissues relax and these energy gateways open.

You can think of the Embrace of the Thighs as a "thigh sandwich." One of you vigorously squeezes the other's thigh(s) between your own. The pressure stimulates acupoints in the inside upper thighs that increase sexual desire. It's a move you can employ standing up or lying down.

Chapter 4: Hug Me, Hold Me, Kiss Me, Lick Me

Embrace of the Thighs

Jaghana Embrace

The *Kama Sutra* refers to the middle parts of your body as the *jaghana*. The Jaghana Embrace is a belly and groin mash fest. Pressing tight against each other, you can remain still or slowly grind in a sensual swivel. All kinds of energy spots light up with this one, particularly along your pubic bone. Aware of the passion this embrace evokes, Vatsyayana recommended that you combine it with "scratching with the nail or finger, or biting, or striking, or kissing." (II-2)

The Embrace of the Breasts is a heartfelt and erotic entanglement. You cradle him between your breasts—the site of your heart chakra, your emotional center. Most commonly it's chest to chest, but he'll welcome the opportunity to place any of his parts in that wondrous valley.

With the Embrace of the Forehead you definitely see eye to eye. Another tender expression of desire, this caress can be a still, face-on, head-to-head connection, or an easy exploration of your lover's face with parts of your own. Touching foreheads together opens your third eye to mystical possibility.

Clever Kissing

Vatsyayana was a big fan of kissing and regarded it as a love art of the highest order. He described and named all manner of ways to kiss, what to kiss, and when to do it. Like passion, kisses can vary in intensity, depending on your nature and your state of excitement.

From Chaste …

When you're just getting warmed up, try some of the kisses that Vatsyayana suggested for arousing the inexperienced young woman. They are a little

Embrace of the Breasts

Embrace of the Forehead

Straight Kiss

Turned Kiss

shy, somewhat tentative, and a pleasant change from either a perfunctory, purse-lipped peck or an off-the-bat, deep-tongue dive.

For the Nominal Kiss you hold your mate's head lovingly in your hands and touch your closed lips to his. It's contact only.

The Throbbing Kiss adds a little motion. He pushes his bottom lip into your mouth. Your bottom lip vibrates against his, but your upper lips remain still.

As your interest and enthusiasm build, advance a little further with the Touching Kiss. Run your tongue silkily along his lips.

Love Bites

Pucker up, allergy sufferers! A Japanese study revealed that 30 minutes of passionate kissing relieved both respiratory and skin reactions for partners with allergies.

... To Challenging

For more experienced lovers, Vatsyayana suggested the following kinds of kisses. The Straight Kiss is a head-on lip collision that can be tender or tough depending on your mutual mood.

With heads angled slightly you give each other the Bent Kiss. Try slowly opening and closing your lips in rhythm. No tongue action yet, just lip connection.

The Turned Kiss adds an element of cherishing affection, as you cup your lover's face in your hand. Turn her tenderly toward you for a kiss of rapture.

Some kisses favor one lip or the other. The Pressed and Greatly Pressed Kisses focus on the lower lip. Pressed is just as its name implies: a kiss pressed with great force against your lower lip. With Greatly Pressed, you catch your sweetheart's lower lip in two fingers, tickle it with your tongue, and then press it very strongly with your lower lip. You perform a Clasping Kiss by taking both your lover's lips between your own.

Stop in the Name of Love

Vatsyayana warned women not to use the Clasping Kiss on men with moustaches.

The Kiss of the Upper Lip is a particularly arousing one for women. In it he presses, nibbles, and sucks your upper lip while you do the same to his lower lip.

A woman's upper lip is one of her major hot spots. In her subtle body a nerve connects her upper lip to her clitoris. It's called the Conch Nerve because at the clitoris it spirals around like a conch shell. Visualize an empty tube running from your top lip up to the crown of your head, down to the base of your neck, through your throat, and down through the center of your body to your clitoris. Now, when

your man nibbles on your upper lip, those marvelous vibrations will zip through you to tingle your clitoris.

Love Bites

Practitioners of Tantric sex believe that saliva produced during lovemaking has powerful properties. In deep kissing, lovers exchange these juices, thereby balancing their masculine and feminine energies.

As you well know, kisses aren't just for your lips alone. Tongues can add lots of fun. When you mingle tongues, or use your tongue to caress your lover's lips, teeth, or the inside of your lover's mouth, Vatsyayana called it the Fighting of the Tongue. He also encouraged you to bring your teeth into the battle.

Kiss of the Upper Lip

Special Kisses

The *Kama Sutra* talks of special kisses that are not the mouth-to-mouth variety. There are "four kinds: moderate, contracted, pressed, and soft, according to the different parts of the body which are kissed, for different kinds of kisses are appropriate for different parts of the body." (II-3)

Sama, Moderate Kisses, are middling kinds of kisses: not too hard, not too soft, but just right. Apply them to the forehead, chest, armpits, thighs, and pubis.

Stop in the Name of Love

When kissing, remember not to tense your jaw, neck, face, or mouth. Learn to keep the muscles here relaxed—giving your lover some lip will be so much more fun.

Pidita, Pressed Kisses, are very firm and accompanied by squeezing the flesh of the places your lips linger: cheeks, breasts, navel, buttocks. Aschchita, Contracted Kisses, are light kisses and tickles for your brow, chin, torso, and belly. Mridu, Soft Kisses, are very tender kisses for your neck, breasts, back, and buttocks.

Kissing Games

Vatsyayana believed that playful competition and mini-quarrels increase a couple's ardor. He proposed betting with your baby on who can catch hold of the other's lips first. If you lose, make a fuss and demand a rematch. Later, catch your sweetie on the sly with your lips and teeth and pronounce yourself the winner.

Kiss your playmate all over from top to toe. Then follow your lips with a Tongue Bath. Lick every inch of your partner's body with slow, thick movements, as if you were slowly licking a giant ice cream cone. Begin with the back then do the front, so you can proceed to oral sex or intercourse if you like. If done by a woman, she can give her lover a special treat by kissing him all over with her yoni lips.

Uncommonly Erotic Zones

Vatsyayana was of the opinion that "even those embraces that are not mentioned in the *Kama Shastra* should be practiced … if they are in any way conducive to the increase of lover or passion." (II-2) With that in mind, here are some suggestions for stimulating particular places that are high in erotic charge. You'll note that a couple of them are about as far away from the genitals as you can get— that's because your whole body can be trained to respond ecstatically. Women especially are aroused by nongenital caresses and by multiple points of stimulation—being caressed in many places at the same time. Studies of women's brains during arousal show that there isn't one single sex center but several that are activated.

Men don't get quite the same thrill from this; that's why it's important to let your man know that *you do*. You can follow the advice of the *Kama Sutra* and use your eyes to tell your beloved what areas want attention. If he's paying attention, he'll read your message, and then "he should always make a point of pressing those parts of [your] body on which [you] turn [your] eyes." (II-8)

Love Bites

Sex researcher Dr. Gräfenberg, of G-spot fame (see Chapter 9), found there were so many women's sensitive spots "that we can almost say that there is no part of the female body which does not give sexual response; the partner has only to find the erotogenic zones."

Bodacious Breasts

Men get really turned on by women's breasts—the sight of them, the feel of them, their smell and taste. They love to ogle them with their eyes, knead them with their hands, rub their faces between and all over them, and suckle and nibble on them with lips, teeth, and tongue.

But during lovemaking, your breasts are not just for your man's pleasure; they're integral to your sexual arousal and satisfaction, too. With the right kind of attention, they can even bring you to orgasmic bliss. Learn to love your breasts for the pleasure they can bring you, not just as a pleaser for him. When your breasts are fully alive and pulsing, their energy spontaneously streams to your vagina, causing it to vibrate with receptive pleasure.

Because every woman's breasts respond uniquely to different types of caresses, it's up to you to let your partner know how you like them to be touched. Direct him with encouraging words or show him by touching yourself first and then asking him to follow suit. Give equal attention to both breasts; focusing mostly on one or the other can bring about an energetic imbalance. Feather-light touches work well here, both on breasts and nipples.

Start paying conscious, loving attention to your own breasts. Think about them throughout your day, not just in sexual situations. Endeavor to feel them from within, from the *inside out*. Gently cup them in your palms. Hold them tenderly as you cross your arms beneath them. Love them as they are.

It's natural for the woman's breasts to get the most attention, but don't forget his. His nipples like a bit of tweaking, too. In Chapter 5, you'll find some titillating ways to give nipples big thrills.

Edible Ears

Your earlobes, and the skin of the neck close to them, are often overlooked but are powerfully erotic spots, especially for women. Acclimate your darling's earlobes to erotic sensitivity by sucking, nibbling, and softly squeezing them during foreplay. Once they're "trained," eventually they can even set off an orgasm just by being played with. Earrings, long and heavy ones that brush the neck, can sustain an unconscious sexual arousal.

Stop in the Name of Love

The sound of deep, raspy breathing directly into her ears can be a sexual downer for some women. So, as always, pay careful attention to her response.

Tender Toes

All toes, but especially your big toes, love to be squeezed, licked, sucked, and gently bitten. Besides the erotic sensations this creates, manipulating toes stimulates many important points throughout the body, because most energy pathways have their terminals at toes and fingertips.

Love Bites

Ancient Eastern theories proposed that passion moves from place to place in a woman's body according to the stages of the moon. It starts in her right big toe at the beginning of the new moon and ends at her left big toe as the moon completes its cycle.

Unlikely as it may seem, your big toe might just become her new best friend. A talented toe can work wonders on her clitoris and vulva, and even act as a honey dipper inside her yoni. For external stimulation, use the flat pad of the toe to gently caress and press her tender parts. Make sure your nails are trimmed and clean.

Love Bites

Erotic Indian paintings show the multiple partner "Herd of Cows" position. The emperor is pleasing five women, one with his lingam, two with his fingers, and two with his big toes.

When you're dining out, thrill her by slipping off a shoe and sock and slowly sock it to her under the table. She'll be squirming with delight and no one will be the wiser. Although every diner will want what she's eating.

Rubs and Tugs

Massage helps create that all-important harmony between lovers. Because there are many different massage techniques, it's a great way to both relax the body and excite it, depending on the effect you want. Massage also helps free up any energy blockages within your system.

As with all touch, your intention is vitally important. Send love, healing, and passion through your hands into your beloved. You can give your partner a full-body massage in under 10 minutes, or you can spend an hour or more thoroughly indulging yourself in this wonderful practice.

Vatsyayana's Perspective on Massage

Although Vatsyayana didn't think of massage as part of a standard amorous encounter, he did consider it necessary for a healthful, sensual life. He numbered scalp and body massage among the 64 arts everyone should know, and instructed his readers to have a massage every 2 days. Most modern couples don't have the time or money to dash off to a masseur every Monday, Wednesday, and Friday, so we're offering you some tips on how to give each other the joys of this healing art.

Shampooing, as massage was known then, was an everyday occurrence. Besides full-body massages, which were often performed by servants, people regularly treated each other to hand and foot massages. Vatsyayana suggested that a new husband shampoo his young bride in order to win her confidence and help her become accustomed to his touch.

Love Bites

Because your hands and feet are microcosms of your entire body, you can influence your inner organs and other body parts by massaging your partner's extremities.

Exhilarating Massage

Because we're focusing on zapping you up for supercharged sex, we're concentrating on massages that animate you. But you can use the same type of strokes for either a relaxing or an exhilarating massage. The main difference between unwinding and charging up is the direction in which you work on the body. To calm your lover, stroke in downward motions. And start at the head and massage each part down to the feet. To enliven, stroke up, moving from feet to head.

Exhilarating Massage

Stop in the Name of Love

Don't create an imbalance in your lover's body by massaging one body part and missing its counterpart. Don't rub one foot, one shoulder, one buttock, without giving the other the same attention.

Basic massage strokes include:

- Firm, smooth, long strokes that follow the muscle lines.

- Circling motions, especially where body parts join.

- Kneading, principally for the large muscle groups of thighs, buttocks, back, and shoulders. For kneading, think of bread dough; slowly squeeze the muscle between your palm and fingers. Relax and repeat.

- Excruciatingly light strokes with your fingertips, also known as feathering.

- Placing one hand on each side of a body part—a butt cheek, for example—and rocking back and forth.

Pala's Perspective

Here's a stroke that's both exhilarating and exotic: curve your fingers and spread them a little, so that your fingernail tips rest on your lover's skin and the heels of your palms push firmly into flesh. As you stroke up the body, lead with a light scratch, followed immediately by the firm palm push—heaven.

As you stroke, breathe in rhythm with your lover. It'll increase your connection. Check in from time to time to make sure you're using the right amount of firm pressure. Ask if there's a particular spot that wants more attention.

Both of you focus fully on the body part being manipulated. Don't allow yourself to be distracted by a busy mind. The masseuse concentrates on her feelings for her partner, and pictures that lusty love spreading out through her fingertips, awakening every single inch of his magnificent body. He puts his attention into each cell of his system, allowing it to relax, expand, and vibrate under her loving touch. He can use visualization—an image of flames,

golden sun rays, neon lights, shooting stars moving through his body—to increase his excitation.

Al's Outlook

A full-body massage before intercourse really helps me delay ejaculation. It relaxes all my muscles so I can stay loose and let the energy flow.

Erotic Massage

Erotic massage is all about arousal, so it can often become increasingly sexual as you get further into it. For women especially, erotic massage helps them get out of their heads and into their bodies. A big part of the thrill of erotic massage is light skin-to-skin contact. Mostly, you don't use the firmer strokes of exhilarating massage. Start with featherweight touches at the extremities of her body and work your way inward. For instance, flutter the tips of your fingers from her toes, over her feet, up her calves, past her knees, along her inner thighs, and stop just before you reach her yoni. Or trace lines of love from her fingers, across her palm, along her inner elbow, through her armpit, almost to her nipple. After some time, as she begins to tremble under your teasing touch, she may want you to go on to titillate her tender hot spots. You'll know by the way she arches up to meet your touch.

Don't just use your hands, but employ all the weapons in your love arsenal: lips, tongue, hair, or your entire body. Also known as Thai massage—because they do it so well in Bangkok—body-to-body massage is exquisitely erotic. Well-oiled, lie atop your lover and slide up and down, back and forth. (If you're really heavy and your darling is quite a bit smaller, skip this one.)

Add other exotic implements to your erotic massage as well, like feathers, silk scarves, and ice cubes. If she's willing, add a little danger with a blindfold or restraints.

Pala's Perspective

MinkgLove.com handcrafts massage mitts from mink and other fine fur. I always appreciate Al's tender touch, but a massage with mink makes my skin sing.

Erotic Massage

Massage Oils

According to the *Kama Sutra*, "massage is usually performed with sandalwood. Other products used are musk, saffron, and aloes, mixed with cream … these ointments make the skin supple and luminous." (Daniélou, I-4, p.60)

Today you have a mind-boggling choice of massage products, including creams and lotions and oil-based, water-based, or silicone-based lubricants. When massaging a woman's yoni, it's best to use water-based or silicone-based lubricants, to avoid vaginal infections.

For pressing caresses anywhere on a man's body and everywhere on a woman's except inside her yoni, you can use massage oils or creams—best are those made with *essential oils*, not chemical scents. Or, make your own with a light oil such as safflower, sunflower, or grape seed and a few drops of your favorite essential oils. For invigorating massage, try eucalyptus or citrus oils. For relaxing, lavender is lovely. Ylang-ylang, jasmine, and rose oils are divinely sensual.

Pillow Talk

Essential oils, highly concentrated oils from plants, are used for scenting, flavoring, and healing. Extracted by distillation, pressure, and steeping, they contain the essence of the plant's aroma and flavor.

If you're using any of these lubricants for intercourse, remember that oil-based lubricants will wreak havoc with condoms. Water-based lubricants are safe with condoms and wash off easily. They tend to get very sticky as they dry out, but can be refreshed with a bit of water. Silicone-based lubricants are also safe with condoms, stay slippery until you wash them off, and aren't absorbed into your skin.

Love Bites

There's a brand of oils and lubricants inspired by the *Kama Sutra*. Completely edible, delicately flavored, light, silky, and nongreasy, Kama Sutra Oils of Love are both scents and sensations.

Genital Massage

Give your beloved a very special treat with a long, loving massage focused solely on his genitals. It can be an arousing and healing experience—physically and emotionally. People can store a lot of sexual frustration and tension in their genitals, either from actual sexual trauma or from any unsatisfying sexual activity. Massaging your partner's genitals can help discharge those blocks, so that his sex centers become vibrantly alive and open to ecstatic sensation.

Although their parts are different, the process for men and women is basically the same. Here's a brief outline with a man as receiver:

1. Your lover lies on his back, a towel-covered pillow under his hips.

2. You sit between his legs, which are apart, knees slightly bent.

3. Looking into each other's eyes, breathe slowly and deeply together.

4. Ask permission to honor his lingam, his "wand of light."

5. Gently massage his legs, belly, and torso, moving leisurely to his inner thighs and pelvis.

6. With a quality lubricant, deeply massage the muscles at the top of his inner thighs, in the crease where his legs and pelvic floor meet. Work along the connecting bone and muscles, releasing tension as you go.

7. Move on to the genitals themselves. For a man, start with the perineum, then testicles, and then the lingam. For a woman, begin at the perineum, and then outer lips, inner lips, clitoris, and vaginal canal.

8. Very, very, very slow is the essence of this entire massage. Proceed delicately, inch by loving inch.

Pay careful attention to any responses—physical and emotional. Stop and wait a bit if there's any unease or discomfort. If he wants to go on to ejaculatory climax, dandy. But perhaps he may want to wait a bit and continue with other sexual activity. Or, he might just want to be held in a loving embrace.

The Least You Need to Know

* There are many varieties of embraces, from mild to manic, from full-body clinches to tender pets with special parts.

* Women are highly aroused by multiple points of stimulation.

* Kissing is an art that, done well, elevates both men's and women's sexual temperature.

* A woman's upper lip, her breasts, earlobes, and big toes are particularly erotic zones.

* Massage before intercourse helps a man last longer.

Erotic Inflamers

In This Chapter

- Artful ways to express intense passion
- The difference between fierceness and violence
- How to scratch more than your lover's back
- Eight teeth techniques to thrill your partner
- *Kama Sutra* love blows
- The erotic potential of sound

Vatsyayana knew that loveplay is the ideal field in which to sow your seeds of wildness and ferocity. Likening sex to a quarrel or a battle, he encouraged his readers to explore the power of passion unleashed. But *Kama Sutra* love battles aren't your usual warfare. They're not self-centered fights for control and domination, nor savage altercations wherein you demoralize your foe. Rather they're joyous, lusty skirmishes between two master combatants who relish the clashing of bodies. As equals with complementary skills, you brandish your finely honed weapons to spur each other into love's delirium.

Vatsyayana figured that when you're both utterly overwhelmed by your desire, the laws of love fly out the window and anything goes at any time. But if your passion is, as he says, "middling," and you'd like to boost it to supercharged, add these sparring practices later in your lovemaking close to and during intercourse. You may be amazed at the intensity they invoke.

You've already got all the armaments you need—teeth, nails, fingers, hands, and voice. Here you'll learn how to flourish them like the champions you are.

The F Word

True warriors of love aren't afraid to be fierce, because they know the difference between fierceness and violence. Whereas violence is cowardly and thinks only of itself, fierceness fights within the arena of love and respect. Fierceness *wants* a matched adversary to duel with, not an opponent to use up and be rid of as quickly as possible.

When you bring fierceness into your lovemaking it's an opportunity to step beyond your domesticated daily self and touch the primordial might at your core. Fierceness is a celebration—of your strength, your heat, your healthy animal who feels the power of its body and flaunts it.

Allowing your magnificent inner animal room to roam doesn't mean you'll become a beast. You'll simply become an uninhibited adventurer. Don't be afraid to lose control. Control is the enemy of ecstasy. Mastery is what you're aiming for. Mastery combines absolute abandon with skill and awareness. That's why Vatsyayana wrote the *Kama Sutra*, to help you join the body's consuming urge to mate and the finer sensibilities of mind and heart.

Love Bites

ABC's *Primetime* revealed that couples who consider themselves adventurous make love more frequently, and are 30 percent more likely to say that their sex lives are very exciting than those who are sexually more traditional.

Sometimes men are reluctant to bring out their splendid warrior of love. And who can blame them, when they're continually admonished to try a little tenderness, to woo their women with sweet words and soft caresses. But, as in much of life, timing is everything. Gentleness fits at the beginning, to tune her mind, heart, and body toward sex. Then, when she's ready, it's time for you to be all man. One of women's most common fantasies is to be ravished by a dashing swashbuckler. Why do you think bodice-ripper novels sell so well? Trust yourself: real, self-confident fierceness is a definite turn-on.

Love Bites

25,000 participants on *Queendom.com* indicated that during intercourse, when the Big O is imminent, women like it at least as rough as men. On a gentleness/roughness scale of 1-10, the majority of women called for a 7½, while men slightly over 7.

Women can also shy away from letting loose their innate sexual power. She may fear that, once awakened, her ardor might devour her lover, or worse, repel him. In her fully empowered sexual state, she embodies the Hindu goddess Kali—the black as night, fearless annihilator of illusion and satisfier of all wants. She is the sexual initiatress who represents the transcendent power of sex. Although Kali is awesome, she is also compassionate. By freeing her fierceness, you can transform both of you. Your passion will feed his and you'll have a full-course love feast. The *Kama Sutra* practices featured in this chapter will completely stimulate your sexual appetites.

These inflammatory arts aren't something one person alone inflicts on the other. It's an entirely reciprocal arrangement. Impassioned lovers match each other—scratch for scratch, bite for bite, blow for blow. And, as Vatsyayana pointed out, the more intense forms aren't necessarily for everyone.

Scratch My Back & I'll Scratch Your …

Your fingernails are exceptionally fine fire-starters. "Nails are used for scratching and scraping in the heat of passion, or, by contrast, to show vigor when enthusiasm is lacking." (Daniélou II-4, p.132) During loveplay, light scratches tantalize, while hard presses punctuate moments of extreme enjoyment.

Marks left by nails carry a lover's touch long after lovemaking is over. Poignant reminders of your intoxication with each other, they proudly proclaim, "You're mine!" An artful, well-placed nail print on your body recalls your interludes of love and makes you long for more. That's why Vatsyayana highly recommended leaving nail marks when you're not going to see each other for a while.

Fingernail Fitness

The characteristics Vatsyayana proposed for well-kept fingernails apply today just as much as they did when he was writing. "They are all of the same length, shiny, clean, without broken edges, strong, smooth, nice to look at." (Daniélou II-4, p.133) Nobody wants their body chafed by nails that are ragged and dirty, so include nail care as part of your regular body-care regimen.

Love Bites

During Vatsyayana's day, exceptionally amorous men and women grew the nails of their left hand long—some even shaped them into two or three points. Because the right hand was used for so many other things, it wasn't practical to try to keep those nails long as well.

Today, women tend to pay more attention to the aesthetic appearance of their hands and nails than men. It's part of their sex appeal. But men should do so as well—it's not effeminate to get a good manicure. In fact, giving your man a manicure (or pedicure) can be a sensuous lead-in to sexual activity. As you're filing and buffing, imagine all the wonderful things those hands will be doing for you later.

Nail Trails

Artful lovers learn that different kinds of scratches work well on different body parts, and the *Kama Sutra* gives you a good indication of where to begin. Vatsyayana then suggested that, after some practice, you should use your imagination and create your own variations. Variety's more than the spice of life; it's also the fuel of ongoing erotic interest. Although you can make nail marks just about anywhere, he recommended that these body parts are especially receptive to scratches: your face, lips, throat, armpits, breasts, belly, buttocks, and inner thighs.

Experiment with these nail trails. They run from exquisitely delicate to acutely sharp, and from easy to intricate. Although passionate Indian lovers prized the marks left by forceful fingers, you don't have to press nearly so hard if you don't want to. You'll get super thrills from each of these nail-biters, even if you apply them with a subtle touch that leaves no sign behind.

Sounding, also known as Ripping Silk because of the sound this move may make on your skin, can be used over your entire body. It's a touch so soft "that no scratch or mark is left, but only the hair on the body becomes erect." (II-4) Trace your nails fast or slow along limbs, back, and torso. Women are particularly aroused by this tingle at any time during lovemaking. It's also a great addition to erotic massage. (See Chapter 4.)

To give him a distinctive delight, apply Ripping Silk to his testicles. Gently, gently cup his testicles in your hand and tighten the skin over one, so that it appears you are holding a silky egg. Now delicately scrape your fingernails back and forth along the skin. It drives most men wild.

The Half Moon, as its name suggests, is a simple curvature, a slight crescent, made by pressing with one finger. Experiment with strength of pressure and with different fingers, as you apply the Half Moon to your lover's throat and breasts.

Love Bites

In Vatsyayana's time, a woman wore clothing that exposed her breasts. Marks of love seen there earned her great favor amongst men.

Love Scratches: The Tiger's Claw

Two Half Moons make a Circle. Combine your thumb with any of your other fingernails to leave your love signature on your playmate's belly, buttocks, and groin creases.

The Line is a short, straight mark made by fingers held loosely together and traced over any part of the body. They make an extraordinary enhancement to nice round buttocks.

Curve your fingers, and press straight down with the tips of your nails, to imprint the Tiger's Claw on breasts, face, or neck. This is also stimulating on the back and buttocks, while you pull your lover close with each powerful thrust of intercourse.

The Peacock's Foot "requires a great deal of skill to make properly." (II-4) It's specifically for the nipples. Catch the entire nipple, areola included, between your five nails and, pulling it outward, leave a "sunburst of delicate red rays." (Sinha II-4, p.54)

If your lover enjoys the Peacock's Foot, the Jump of a Hare might be even more thrilling. It's a harder, stronger pull, toward the nipple tip, made first on one breast then the other.

A very adept nail wielder learns to make a mark that looks like the Leaf of a Blue Lotus. These emblems of love are left on the breasts or hips. They require such skill that they were considered "a compliment equivalent to giving a lady jewels." (Sinha, II-4, p.54)

Chew on This

Vatsyayana told lovers that everywhere you kiss you can bite, except "the upper lip, the interior of the mouth, and the eyes." (II-5) Perhaps you already employ your teeth when you're engaged in loveplay. If so, these *Kama Sutra* bites will add polish to your pearly-whites' performance. If not, you may be inspired to try a nibble or two.

Sometimes people are put off when they hear the words bite and lovemaking in the same sentence. They imagine cruelty, torn skin, and pain that's decidedly not pleasurable. But those are not the kinds of bites Vatsysyana suggested. We're speaking

of connoisseurs of love, after all. Although a skilled lover's bites range from gentle to intense, they never break the skin. And they're only given if your partner likes them.

Stop in the Name of Love

Exercise extra caution about biting as you approach orgasm. If it's a particularly intense one, your jaws might go into spasm and you could literally bite off more than you'd ever want to chew.

Tooth Technique

Modern lovers, especially young ones, commonly give each other versions of bites called hickeys. Produced by forcefully sucking and teething the skin, they leave a red or purplish mark that can last for days. Necks seem to be a favorite spot for hickeys—with shades of the erotically charged danger of vampires—but enterprising lovers leave them all over the place.

Love Bites

Bites on the cheeks of the face were always done on the left cheek—the feminine, receptive side of the body. Bite and nail marks on the face were considered to be sensually ornamental.

Expand your toothsome technique with these eight bites practiced by ancient sexual playmates.

- The Hidden Bite, a kind of mild hickey, isn't very forceful. It doesn't leave a lasting mark, but only causes "excessive redness." Your lower lip responds well to Hidden Bites.

- Pressing harder, until you make a soft bruise, produces the Swollen Bite. Vatsyayana especially liked this bite for the lower lip and for cheeks—face cheeks, that is, although it could be quite dandy for butt cheeks, too.

- You make your Point by lightly nipping the skin. Seize a small spot of skin between your teeth and quickly pull, leaving a dot "no bigger than a sesame seed." (Sinha II-4, p.56)

- String together a series of Points and you've got a lovely Line of Points. They'll "look beautiful in the soft skin of her neck, breasts, and the hollows of her thighs." (Sinha II-4, p.56) They make a marvelous badge on the forehead, too.

* You use teeth and lips to create the design of the Coral (lips) and the Jewel (teeth). Squeeze the same bit of skin several times between your top teeth and your bottom lip.

* Coil a chain of Coral Jewel imprints along the throat or thighs and you've patterned a Line of Jewels, also known as a Necklace of Gems.

* Breasts are favored sites for the Broken Cloud, a circle of irregular small tooth marks, "which comes from the space between the teeth." (II-5)

* Broken Cloud and the Biting of the Boar are only made when you're very, very fired up. Boar Bites consist of wide rows of deep marks, close to one another with reddish bruises in the center. They're perfect love brands for firm shoulders.

Indian lovers didn't just bite each other. They'd also place alluring teeth marks on personal items, such as a flower a woman might wear on her ear, or the palm leaves that love letters were written on. They were indications of appreciation for past erotic adventures and signals of joys to come, in much the same way that today's lusty ladies imprint lipstick kisses on love notes.

Dental Hygiene

Just as Vatsyayana suggested you should look after your nails, he also advised maintaining healthy teeth. His ideal teeth were "clean, shiny, even, sharp, well-shaped, and easily colored" with *betel*. (Sinha II-4, p.56) *Kama Sutra* gentlemen were to clean their teeth daily with an exotic mixture that servants made a week ahead of time. Special sticks for brushing teeth were collected in accordance with the cycle of the moon. They were then soaked in a concoction of sandalwood and cow urine, and finally dipped in a blend of black pepper, honey, cinnamon, and cardamom.

It's a lot easier and more appetizing to maintain healthy teeth today. In addition to brushing your

teeth, floss them. It helps prevent bad breath and gum disease. Your lover will be much more inclined to kiss you and consider allowing some love nips if your teeth are appealing.

Pillow Talk

Betel is an evergreen shrub whose leaves have been used for thousands of years to wrap spice mixtures, which, when chewed, produce a red stain. Betel has a wide range of uses: sweetening breath, stimulating heart rate, preventing infection, and treating headaches.

Love Taps

In these times of increased sensitivity to all sorts of violence against women, people tend to steer clear of discussions about smacking each other in bed. Unless, of course, you're talking about the more exotic life of BDSM (bondage, domination, sadism, masochism). Actual BDSM is a well-structured world. And although many people like to flirt a little on its milder edges, like tying each other up so they're at each other's mercy, BDSM is not exactly what Vatsyayana had in mind when he wrote about love blows.

Love Bites

Both pleasure and pain call forth your body's stimulators of natural highs, endorphins.

Kama Sutra hitting practices sound much more violent than they feel when you're fired up for love. Your body's in an entirely different state than it is now, when you're relaxed and reading this book. During supercharged sex, you're more like an athlete who's energized by the bumps and bruises received during the heat of competition. They give you the desire to bump and bruise more. Afterward, any tender twinges you feel are sweet reminders of your all-consuming clash.

Blows are both excitants and expressions of excitement. They extend from mild to wild, just like the

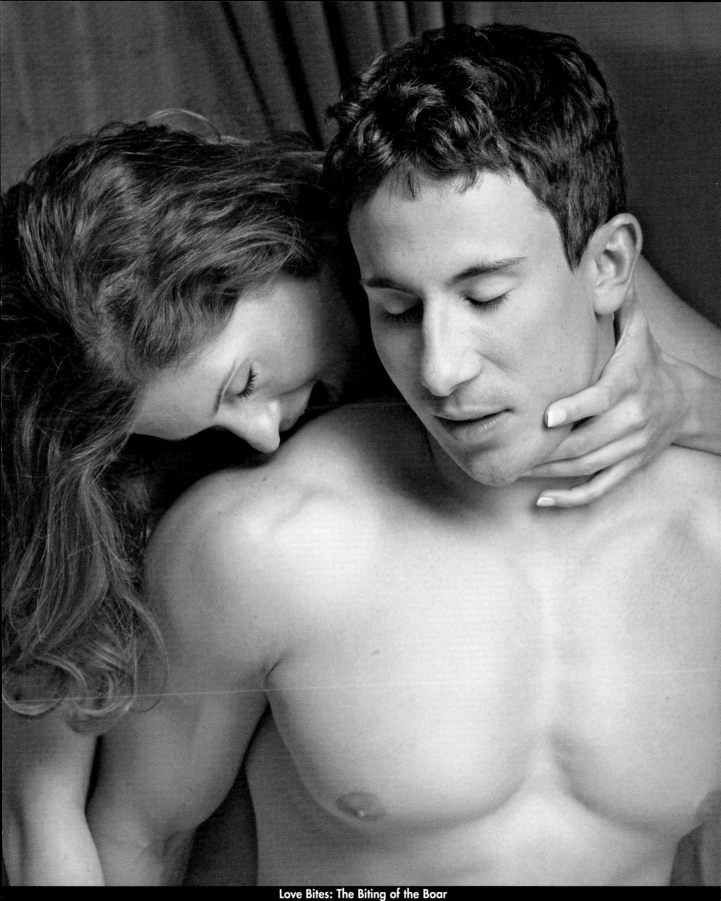

Love Bites: The Biting of the Boar

lovers who apply them. According to Vatsyayana you should introduce love blows during intercourse when you want an extraordinarily explosive outcome. Driven by love's zeal, you might strike each other on the shoulders, head, center of the chest, back, sides, and groin.

Love Bites

Research has shown that during G-spot stimulation women's pain threshold rises by 50 percent. During an orgasm it's increased by a whopping 100 percent.

Love blows are especially effective when combined with particular sounds; in fact, you're listening for certain kinds of responses when you give them. See the next section for what those sounds are and how to make them. Here are a few *Kama Sutra* love taps that you may wish to explore.

There's Apahasta, slaps with the back of the hand, which you begin very slowly and increase in speed and pressure as excitement mounts. An effective spot for this type of blow is the center of the chest. Taps here stimulate your heart energy center, increasing your emotional interaction.

Prasritaka is a special type of tap to the head. You curl your fingers in the shape of a cobra head, and lightly (or more forcefully, depending or your sweetheart's tastes) rap your lover's skull with it. Vatsyayana suggested using it as a special ecstasy wake-up call if Apahasta hits don't deliver quite enough gusto.

Love Blows: Samatala—The Open Palm

Samatala is an open-palmed slap, the kind used for spanking. Depending on the vigor of your loveplay, it can be relaxed or raunchy. The crisp sound of palm to skin is extremely erotic, and you don't have to hit hard to make big noise. You can give one light spank on the buttocks, or a whole series, like the rhythm of a snare drum, first one cheek then the other. Women may find they enjoy Samatala most during rear-entry positions. It's easiest to give a man these love smacks when he's in man-on-top poses or when you're standing up.

You can also pummel your partner lightly with your closed fists. Buttocks, back, and thighs are partial to such treatment. Think of a really good Swedish massage, with its thorough thumping of big muscle groups, and you'll get a good idea of the proper technique. Appendix D teaches you four more love taps from the *Ananga Ranga*.

Aural Sex: Sounds and Sighs

Ah, the sounds of love! From sighs to cries, each makes its own music to our ears. Women, particularly, are affected by sounds; that's one of the reasons Vatsyayana attributed such importance to hearing. According to the *Kama Sutra*, "women find an emotional attraction in the sound of their lover's voice [and] can be hypnotized by" it. (Daniélou II-10, p.211)

Making sound while you're making love serves more than one purpose:

* It lets your partner know your state of arousal.

* It helps you let go of control.

* It facilitates moving your sexual energy throughout your whole body.

* It releases emotional blocks.

Depending on the particular sound you're making, it brings different emotional and energetic qualities to your experience.

To Moan or Not to Moan

Some people just naturally let loose their voices when they're having sex. They moan, whimper, roar, laugh, and sing. Others are much quieter. Muted murmurs and the occasional grunt are all that pass by their lips. It doesn't really matter the amount or level of noise you make; there's no absolutely right degree of sound. What's important is that you be real and free with your noise effects. If being quiet is your true nature, rest easy with it, as long as you make sure your lover can tell what's pleasing you. But, if you're suppressing an innate boisterousness because you're afraid, ashamed, or embarrassed, it's time to reassess your approach. Remember, sex is good, and if even a small part of you holds something back out of shame or guilt, you won't receive the pleasure you deserve.

Pala's Perspective

I'm often astounded that couples allow themselves to argue, sometimes loudly and vehemently, in front of family and friends. Yet heaven forbid those same people should hear them making the life-affirming, relationship-building sounds of love.

It can be difficult to begin making sounds or to increase their frequency and volume. After all, like many others, you've probably been conditioned to be fairly quiet and self-responsible, to act like a grown-up in most aspects of life, not just during sex. But a thoroughly enjoyable sex life doesn't allow itself to be limited by those anti-pleasure rules.

If you would like to become more vocal but are uncomfortable about it, practice first in sensual, but nonsexual, situations.

* **Breathe out loud.** Take a deep breath and, as you exhale, let the air ride out on a sonic wave.

* **Eat something irresistible.** Savor the flavor and hum your appreciation.

* **Stretch your body.** Feel the pleasure of release and relaxation. Let it rise up from your belly and out through your lips.

As you become more at ease making pleasure sounds, gradually add them to your lovemaking.

Love Bites

In a *Cosmopolitan* survey, 47 percent of men said that the way their partners could make intercourse "mind-blowing" was to make sounds.

Although we encourage you to make sound during lovemaking, we aren't suggesting you abandon common sense or consideration for others. It's not a good idea for apartment dwellers or couples with children to have screaming sex at 3 o'clock in the morning. In the daytime and early evening, let yourself go—there's often lots of other sound going on around you—TVs, radio, traffic. If you want to camouflage your fanfare, play music. It adds ambience as well. You can also deaden your din with thick rugs on bedroom walls and ceiling, not only floors. You can squeal into a pillow, press your face into your lover's chest, or cover your mouth with your hands.

Stop in the Name of Love

Court cases in Sweden, England, and Canada affirmed the rights of lovers to make lots of sound during the day or evening. But the judges also ruled that, if excessively loud at night, such noises were cause for eviction.

Sexy Talk

Lovers' vocalizations needn't be restricted to inarticulate sounds; words have their ways of arousal and release, too. At the moment of orgasm, throughout the ages and around the world, lovers have consistently called on their parents, wailed of death, or referenced religion. Whether whispered in an ear or cried out into space, words can take your lover's breath away and yours with it. Thrill your mate with erotic fantasies as you're caressing private places. Combine words of endearment with words of excitement. Appreciative words, affirming words, crude words all have their place in the adventurous lover's vocabulary. You'll never know what works for you until you try it.

Stop in the Name of Love

Never, never discourage your love's uninhibited wordplay by later referring to what was said in the bedroom in a negative or ridiculing way.

Conscious Sound

In addition to wails and words that escape unbidden from your lips, you can further refine your aural art by consciously making specific sounds. Vatsyayana listed the following sounds for a woman to articulate during intercourse, building up to orgasm. "The sequence, which should be learned, shades from pleasure to pain to deeper pleasure." (Sinha, II-7, p.80)

* Hinkara, a ragged, indrawn, nasal breath accompanies Apahasta slaps to the heart center.

* As excitement continues to build, she emits Kryita, a sound like doves cooing.

* Then Stanita, the "roll of thunder," a deep and resonant haaaa.

* Prasritaka strikes call forth Phutkrita, a forceful expulsion of breath like the sound of a "berry falling in water."

* Dutkrita is a cry of painful pleasure, like the "sound of bamboo splitting."

- Rudita, the weeping sobs of orgasm, are followed by …
- Sutkrita, the panting sighs of satisfaction.

This sequence of sounds indicates to her lover where she is on her path of passion, which is a really good idea. Extraordinary lovers give each other recognizable signals. They also pay very close attention to those markers along the road to bliss. A man can respond to such cries with similar sounds, teasing her on to greater heights. Or he may utter his own special brand of love language.

Love Bites

If you'd like some inspiration for your noisemaking, you can purchase CDs of recorded sex sounds. There are also entire music CDs, by artists like Jessica Vale and the Venetian Snares, that include actual lovemaking sounds as integral parts of their tunes. For those times you're on your own and want some aural sex to augment your self-pleasuring, there's the Talking Head Vibrator. It comes with audio chips of pre-recorded erotic scenarios.

Both Indian and Chinese erotic manuals focus quite a bit on women and sound. That's because hearing sound turns women on and making sound urges them toward euphoria. In those texts women were encouraged to mimic the songs of birds. In addition to the cooing dove, the *Kama Sutra* suggested the sounds of "the cuckoo, the green pigeon, the parrot, the bee, the sparrow, the flamingo, the duck, and the quail." (II-7) Making bird sounds carries your spirit upward toward the heavens.

As with all the techniques we mention, if you feel a little self-conscious about warbling in your lover's ear, practice beforehand. Get a feel for letting your vocal chords soar. You'll be surprised, though, at the difference in quality when you're only practicing and when you're actually making these sounds in the throes of ecstasy. You'll truly hear the music of the spheres.

Chanting is another way to channel sound during lovemaking. Focus and direct your sexual charge with chants, either when you're relatively still in sitting postures, or match them to the rhythm of your thrusts. Chanting together will harmonize and unite you with your beloved. Try the simple, yet powerful Om, the supreme mantra of meditation.

Silence Is Golden

Amidst all this talk of sighs, cries, and coos, let's not forget silence. Sometimes it's astounding to consciously contain your sound. We're not talking about repressing it for fearful reasons, but about tapping into the power of that internal tumult. Feel the beat and direct the vibrations throughout your body. You'll heighten your touch sense both inside and out. And when you're quiet, your ears can tune into other tones, like the scintillating slide of skin against skin.

The Least You Need to Know

- As they approach orgasm during intercourse, both men and women can enjoy a fairly high degree of roughness.
- Always, always consider you partner's desires when introducing fiercer play into your lovemaking.
- Using your teeth and nails is both an expression of your excitement and a way to increase your passion.
- Scratching, biting, and striking are refined love arts.
- Making sound during lovemaking enhances your experience on many levels.

Lickable Lingam and Yummy Yoni

6

In This Chapter

- Common concerns about oral sex and how to overcome them
- The three keys to pleasing him orally
- Eight *Kama Sutra* techniques for fabulous fellatio
- Explore the most comfortable positions for oral sex
- The three most important factors for giving her great genital kisses
- The ancient Indian love manual techniques for clever cunnilingus

Oral sex—the sensual gourmet's favorite feast. Most modern bedmates include it as part of their banquet of love, at least occasionally. And for some, oral sex is more intimate than intercourse. Whether you're an habitué of your beloved's body buffet or just an occasional visitor, you'll find morsels on our menu to whet even the most sophisticated appetite.

All About Dining Out

Although oral sex has probably been around since people discovered their mouths could do more than grunt and chew, cultural attitudes about it certainly haven't remained constant. Like many sexual acts, it's been reviled as well as applauded. These days oral sex is more than just accepted, it's sexually fashionable.

Love Bites

A U.S. government study revealed that over 50 percent of teenagers aged 15 to 19 have participated in oral sex. That includes almost a quarter of those who haven't yet had intercourse.

Women certainly agree that, for most of them, it's the easiest way to reach orgasm. And that's probably one of the reasons they prefer being on the menu to being the diner. Men, on the other hand, are about equally turned on by devouring as by being devoured.

Vatsyayana's Views

Auparishtaka, or "mouth congress," also translated as *superior coition*, was considered improper in most, but not all, areas of the country during Vatsyayana's day. According to standard Holy Writ, oral sex was "contrary to morals and is not a civilized practice. One is defiled by the contact of the sex with the face. … The manner of embracing the vulva as one embraces the mouth is not recommended." (Daniélou II-9, p. 188, 192) It was also deemed abnormal for the mouth to do the "work of the vagina."

Pillow Talk

Superior coition refers to the fact that your mouth is higher up your body than your genitals. It doesn't imply more pleasure or higher moral value.

Surprisingly, in a society with so much sexual tolerance, mouth congress was regarded as a pastime of disreputable characters, not something respectable men and women should practice. That sure didn't stop people from enjoying it, though. (Has it ever?) Women in harems shared it with each other. Regular citizens received oral sex from eunuchs, serving girls, prostitutes, and "corrupt" women. And no matter how indecent it may have seemed, people were well aware of the persuasiveness of outstanding oral sex. "For the sake of such things courtesans abandon men possessed of good qualities, liberal and clever, and become attached to low persons, such as slaves and elephant drivers." (II-9)

Because there was such difference of opinion in moral codes, local customs, and personal preferences, open-minded Vatsyayana suggested that, "in all these things connected with love, everybody should act according to the custom of his country and his own inclination." (II-9) Words to live by!

Modern Perspectives

Acceptance of oral sex came slowly into the mainstream of Western culture. John Cleland's classic erotic novel *Fanny Hill: Memoirs of a Woman of Pleasure* (1749) included lesbian and homosexual coupling, but no oral sex. Even up into the twentieth century, sexuality guides, modestly referred to as "marriage manuals," excluded any discussion of it at all. Alex Comfort's *The Joy of Sex*, published in 1972, was the first widely distributed manual to present oral sex as a normal part of healthy sexuality for heterosexual couples. Now there are innumerable books, ebooks, audio and video recordings, Internet sites, and personal seminars devoted to the fine art of making mouth music.

Love Bites

If you want to add some savor to the flavor of your semen, eat pineapple, strawberries, melons, celery, or pears a few hours before lovemaking.

Common Concerns

Although people are generally pretty enthusiastic about it, they can also have a few reservations. Here are some common reasons why you might refrain from asking for or offering to perform oral sex.

- "I don't know how." After reading this chapter, you'll certainly know enough to get started on an exciting learning journey.

- "It's disgusting." This usually means that somewhere along the way you've picked up the erroneous idea that genitals are dirty. Actually they're cleaner than your mouth, unless you simply don't take care of yourself. Wash well and remember not to apply deodorizer to your genitals. It'll cover your natural musk—nature's sexiest scent.

You could also be put off by the copious fluids involved—saliva, vaginal lubrication and ejaculate, and male semen. If so, you might try to shift your perspective and experience them the way Tantric and Taoist sexual masters do: as the juice of life, divine nectar packed with all manner of beneficial goodies.

- "I'm embarrassed or ashamed of my body down there." Generally, this is the case more for women than men. A man could think his penis is too small, or crooked, or his testicles are odd, or his foreskin (if he has one) isn't attractive. But there's an overall societal acceptance of phalluses as powerful and awe-inspiring. Sadly, this isn't the case for women's genitals. Although long ago they were honored as the gate of life, more current perception has been that they're smelly, dirty, and ugly.

It's up to you to relearn respect and appreciation for this pleasure-giving part of you. Take a long, loving look at yourself with a mirror and admire your uniqueness. There are lots of differences among genitals—size, color, shape, scent—but there's no ideal penis or vagina. Love mates can help their partners be more comfortable with their genitals by showing appreciation and desire for those sensitive, sexy spots.

- "It's physically uncomfortable for me." This is usually an objection that women make about giving oral sex, and it's mostly because they haven't learned the intricacies of accepting such a large object into their mouths and keeping it there for a while. After you read this

chapter (and practice a little), you'll find you're not only more comfortable, but you're actually enjoying the action.

Pala's Perspective

I'm appalled that the most recent cosmetic surgery fad is designer vaginas. Sure, some women have problems that require surgical intervention, but most of us are functional and beautiful as we are. We don't need to be nipped and tucked to meet some artificial, symmetrical ideal.

Preparing for the Party

Any great dinner party demands at least a little preparation. Well, the same is true for your oral sex feast. If you're receiving, there's the all-important washing up, a quick and simple procedure with mild soap and water. The inside of the vagina doesn't need any purifier, by the way; it's self-cleaning. But you might also entertain the idea of trimming, shaving, or waxing pubic hair. It's an entirely personal preference. Why not ask your darling for an opinion? Vatsyayana suggested that well-bred townsmen should shave their pubic hair every 5 to 10 days.

If you're the giver, think about doing a few jaw, mouth, and tongue stretches to loosen your facial muscles before you begin. You'll be able to pleasure your lover longer if you can keep these muscles relaxed.

Love Bites

For the eager oral-sex aficionado, there's Tongue Kung Fu, a series of tongue exercises that strengthen this amazing muscle. Mantak Chia's *Taoist Secrets of Love* provides detailed instructions.

For those practicing safer sex, there's also the question of dental dams and condoms. If you don't have a dental dam for vaginal or anal kisses, plastic food wrap will do in a pinch. And a woman who's well versed in the arts of love will know how to put a condom on with her mouth. It's not a difficult skill to master.

Saliva is the best lubricant for any kind of sex action, but sometimes you need a little extra wetness. You might also want to experience different flavors, especially if you're using a condom. Many water-based lubricants have flavors like Piña Colada, Vanilla, and Berry, which can add sweetness and spice to oral sex.

For Him: Fellatio

Men are full of contradictions when it comes to oral sex. They long for it, dream about it, even wet-dream about it, and never seem to get enough, but at the same time they can fear the very thing they desire. For one thing, fellatio could bring him to almost instant ejaculation, which can be extremely frustrating and downright embarrassing, or it might make him too self-conscious to reach orgasm. He might even have a subconscious fear of being devoured by an insatiable woman.

So men, it's important for you to find ways to communicate to your lady what you like and don't like—talk about it beforehand, make sounds, use body language, or even get a dildo and show her. Whatever works to get your message across in a manner that's respectful, encouraging, and good-humored. If you reveal all your feelings about fellatio, not just your aching desire for it, she'll be much more inclined to give you just what you want.

Sometimes women are reluctant to play their lover's flute because they regard it as a submissive act. They feel dominated and used. But such sentiments have as much to do with your perception as it does with his. If you learn some sucking skills and take an assertive, playful part, you'll soon find that you're the one in charge, orchestrating his pleasure.

Occasionally live out his fantasy of fast and furious fellatio. But most of the time, he'll probably prefer a slow, seductive sucking that lasts and lasts and lasts. When you take him into your luscious mouth, exploring with pouty lips and probing tongue, beware of frightening him with an immediate, voracious, gobbling hunger. If your man tends to come very quickly, pace him with a leisurely, tender build-up. Pay attention to his signals so you'll know right where he's at, all the time.

The Three Keys of Male Mouth Music

Giving great head is just about as easy as one, two, three:

1. **Show your enthusiasm.** He loves his big fella and he wants you to love him, too. A good start is to undo his pants, reach in, and take hold of his testicles in one hand and his penis in the other. Then, while holding his precious jewels, rise up and kiss him passionately on the mouth. Don't dive right in just yet; take a good long look at his penis, not as if it were a specimen in a medical examination, but, rather, candy for your eyes. Let him know how you appreciate and admire his manliness and beauty. Talk directly to his lingam, as if it were a person, and tell him about the wonderful pleasure you're going to give him.

2. **Make eye contact.** Sometimes he'll close his eyes and savor the sensations. But men love to look, so he'll be watching you a lot. It'll blast him bone deep if you occasionally look up from your ministrations and meet his eyes. Be bold and sassy. Let him see how well you handle things and how much you're enjoying it. A few happy, slurping sounds are good indicators, too.

3. **Use more than your mouth.** Mouth and hands together can accomplish much more than your mouth alone, no matter how deep you can swallow. Hands can tickle his testicles, stroke his anus, massage his perineum, press acupressure spots. And if you're worried that he wants to go farther in than you're comfortable with, wrap your hands firmly around the shaft and you can guide him to just the right depth.

Love Bites

Cosmo asked men, "What's the biggest mistake a woman can make when performing fellatio?" The most frequent response (32.3 percent) was, "Not incorporating her hands."

Boys' Anatomy Just for Girls

If you want to make really magnificent mouth music, it's important to know the instrument you're playing. Learn these parts and their role in his pleasure.

glans penis   Head of the penis.

foreskin, or **prepuce**   Layer of skin covering the glans in men who are not circumcised. It pulls back when he's erect.

corona   The ridge of skin near the tip of the penis where the glans joins the shaft of the penis.

frenulum   A layer of loose bunched flesh on the underside of the penis at the point just below the corona that connects the glans and the shaft of the penis.

The glans, corona, and frenulum are the most sensitive parts of the entire package. If you focus all your handiwork here, especially licking or sucking hard, he'll be finished before you know it, so spread your attentions around.

urethra   Tube through which urine and semen leave the body.

meatus   Opening of the urethra at the tip of the penis. Don't blow or put anything into the meatus, except maybe the tip of your tongue.

shaft   The body of the penis, whose spongy tissue engorges with blood during arousal and becomes rigid. There aren't many nerve endings in the shaft, so it's much less sensitive. A firm handgrip does wonders here.

testes, or **testicles**   Male sexual glands that produce testosterone and sperm. Testicles love the right kind of attention—gentle, gentle, gentle tugs, kisses, and scratches. Many men love to have their testicles licked and then taken into your mouth. They pull up close to his body just before he's going to ejaculate, so this is a good signal for you.

scrotum   The sac containing the testicles, which maintains their temperature at approximately 93.2° Fahrenheit (34° Celsius) to keep those sperm happy and healthy.

anus   The muscular ring at the entrance to his rectum. There's lots of nerve endings here; try a few light tickles. Some men enjoy penetration with a playful pinky finger.

prostate   A gland that produces part of the ejaculate fluid. During ejaculatory orgasm it goes into spasm, causing that fluid to be forcefully expelled.

perineum   The patch of skin between the testicles and anus. The prostate's right under here. Firmly massaging this spot will feel good, and it can help keep the prostate relaxed so he might last longer.

Love Bites

During Vatsyayana's time, many men were treated to oral sex during their regular massages. Masseurs were often gay men or eunuchs.

Lickable Lingam

Positions for His Pleasure

Because he'd love it if you'd lick his lingam for more than a minute or two, it's really important that you're both comfortable. You want to focus on pleasurable sensations, not be distracted by a cramp in your neck.

Experiment with these positions to determine which work best for both of you.

- He stands and you sit. A low stool or ottoman can put your head at exactly the right height. Your hands are free to pet him—you can reach just about anywhere—and to hold his hips in case he wants to thrust more than you'd like.

- He sits, you kneel. Although not quite as comfortable because of the slightly different angle of your neck and head, it's definitely a very workable pose. You'll also have great control of all the action.

- You lie on your back with your head over the edge of the bed and he stands behind your head. This is a fabulous position for deepthroating, because it puts your mouth and throat nearly in a straight line, rather than the usual 90 degree turn. But it's a vulnerable position in which you have very little control. You need lots of trust. He needs some restraint.

- He lies on his back, you sit or lie between his legs. It's a pretty easy pose for both of you, especially for longer bouts, and he can have a good picture of the proceedings.

- He lies on his back, you kneel by his head. This reverse pose makes it easier for you to take him farther into your mouth. Plus, he may like seeing a different side of you.

- You lie on your back, he kneels over you, his thighs straddling you. Although fairly comfy for your body, it's another position that requires lots of trust and communication, so you won't feel as if you're going to be smothered.

Stop in the Name of Love

No matter how overwhelming the urge may seem, unless she's given you the okay, don't grab her head and thrust deeply down her throat. It can make her choke and gag and it's one of the reasons women aren't always keen on fellatio.

Kama Sutra Sequence

The forms of fellatio are as varied as the people who practice it. Vatsyayana's take on this ancient art was a series of eight movements. After starting out soft and slow, each ensuing action adds more gusto. "Striking, scratching, and other things may also be done during this kind of congress." (II-9) You can follow the sequence in part, selecting one or more mouth moves, or you can nudge him all the way through to the climactic finale. Take a short break between each maneuver, time for him to calm down and long for more, and for you to rest.

Love Bites

Add flavor and sensation to your sucking with an Altoid mint or two, an ice cube, a frozen berry, a small mouthful of warm cognac, or bubbly champagne.

1. **Nimita, Nominal Congress:** After your admiring and enthusiastic inspection, begin by holding the shaft of his lovely lingam firmly, but gently, in your hand. Make an appealing O with our mouth—your lips are a soft circle, relaxed and wet. Slowly slip the glans of his penis between your lips. Keeping your mouth loose, circle your head around his "head." Or, you can remain still and tenderly twirl his penis inside your mouth.

2. **Parshvatoddashta, Biting at the Sides:** Curl your supple fingers around the head of his lingam, "like the bud of a flower." (II-9) Moving your head up, down, and along the sides of his shaft, cover it with firm kisses. Incorporate your teeth, but do it very carefully. As you press with your open mouth, bear down ever so lightly with your teeth. You may have to

switch hands to be able to cover all sides with your kisses.

3. **Bahiha-samdansha, Pressing Outside:** Move your hand back to holding his shaft and slide his glans into your mouth. Glide your hand up and down in leisurely movements, as you press your lips around his head just below the coronal ridge. Then add a minimal sucking motion. Alternate—slight suck, lip press, slight suck, lip press. Don't use your tongue or teeth, just your lips.

Pala's Perspective

There's an exciting energy spot where the soft and hard palates meet at the roof of the mouth. When I'm really, really excited and charged up with sexual energy, holding the head of my love's penis against this spot, in the Pressing Inside move, sends waves of electric pleasure from my mouth through my entire body.

4. **Antaha, Pressing Inside:** Settle your mouth down a little farther so that you're surrounding all of his head and part of the shaft. Firmly tighten your mouth around his mighty member and hold it for a few seconds. Then, with your lips exerting medium pressure, slide back so that only his very tip remains between them. Glide back down, hold, and repeat. You're mimicking the vaginal Mare's Trick with your mouth. (See Chapter 7.) Add a little extra by lazily pulling his testicles down in rhythm with your mouth slides.

5. **Chumbitaka, Kissing:** To give him a little respite from the intensity of your attention to his glans, switch your focus once again to his shaft. Cradle him in your palm and kiss him all up and down his length, only this time much more ardently. Suck his sides as if you were drawing his lower lip into your mouth. Use your other hand to massage his perineum.

6. **Parimrshtaka, Rubbing:** Your speed and zeal are building along with his excitement, as you switch from lips to tongue. Lave his shaft with a variety of licks—long, flat-tongued slurps; short, firm-tongued flicks; circles around; or

slitherings up and down. Remember to include his glans, coronal ridge, and frenulum in your frenzied flickering. Try licking in one continuous motion from the skin between the two testicles all the way to the meatus. Hold the base of his penis in your hands and press the edges of your little fingers against his pubic bone. You're activating Crooked Bone and Transverse Bone, acupoints that will increase his sexual energy.

7. **Amrachushita, Sucking a Mango:** You've moved back again to taking his penis into your mouth. This time endeavor to take half his length comfortably inside you. Squeeze sturdily with your lips and, using the base of your tongue, suck him sweetly "as when sucking the juice of a mango." (Daniélou, II-9, p.187) Steady his penis with your fingertips as you press the heel of your palms into his groin creases. In the middle of these creases, where his legs join his body, are the acupressure points Rushing Door and Mansion Cottage. They perk up sensations throughout his genitals.

8. **Sangara, Swallowed Whole:** Just as its name implies, this move involves taking his penis as far into your mouth as you can. Circle your hands round the base of his shaft if you can't fit all of him in. Press hard with your lips. Lick and suck rapidly. Move your hands up and down as your head bobs up and down. This can be his explosive finale. You can continue on until he comes, or stop, let him calm enough so he won't fire off immediately, and move on to some other engaging activity—like intercourse or mouth congress for you.

Love Bites

For monogamous lovers who don't need to use protection, besides making him feel like you love every bit of him, here's added reason to swallow. Seminal plasma contains calcium, zinc, and other minerals shown to help prevent tooth decay.

For Her: Cunnilingus

Because her clitoris is directly stimulated during cunnilingus, it's the most surefire way to bring a woman to climax. You can understand why women rate it so high on their list of sexual pleasures. But despite their delight about receiving oral sex, they can also have a few fears about it. Mostly they worry about their partner's enjoyment and the length of time he must spend giving them oral caresses so they can reach orgasm. Due to that "dirty, smelly, ugly" training, they wonder, "How can he possibly like staying down there so long?"

Well, ladies, if you're concerned, remember in Chapter 3 we told you that your vagina produces female pheromones that he senses through his nose. Relax and enjoy every minute of his attention. He's chemically programmed to want to have his face at your pleasure-treasure cove.

Love Bites

Wu Zetian, the only female Chinese emperor, instituted a law in the seventh century requiring all court appointees and visiting dignitaries to worship at her throne by performing cunnilingus on her royal yoni. Paintings still exist showing the empress holding her robe open while a dignitary kneels before her to lick her genitals.

Women can also be shy to ask for precisely what they want you to do with your magic tongue. Let her know you'd love her to give you a few pointers. Then listen closely and follow her suggestions.

The Three Keys of Female Mouth Music

You'll please her always if you remember these three simple oral sex suggestions:

1. **Let her know you like it.** Reassure her before, during, and after. Tell her you love her succulent peach, that her juices are ambrosia. Make contented m-m-m-munching sounds as you lick and kiss her.

2. **Take your time.** Eating your goddess is one of the great banquets of your life—not a fast food sprint, but a gourmand's spread. Start out slowly and gently, and then gradually, gradually, gradually build up speed and pressure.

3. **Find the right move and keep at it.** When you find a stroke that's working, keep on doing it exactly the same way; don't change a thing. After you've been pleasuring her for a while and you can see she's building toward an orgasm, settle on a tongue stroke that she really seems to be enjoying. Continue that same movement, over and over, without any variation in speed, pressure, or location.

So often a woman will be close to coming, and her loving partner, eager to please thinks, "Wow, if this is so good, I bet a little harder, a little faster, or a little over here will be even better." But, when he makes his shift, instead of falling over the edge into ecstasy, she falls back down to ground zero. Stand fast and be consistent.

Girls' Anatomy Just for Boys

The lover's art of cunnilingus requires that you know your way around the yoni, including all its juicy pleasure places. You'll be well rewarded if you linger to play at all of them.

mons veneris The soft mound of fatty flesh that pads the pubic bone. It responds well to pressure with your fingers or palm.

labia majora and labia minora In Latin *labium* means lip; two of them are labia. Labia majora are the two large, lip-like bulges on both sides of her vaginal opening. Spread them apart and you'll see her labia minora, her inner lips. Both sets become engorged with blood as sexual arousal builds. They love to be licked, sucked, and nibbled on.

clitoris It's at the top of the vulva, above the opening of the vagina. If you were looking at the vulva as if it were a clock, the clitoris is at 12:00. Its only function is pleasure and it's a lot bigger than you might think. The visible tip of the clitoris is called the glans clitoris, which is normally covered by a

layer of tissue called the prepuce, hood or clitoral hood. The prepuce is similar to the foreskin of a man's penis.

The clitoral shaft extends into the body, angling down toward the vagina, where it splits into the two roots known as *crure* (crura is singular), composed primarily of erectile tissue. The crure extend around both sides of the vagina and end in two lubricating bulbous glands (vestibular bulbs). The entire length of the clitoris ranges from 3½ to 7½ inches (10 to 20 centimeters).

The absolutely best way to stimulate the clitoris is with the mouth, particularly the tongue, which is closely matched to the clitoris in texture, moisture, and sensitivity.

vagina The elastic muscular tube, the internal part of the vulva, where a lover will insert his tongue, fingers, or penis for erotic stimulation.

urethra The tube through which urine and female ejaculate leave the body. It's the small opening that lies just below the clitoris and just above the opening of the vaginal canal.

perineum The patch of skin between the opening of the vaginal canal and the anus. It's an often-overlooked pleasure point that responds well to massaging or tapping with fingers, as well as sucking and licking.

anus The muscular ring at the opening of the rectum. It's host to a large number of nerve endings, so it likes to be licked, too. Pleasuring the anus with your mouth is referred to as anilingus or rimming.

Stop in the Name of Love
Although yonis like you to breathe hotly all over them, never, never blow into her urethra or her vagina. You could cause serious damage.

Positions for Her Pleasure
Proper positioning for superb cunnilingus is imperative. The angle of your head will affect how your tongue strikes her clitoris—from above, below, straight on, or sideways. And that can make all the difference between a happy "Oh yes" and a

frustrated "Oh no." Experiment with your lady love to see which angles work best for her.

* She lies on her back and you lie between her legs. This may well be the most comfortable position for both of you. And, you've got good access to all her lovely bits. Try putting your hands underneath her buttocks to lift her in extra close.

* She lies on her back with her buttocks at the edge of the bed. You kneel on a pillow between her legs. She can place her legs over your shoulders or bend her knees and put her feet flat on the bed.

* She stands and you kneel in front of her. Because you'll probably have to tilt your head back a little to reach everywhere, it can become uncomfortable after a while. Plus it's harder for her to really relax standing up.

* She sits in a chair and you kneel or sit before her. This is a pretty comfy pose for both of you.

* You lie on your back and she kneels over your face. Many men get quite a thrill from this more assertive genital kiss. She has much more influence over the action as she positions her yoni for maximum pleasure.

Ancient Ways of Cunnilingus for Modern Lovers

Vatsyayana didn't have a lot to say about cunnilingus other than that, "the way of doing this should be known from kissing the mouth." (II-9) Fortunately a later Indian love manual, the *Ratiratnapradipika*, went into great detail on the subject. Composed during the fifteenth century by the Maharaja Praudha Devaraya, it gives you as much to play with as Vatsyayana did with fellatio.

Like the fellatio series, these genital kisses can be given in stupendous sequence or as one-at-a-time thrills. Although her clitoris is her magic button, don't immediately start waving your wand over it. Make her clitoris ache for your touch by warming up all those other enchanting elements of her yoni. Keep in mind the effects of multiple points of stimulation and put your hands to good use all over her body.

1. **Adhara-sphuritam, the Quivering Kiss:** Using only the very pads of your fingers, gently and extremely slowly, squeeze her vaginal lips together. Give them a kiss as if they were her lower lip—just like the Throbbing Kiss, tender, tentative, and hopeful.

Yummy Yoni

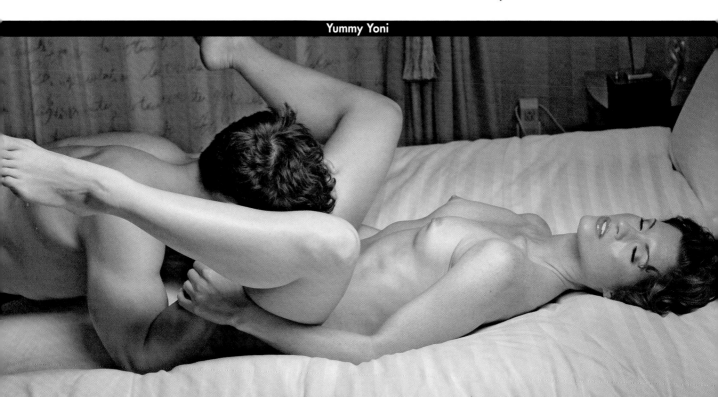

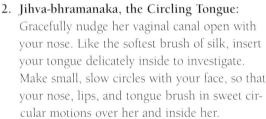

Worshipping Your Goddess

Stirring Mouth Music

2. **Jihva-bhramanaka, the Circling Tongue:**
Gracefully nudge her vaginal canal open with your nose. Like the softest brush of silk, insert your tongue delicately inside to investigate. Make small, slow circles with your face, so that your nose, lips, and tongue brush in sweet circular motions over her and inside her.

3. **Jihva-mardita, the Tongue Massage:** Rest a moment and wait as she quivers and shivers for more. Then slip your tongue authoritatively inside her yoni. Dart it in and out and all around, fervently and powerfully. Remember that your tongue's purpose is to give her pleasure, not to just lap it up for yourself.

4. **Chushita, Sucked:** Push your mouth and lips firmly against her vaginal lips and kiss them as you would her mouth in a deep kiss. Incorporate gentle nibbles with your lips as well. Now you can begin to pay attention to her clitoris. Alternate your lip kisses with light

sucking on her clitoris. If you rest your forehead along her pubic bone, you'll be stimulating the energy spots there, boosting her sexual charge.

5. **Uchchushita, Sucked Up:** Bring her closer for stronger sensations. Lift her buttocks with your hands. As you grip her butt, put your fingertips in the indentations of her tailbone. Her body weight will increase the pressure on these acupoints and she'll feel a tremor right through to her clitoris.

Start at her belly button and slick your tongue lightly down over her belly. Lick light circles on her clitoris and then switch to giant ice-cream cone licks, up from the bottom of her vagina to the tip of her clitoris.

6. **Kshobhaka, Stirring:** Now she wants to open as wide to you as she can. She spreads her thighs and holds them apart with her hands so you have as much room as you need. You press

Congress of a Crow: Sideways

your palms into her groin creases, sending sensation deep into her genitals. Now curve your tongue and tantalize her clitoris with rapid flicks of bliss.

7. **Bahuchushita, Sucked Hard:** Bring her feet to rest along your shoulders. Hold her by the waist and draw her yoni tight to your mouth. Combine powerful, satisfying sucks of her clitoris with steady, lingering licks of it. You'll make her a very happy woman.

Love Bites

The term "69" refers to the shape your bodies assume when you're performing oral sex on each other at the same time. You can also try "68," which means, "you do me and I owe you one."

Kokila: Congress of a Crow or the 69 Position

Kokila, both of you making mouth music at the same time, can be a source of extraordinary pleasure all round. The main requirement is that you're completely tuned in to each other. It's a great position for coming together, but you've got to be paying exquisite attention, rather than losing yourself in your own gratification and forgetting your partner's. One of the special advantages of the Crow is that the alignment of her mouth and throat allow deeper penetration.

There are three basic positions for the Crow. You can both lie on your sides, facing each other. Rest your head on your lover's thigh as you pleasure your beloved tenderly with your mouth. You'll be quite comfortable to stay together this way until you get your fill.

Another snug and fairly relaxed version occurs when one partner lies flat on the bed with the other over top. You can experiment with man or woman on top to see which best suits your body shapes and your temperaments.

An extremely challenging adaptation is the Standing 69. You have to be strong and she needs to be light to be able to do it. Even then it will likely be difficult to maintain for long. To begin, she lies on her back, with her head hanging over the bed's edge. You stand with your legs on either side of her head. Bending over you pick her up and position her so that her yummi yoni is at your mouth and your luscious lingam is at hers. In this pose, your male-female energy circuit is further complemented by the tension required in your body and the deep relaxation in hers. It's a magnificent melding.

The Least You Need to Know

* Enthusiasm is almost as important as technique when it comes to giving your lover oral sex.

* Get to know intimately each pleasurable part of your lover's genitals, what it does, and what it wants you to do.

* Positions with one lover lying flat on the bed and the other between the legs are the most comfortable for oral sex.

* Use your hands, as well as your mouth, to give him great satisfaction.

* For her, when you find a tongue stroke that's building her forcefully toward orgasm, keep doing it exactly the same way until she lets you know differently.

PART
THREE

In the Heart of the Fire

There are so many ways to join your bodies for the ultimate union of intercourse. Varying your positions changes not only your physical sensation but your emotional and energetic experience, too. With the *Kama Sutra* love postures and their optional thrusting maneuvers, you can consciously generate the kind of connection you want.

You might be aching to elevate your emotional bond. Perhaps making your G-spot sing is on your agenda. Reaching a maximum erection and maintaining it could be what you're interested in. Or going to that place of fever and passion so intense that you become lost in each other. You can create all these encounters, and more.

In & Out, Up & Down, All Around

In This Chapter

* Understand a simple way to classify *Kama Sutra* intercourse positions
* Be familiar with the main characteristics of face-to-face lovemaking
* Recognize the main characteristics of opposites positions
* Discover Vatsyayana's thrusting techniques that add more pleasure and variety to your lovemaking
* Learn how exercising your genital muscles leads to better sex

This is it, the part of the book you've been eagerly awaiting: an introduction to those exotic *Kama Sutra* intercourse positions you've heard about. By our count, excluding postures for group sex, the *Kama Sutra* lists 34 positions that can be used during intercourse. As you'll see, some are indeed exotic, and others quite plain; some are very distinct poses and others are just subtle variations. When combined with different methods of thrusting, kissing, and caressing, the possible permutations are countless. With a little imagination you can mix and match them into many versions of both basic and complex love dances, as Vatsyayana encouraged you to do. "For these different kinds of congress ... generate love, friendship, and respect." (II-6)

Vatsyayana believed that nicely matched lovers are most able to celebrate all the postures of love and would reap great pleasure from just about all of them. But he wanted to make sure that lovers who aren't quite a natural fit would get the most from their time between the sheets, too. So he took great care to point out positions that will suit lovers of varying genital sizes. We'll help you learn which ones are right for you.

To ease your exploration, we've sorted Vatsyayana's lovemaking postures into a simple classification that will be intuitively obvious to you. We've also expanded on the very brief original description of each posture, adding technique details, benefits, and cautions. So that you'll have a visual reference to inspire your own experiments, most poses are illustrated with color photographs.

How Many Ways Can I Love You?

To help distinguish one love posture from another, the ancient sages gave each a name according to the images they evoke and the shapes lovers' bodies assume during intercourse. Positions may be named after animals (the Cow), plants (the Lotus), or the effect they create (the Half Pressed). While it can be exotic fun to remember some of these names and use them during your love play—"Oh baby, split my bamboo!"—you certainly don't have to memorize a position's name to thoroughly enjoy it. In the following chapters, as we're describing the positions, we give you their names as translated by Burton, followed by Sinha's version if it's noticeably different, and then the Sanskrit term when it's available.

Besides learning their names, a simpler way to understand and play with the *Kama Sutra* intercourse postures is to divide them into two main categories: face to face and opposites. All positions fall into one of these two main classifications. Both have distinct characteristics and particular benefits for lovemaking. Depending on the effect you want to create at any given moment, you can position your bodies accordingly.

Face to Face

Face-to-face positions with similar body parts facing or touching (mouths kissing, hearts together, hands linked) encourage emotional union and circulation of your sexual energy. You look deep into each other's eyes, you breathe your lover's breath, your hearts melt. Face-to-face positions naturally activate primary acupressure points on your pubic bone, your groin, and the inside of your thighs. As you move and press your bodies together stimulating these acupoints, blood circulation to your genitals increases. More circulation brings more sensation.

Sexual excitement builds more slowly when you're face to face than in positions that bring together opposite parts of the body. Use more face-to-face positions when you want to:

* Extend lovemaking for longer periods of time.
* Open your hearts to deep connection.
* Focus on flowing energy between you.

Face to Face

Opposites

Postures that combine opposites (rear entry, head to feet) build erotic excitement and generate a high sexual charge very rapidly. You can't really see each other's faces, so opposites are more impersonal and animalistic. You might find yourself focusing more on your sensations rather than what's happening for your partner. Opposites positions offer men, who are highly visual creatures, unusual and exciting views of their lovers' bodies.

Because they are so arousing, reverse positions are helpful for men who have difficulty getting and maintaining an erection and for those who find it hard to reach a climax of ejaculation. On the other hand, men who ejaculate too soon should avoid these fiery postures.

Use opposites positions when you want:

* A passionate quickie.
* A stimulating interlude between slower postures.
* To build a high sexual charge.

Remember that quickies are fantastic as long as they're not the only item on the menu. A sexual diet of strictly quickies becomes repetitive and boring. It's anorexic sex, without enough juice to sustain life or love. Quickies alone won't maintain your interest in sex with the same partner over the long haul. They're one reason why increasing numbers of couples become sexless, making love infrequently or not at all.

Love Bites

Newsweek magazine defines a sexless marriage as one in which a couple makes love 10 or fewer times per year, a situation which they say describes at least 15 percent of all married couples in the United States.

Although men, whose nature is considered to be like fire, heating up fast and burning out quickly, can be fairly satisfied with frequent bouts of brief sex, most women definitely aren't. Women are like water. They need time to come to a full boil, and once steamed up they can go on boiling for a long time. They'll lose interest and become increasingly frustrated if fast and furious is all you offer. Vatsyayana knew this well and throughout the *Kama Sutra* he admonished men to be certain that their lovers are thoroughly pleasured. If you want lots of sex, your lady

must get satisfaction, and quickies alone, even with fierce, body-pounding thrusts, will not give her that.

Lovers sometimes mistakenly believe that it's the length of time you spend thrusting that will enable a woman to have an orgasm during intercourse. But actually it's her level of arousal. If she's not sexually excited, you can bop away for an eon and not much is likely to happen. On the other hand, if she's tuned tight as a top, even the mere act of penetration can send her to heaven. Part 2 gave you all the essentials you both need to set her heart racing. Use them before you dive in.

Opposites

Experiment with this oh-so-satisfying dance of love: fire up your sexual charge with a rapid, come-from-behind pose, then move round to face each other and in slow sensuality concentrate on spreading the heat throughout your bodies. As you begin to cool

down, switch again to the passion of a reverse pose, and so on, and so on ....

For an even clearer understanding of the *Kama Sutra* positions, you can divide the two major categories (face to face and opposites) into the following easy to picture subclasses:

- Man on top
- Woman on top
- Sideways
- Sitting
- Standing

Man on Top

Man on Top and Woman on Top

The person who is on top during active lovemaking generates the most energy, which is naturally passed to the partner on the bottom. To balance the yin yang/masculine feminine energies within each of your bodies, take turns sending and receiving by switching top and bottom throughout your loving. If one of you is tired or recovering from an illness or injury, then spend most of your time on the bottom. If you want to feel more empowered or in control, take the top position. When you're on the bottom, you willingly surrender to your lover.

In relationships where one or the other partner is particularly dominant, an excellent way to give up the lead is to allow the lover who is normally less active and more passive to assume the top position, at least sometimes. Both men and women may have difficulty opening their hearts, allowing themselves to be emotionally vulnerable and transparent, but it seems most challenging for men. In face-to-face, woman-on-top positions, the man must surrender to his lady. You let yourself be vulnerable to her. Once you understand that control is the enemy of ecstasy, you may begin to appreciate the benefits of complete surrender during lovemaking.

Al's Outlook

When the heart opens, energy moves freely from the lower chakra centers in the genitals, belly, and solar plexus through it to the higher chakra centers in the throat, third eye, and crown. You may discover, as I did, that simply opening your heart, allowing yourself to feel everything, to freely give and receive love, accomplishes what sexual technique alone can never do: it cleanses your doors of perception, accelerates your consciousness, and prepares you for the gift of ecstasy.

The men for whom Vatsyayana wrote the *Kama Sutra* were pretty much masters of all they surveyed. Perhaps because of their dominant role in life, as well as the Eastern perception that men are associated with the sun and goal-oriented energy and women with the moon and receptive energy, it was very unusual for a man of Vatsyayana's time to allow himself to be submissive. Man-on-top positions were the norm. Woman-on-top positions were a delicious and naughty deviation—in fact, Vatsyayana referred to such positions as "woman acting the part of the man." If both lovers were curious, or if he got tired out before he came, she could, "with his permission, lay him down upon his back, and give him assistance by acting his part." (II-8)

But generally men were supposed to do the majority of the work, so Vatsyayana gave most of his attention to describing the many versions of man-on-top. In this lovemaking posture, also known in modern times as the "missionary" position, the woman generally lies flat on her back with the man on top of her. Then, depending on how you move your legs, arms, and pelvises, you can create a myriad of fascinating, pleasurable variations.

Woman on Top

Sideways

For instance, when a woman raises her pelvis and/or spreads her thighs, her vagina opens and expands. This helps make a better fit when the lingam is larger than the yoni (high and highest congress). Positions with pelvis lifted also tilt the vagina so that friction contact between G-spot and penis is easier to achieve. Positions in which the lady keeps her hips lowered and/or pushes her thighs together will tighten the vagina, providing more pleasurable friction for a smaller lingam inside a larger yoni. If your yoni is large and your lover's lingam is small (low and lowest congress), it's also important to develop the power of your vaginal muscles. No matter what position you're in, you'll be able to warmly grasp his lingam and hold it snugly inside (see the Mare's Trick later in this chapter).

Love Bites

Research shows that man on top, followed closely by woman on top, are the most-used positions. Interestingly, most men and women prefer to be on the bottom.

While many women today enjoy being on top (and their men like it even more), it's particularly appealing if you're a woman with a small yoni whose partner has a large lingam. You can safely control the pace, angle, and depth of penetration. Many men find that they can delay ejaculation more effectively when their lover is on top. It's easier to stay relaxed and to direct your hot sexual energy away from your penis, testicles, and prostate gland.

Sideways

Sideways positions (both of you lying on your sides) tend to be gentler, slower, and quieter. Although less physically stimulating than other positions, they can be powerfully emotional, even during rear entry. There's a deep sensual connection as every inch of your skin stretches out and presses against your lover. Sideways poses are also well suited to sharing sexual/spiritual energy.

Sitting

True face-to-face sitting positions, with the woman perched on her man's lap or upright between his legs, are best suited for heart connecting and energy sharing. Stimulation doesn't primarily come from genital thrusting because most people aren't physically strong or flexible enough to get a big range of motion. But you can generate a certain amount of heat in seated postures by rocking your pelvis and breathing rapidly together. If you lean back on your arms you can get more support for thrusting movements and you can both influence the tempo.

You can explore rear-entry seating as well. She's on your lap, but this time facing away from you. If her legs are bent beneath her she can use the strength in them to move up and down quite powerfully on your lingam. Your hands are free to reach round and caress her breasts or titillate her clitoris. Listen for the change in her breathing that tells you her passion is ripening.

In his chapter on intercourse, Vatsyayana didn't include seated postures, but he did describe a sitting embrace, Milk and Water, that he suggested should "take place at the time of sexual union." (II-2)

Sitting

Standing

Standing

Face-to-face standing positions are not usually held for long periods because of the physical strength required. They also don't give much range for thrusting, but because you're in an upright stance, there's lots of potential for energy circulation.

Standing opposites positions are a little easier to maintain, particularly if she has some support to lean on, like a wall or table, as you bend her over a little to take her from behind. You'll find there's much more space for thrusting, too. Standing poses are ideal for lovemaking "quickies," for instance, when you're being discreetly daring in some semi-public place such as an out-of-the-way washroom in an art gallery.

Exploring Basic and Advanced Postures

Many of the *Kama Sutra* positions are suitable for modern lovers of all ages, and with some selectivity, in various stages of physical fitness and health. You don't have to be a young, perfectly fit gymnast to enjoy them. Other poses require much higher degrees of strength and flexibility. As you read about them, if you're wondering how on earth lovers could perform such feats, remember that when the *Kama Sutra* was written, people spent their time much closer to the ground than we do. Our common elevated chairs that hold bottoms 18 inches or more above the floor were rare. Accustomed to squatting, crouching, or sitting on mats, cushions, or low divans, those ancient lovers had greater lower-body flexibility than most modern Westerners.

In the chapters that follow, you'll find positions that increase emotional connection, stimulate her G-spot, help arouse and maintain his erection, boost excitement for both of you, and open her up for deep penetration. You'll get detailed instructions on how to try all of them. Right now we'd like to let you know which ones are easiest and which more difficult.

Love Bites

In a footnote to his translation of the Indian love manual the *Ananga Ranga* (see Appendix D), Burton made this comment on the difference in flexibility between people of India and those in the West: "the exceeding pliability of the Hindu's limbs enable him to assume attitudes [positions] absolutely impossible to the European."

The Basics

These first two lists cover the easiest face-to-face and opposites positions, probably the best for you to start with as you begin your exploration of the *Kama Sutra*'s intercourse practices. You likely won't find them too daunting and may well be encouraged to try more challenging poses. Most lovers should be able to comfortably manage the majority of these variations, regardless of their age or condition—within reason. Some that include raising and stretching legs or bending way over might be a bit challenging if the lady needs to work on her flexibility. If one or both lovers are seriously overweight, some of these positions will definitely be more difficult. (We've referenced the chapter in which you'll find each position explained.)

Easiest face-to-face positions:

- Clasping Supine (*Jewel Case—Samputa*)—Chapter 8
- Clasping Sideways (*Jewel Case—Samputa*)—Chapter 8
- Sesame Seed with Rice (*Tila-Tandulaka*)—Chapter 8
- Pressing (*Pidita*)—Chapter 9
- Twining (*Veshtita*)—Chapter 8
- Widely Opened (Flower in Bloom—*Utphallaka*)—Chapter 11
- Yawning (Widely Yawning—*Vijrimbhitaka*)—Chapter 11
- Rising (*Bhugnaka*)—Chapter 11
- Packed (the Squeeze—*Piditaka*)—Chapter 9
- Half Pressed (Half Squeeze—*Ardhapiditaka*)—Chapter 9
- The Crab (*Karkata*)—Chapter 8

* Pair of Tongs (*Samdamsha*)—Chapter 10
* Milk and Water (*Kshiraniraka*)—Chapter 8
* Standing Supported (*Sthita*)—Chapter 11

Easiest opposites positions:

* The Ass (*Gardabha*)—Chapter 10
* The Dog (*Svanaka*)—Chapter 10
* The Elephant (*Aibha*)—Chapter 8
* The Deer (*Harina*)—Chapter 11
* The Boar (*Varaha*)—Chapter 10
* The Horse (*Ashva*)—Chapter 9
* The Mare's Position (*Vadavaka*)—Chapter 9
* The Tiger (*Vyaghra*)—Chapter 11

Degrees of Difficulty

These two lists cover the more difficult face-to-face and opposites positions. By all means, try some of these advanced arrangements. They can add an extra dimension of excitement and challenge into your lovemaking. But don't be in a hurry to master the more sophisticated poses. Allow your sexual skill and mastery to develop over time. When it comes to lovemaking, are you really in a hurry? Keep in mind that this is learning for lovers and lovers for life.

Love Bites

Have you heard of the Plumber's Position? It's one where you wait all day and no one comes!

More advanced face-to-face positions:

* Pressed (High Squeeze—*Utpiditaka*)—Chapter 8
* Position of Indrani (*Indranika*)—Chapter 11
* Splitting Bamboo (*Venudaritaka*)—Chapter 9
* Fixing a Nail (Spit-roast—*Shulachita*)—Chapter 10
* The Lotus (*Padmasana*)—Chapter 8
* The Swing (*Prenkholita*)—Chapter 9
* Standing Suspended (*Avalambitaka*)—Chapter 11

More advanced opposites positions:

* The Cow (*Dhenuka*)—Chapter 11
* The Goat (*Aja*)—Chapter 10
* The Cat (*Marjara*)—Chapter 9
* The Top (The Bee—*Bhramara*)—Chapter 10
* The Turning Position (*Paravrittaka*)—Chapter 10

Remember, as you experiment with these poses, to take your time and really feel each delightfully different sensation that even the slightest shift can bring. Pay attention to the subtle changes you feel in your genitals and throughout your body, as well as those big differences that happen when you change from one position to another.

After you've experienced the delights of the *Kama Sutra* positions, you might be stimulated to continue expanding your horizontal horizons. If so, we're ready to help you with nine positions from the *Ananga Ranga* (Appendix D) and twelve from the *Perfumed Garden* (Appendix E).

Love Bites

Durex condom's Global Sex Survey revealed that experienced lovers reach orgasm more often. Forty-eight percent of those over the age of 35 claimed they have an orgasm every time they have sex, compared to only 32 percent of those under 20.

Thrusting Techniques and Rhythms

There's a lot more to great intercourse than exploring interesting positions to put your bodies in; there's also moving in those positions. Thrusting, or how you slide your two wonderful body parts together—his and hers, penis and vagina—can offer extraordinary varieties of sensations. Although straight in and out is quite pleasing, there's a whole other world of penetration play. And, of course, Vatsyayana had something to say about how to use your equipment to the ultimate advantage.

One key point to remember is variety—changing your love strokes gives her different sensations and helps you last longer. Rhythm is also important, matching the pace and selection of strokes to bring her maximum enjoyment and to keep you in a zone of pleasure plus staying-power. Vatsyayana listed nine ways to move your magnificent member—each one offering different delights.

Moving Forward (Natural—Upasripta)

Moving Forward *is* your standard in and out, what Vatsyayana described as bringing the organs together "properly and directly." (II-8) Moving Forward is so natural that it's "instinctive even to untutored cowherds." (Sinha II-6, p.74) Although this is a very basic, straightforward stroke, it lends itself to a range of subtle or strong passions depending on how deep you drive and how fast you move.

Pala's Perspective

Although we most often think of the man doing the thrusting movements, he might try staying still while *you* do the moves. I love to take control this way and make swallowing my lover's penis with my yoni subtle or strong depending on my mood.

Churning (Manthana)

Churning involves holding your penis in one hand as you turn it around inside her vagina. To do this well, you need to be in positions where you are balanced or supported enough to have a free hand. Give her added pleasure before you insert your lingam into her yoni by rubbing it over her clitoris and vaginal lips. Such teasing will have her aching for you to come inside. Penetration won't be very deep because your hand's holding you back, but as you're stroking you can angle your lingam up to sweep past her G-spot. Churning's also good if you've got a large lingam/small yoni combo. Holding your penis firmly will give you more enveloping sensation throughout your entire length.

Piercing (Double-Bladed Knife—Hula)

"When the yoni is lowered and the upper part of it is struck with the lingam, it is called Piercing." (II-8) This is a thrust that is best when you work together. She tilts her vagina down by pressing her hips into the bed and arching her back a little. This brings her clitoris out for attention. You start your thrust with your body a little higher on hers and then slide down and in. As you do, the shaft of your penis will slide past her clitoris. Do this enough and she may come to a blended climax of clitoral and intravaginal orgasm.

Rubbing (Avamardana)

Rubbing is the opposite of Piercing. For this stroke, your lover angles her hips slightly upward and you push up into her from below. Rubbing is a great stroke for G-spot stimulation.

Pressing (Piditaka)

Entering her as deeply as you can and then staying there for a while is the essence of Pressing. Every inch of her yoni is pleasurably full. This is a great stroke for her to practice squeezing you tight with her vaginal muscles. With your body tight against hers, those acupressure spots in her groin will be sure to awaken. If you rub your bodies lightly together, you may also stimulate her clitoris. When you feel like you're getting too close to the edge of ejaculating before you want to, switch from other thrusting patterns to Pressing. The relative stillness will help you to calm your excitement.

Giving a Blow (the Buffet—Nirghata)

To Give a Blow, you remove your penis completely from her vagina then enter forcefully all the way to her depths. Tease her by varying how quickly you dive in—exquisitely slowly, and then pulsatingly fast. Because it involves such strong and deep penetration, Giving a Blow is a good technique to employ later in your lovemaking when she's very wet and very open. It also works well with rear-entry positions.

Stop in the Name of Love

Whenever you're trying thrusts that bring your penis fully out of her vagina, you both must be careful to make your re-entry a smooth one. A misplaced thrust can bend your penis and cause you injury.

Blow of a Boar (Varahaghata)

As you are inside her with Blow of a Boar, you adjust your angle of penetration so that your strokes focus on only one part of her vagina. Pleasure her this way and then move your attention to another spot—sides, top, bottom. See if she likes one spot better than others.

Blow of a Bull (Vrishaghata)

With Blow of a Bull, you're endeavoring to come into contact with all parts of the vaginal canal during your stroke. If you rotate your hips in a circular "screwing" motion, you've got the best chance to succeed. Stroke some spots on the way in and others on the way out.

Sporting of a Sparrow (Chatakavilasa)

Sporting of a Sparrow strokes are light and fast. Your lingam doesn't leave her yoni as you plunge in and pull back. Vatsyayana suggested making most use of this thrusting pattern at the end of lovemaking. That's because it's a consistent rapid stroke that can build you quickly to climax. Sporting of a Sparrow is good for men who have difficulty getting or keeping erections.

If you'd like to hone your thrusting skills even more, check out the six moves in Appendix E, *The Perfumed Garden*.

The Mare's Trick

The Mare's Trick isn't really a trick at all, but it's definitely a talent. It's the fine art of squeezing the muscles in your genitals—the PC or *pubococcygeous* muscles (pronounced pew-bo-cox-e-g-us). This group of muscles extends from your pubic bone back to your coccyx and acts as a lower diaphragm supporting your reproductive organs. When a woman squeezes these muscles during intercourse and "forcibly holds in her yoni the lingam after it is in," it's called the Mare's Trick. Vatsyayana cautioned that this skill "is learnt by practice only." (II-6) But it's definitely well worth the practice.

The easiest way to discover which muscles to squeeze is to stop your flow of urine in midstream. Then you can squeeze and relax them at any time. Practicing PC squeezing by starting and stopping your flow of urine isn't the best—it can lead to infection, particularly for women—but it's a great way to identify the muscles. You may already have heard of this practice as Kegel exercises, named for Dr. Arnold Kegel, who prescribed them to women suffering from incontinence. Now they are regularly taught to women in preparation for childbirth. But they're also a must for anyone who wants a truly extraordinary sex life.

When you first begin these exercises, you might involuntarily tighten other muscles besides your PCs—your shoulders and belly for instance. But after awhile, you'll be able to keep the rest of your body relaxed and just tighten your PC muscles. In fact, you can learn to isolate the individual muscles within the vaginal canal—tensing and relaxing them from your vaginal opening all the way back to your cervix.

Al's Outlook

When Pala does PC muscle squeezing while I'm inside her, I call it "riding the elevator." It's the best elevator!

When your lover is inside you, you can thrill him with rippling waves ("milking" his penis) or simply squeeze along his length, holding him very firmly.

This art is especially helpful when you're in still or resting positions. It can help to keep a man hard when he might begin to lose his erection because he's stopped moving. It's also a great way to hold him inside when you're moving from one position to another and you want to maintain that wonderful contact. You can build great power in your yoni muscles and feel the excitement of actively enveloping your lover's penis rather than just passively opening to his penetration. The more adept you become at squeezing and relaxing, the more sensation you'll feel, too.

Love Bites

Do this simple exercise 50 times a day to strengthen your PC muscles: inhale and focus on your genitals. Exhale and squeeze your genital muscles, holding the contraction for a slow count of five. Inhale and relax your genital muscles. Repeat.

Vatsyayana reported this practice as a female activity, but men can learn to PC squeeze as well. Like women, they can isolate different muscles in their genitals, ultimately learning to keep their whole body relaxed as they just tighten their anus, or pull up on their perineum, or lift their testicles, or dance their penis. Besides being a great conversation stopper at parties, this skill has some powerful benefits for both sexes:

* Helps men get and keep strong erections.
* Women's orgasms become stronger and more frequent.
* Assists men to delay ejaculation.
* Women avoid incontinence and prolapsed uterus.
* Maintains a man's prostate health because each squeeze gives it a mini-massage.
* Tones and strengthens your uro-genital muscles.
* Locks your sexual energy inside and helps push it up through your system.
* Feels really, really good when you do it during intercourse.

For physical sexual fitness and to soup up your sex life, do PC squeezes daily. You can do them anywhere, anytime—while waiting in line, while stopped at a traffic light, while watching TV, or as part of your regular fitness routine. No one will know what you're doing, unless they wonder why you've got that big smile on your face. After you've been practicing these exercises for a few weeks, you'll begin to notice a very pleasurable difference in your lovemaking.

The Least You Need to Know

* Face-to-face postures create more emotional connection.
* Opposites positions build sexual excitement very quickly.
* Because he considered them the most natural form of intercourse, Vatsyayana mostly described man-on-top positions.
* Try matching different thrusting rhythms to your positions for added variety.
* Both men and women benefit from regularly exercising their PC muscles.

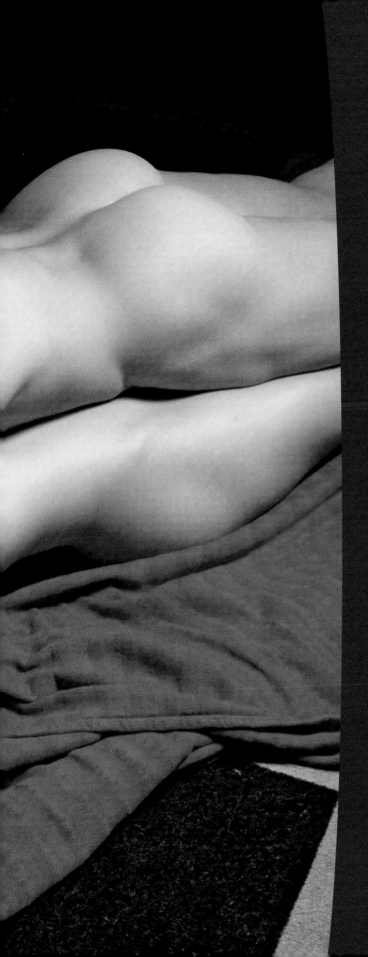

Hearts Wide Open

In This Chapter

- ❧ Seven specific practices that build intimacy during intercourse
- ❧ *Kama Sutra* love postures that intensify emotional connection
- ❧ The power of slow rhythms and stillness
- ❧ The difference between Peak Orgasms and Valley Orgasms

Lovemaking—not just spectacular sex, but sweet, sweet love—is what the positions in this chapter are all about. These positions are perfect when you want to melt into a slow, soulful, sensuous connection—or when your hearts are full and you want to fill them even more, so that your love runs over, bathing you in emotion's warm waves.

Here you'll find out how to create that poignant heart coupling, not only through particular postures, but also with all the added accessories that cement your bond. You'll discover which thrusts, in what rhythms, will fuse your willing bodies with your innermost affections; what caresses, kisses, and cries will open your hearts so wide as you invite your lover in, that you'll feel each other as your very self.

Love Me Tender

Emotional intimacy is inherently important to most women. They want it before, during, and after sex, but especially in the early stages of loving, so that the warmth in their hearts can start a blaze in their yonis. In Part 2, we shared with you Vatsyayana's many methods for setting her feelings aflame, to fire her desire for intercourse. Well, when she's finally fueled up for genital connection, you don't suddenly shift all your attention away from affection and on to action. Maintaining your emotional union will build her passion and will add enormously to the intensity of your sexual experience. All of you will be involved, not just your lusty lingam.

As you're exploring the positions in this section, incorporate some, or all, of the following practices. You'll find your hearts will fill with gladness.

Kissing

Kissing, as noted in Chapter 4, is one of the best intimacy builders, particularly for women. Because most of the positions here are face to face, they lend themselves very well to lots of kissing. Commence with the delicate probing of the Throbbing Kiss, push on to the firmer explorations of the Kiss of the Upper Lip, and culminate with the intense ownership of the Clasping Kiss. Be sure to kiss various parts of your lover's body, not just the mouth, but also throat, ears, chest, shoulders, armpits, and fingers. Add in a bit of light nibbling or tender biting with your kisses, like lingering Hidden Bites, or a velvety version of the Coral and the Jewel.

Skin Connections

Create connection through skin, skin, and more skin—all those lovely sensual receptors are just aching to awaken at your touch. Caress each other with your whole bodies. A number of these poses include full body contact from top to toe. In them, your hands are free for teasing tickles with Ripping Silk, as you barely brush your fingertips or fingernails over sensitive spots like the inner thighs,

the elbow creases, and the cleft of the buttocks. Remember that women respond to multiple points of stimulation, so use your clever hands and mouth to intoxicate her everywhere.

Love Bites

Neurobiologist Candace Pert has proven that emotions aren't just created in your head; they're the result of complex electrochemical and biochemical interactions that occur all over your body. Emotions are felt and stored in cells throughout every inch of you.

Words of Love

One of the most intimate things you can do during sexual intercourse is to talk to each other. Whisper sweet words of endearment, adoration, and appreciation into your mate's ears. Share what you're feeling, and let your lover know you want this to go on forever. Don't be shy—let your heart sing its song of love.

Take It Slow

Slow everything way down. Winsome waltzes are just as much a part of a skillful lover's horizontal bop as a playful polka or a rollicking rhumba. Well-timed, deliberate thrusts engender intimacy much more readily than rapid, fierce, or pounding strokes. Most intimate of all is complete stillness while you're connected in intercourse. Focus your attention on your genital bond and become aware of the subtle exchange of energies that happens between lingam and yoni, without any motion whatsoever.

Let Your Eyes Meet

Eye contact is a simple but powerful aid to emotional closeness. If you open your eyes and gaze softly at each other, your hearts are sure to crack open. Allow your lover's image to come into your eyes, rather than grabbing each other in with your look. Out will pour amazingly tender feelings of affection. When you combine these looks of love with stillness, you double your intimacy potential.

Stop in the Name of Love

Eye gazing is not a staring contest. It isn't about domination, control, or power—other than the power of love.

Breathe

Breathe in harmony together. Make your breath as one, a perfectly matched flow of united inhalation and exhalation. If you're also motionless and have your eyes open while you harmonize your breath, you're in for a treat. Sometimes the feelings of intimacy this trio elicits become so strong that you'll find yourselves crying with sheer, overwhelming joy.

Stop and Start

For many lovers, intercourse is the beginning of the end. Once intercourse starts, they press on until the man ejaculates, effectively ending their lovemaking. Instead, experiment with interrupting intercourse before he has an ejaculation. Take a break and engage in other sensual and sexual activities, and then resume intercourse again. If you repeat this several times over the course of your lovemaking, you'll find it easier to relax during active intercourse and be fully present in the moment. You won't be so goal-oriented toward reaching orgasm. Your pleasure and your intimacy will increase dramatically.

Positions for Emotional Intimacy

Are you ready to open your hearts and satisfy your souls? Then take your sweetheart by the hand and head off to a secluded, romantic bower for these incredible poses:

* Clasping Supine (Jewel Case—*Samputa*)
* Clasping Sideways (Jewel Case—*Samputa*)
* Milk and Water (*Kshiraniraka*)
* Sesame Seed with Rice (*Tila-Tandulaka*)
* Pressed (High Squeeze—*Utpiditaka*)
* The Crab (*Karkata*)
* The Elephant (*Aibha*)
* Twining (*Veshtita*)
* The Lotus (*Padmasana*)

Clasping Supine

Clasping Supine (Jewel Case—Samputa)

You lie stretched out flat on your back, your arms overhead, languorous, lovely, quivering with subtle expectation. He eases himself on top of you and stretches out, covering your entire body with his. Your legs are closed, thighs just open enough for his lingam to pass between them and into your yoni. The Piercing thrust works wonders in this position, as he slides slowly up and down your body, stimulating your clitoris and turning your temperature higher for more intense pleasure.

If he supports himself a little above you with his arms, you can gaze into each other's eyes with love and longing. You can exchange tender, tentative, teasing kisses, like the Touching Kiss. He can playfully lick and nibble your ears and neck. Or he can whisper heart-melting words of adoration into your ears. With your hips down and your legs together, your vaginal canal is narrowed and shortened, so Vatsyayana suggested Clasping positions for larger yoni/smaller lingam matches.

Pala's Perspective

You'll find Clasping is great for larger lingam/smaller yoni connections, too. Your thighs enveloping his lingam make him feel like he's going a lot deeper than he is.

Clasping Supine is a gentle position: slow, basic, and easy. But don't let its simplicity fool you: it has many roles in your lovemaking repertoire. It's perfect for tuning in completely to each other at the beginning of intercourse, when a woman's passion is still building and her yoni hasn't expanded to its full capacity. It's also great for resting and recharging between more vigorous postures while still maintaining your connection, and for a delicious ending when you're so content and want to stay in that place of sensual satisfaction.

While Vatsyayana confined his description to the "normal" male dominant pose, we suggest you try this with woman on top as well. For as he said, "though a woman is reserved, and keeps her feelings concealed; yet when she gets on the top of a man, she then shows all her love and desire." (II-8) You can relax a little and allow her to pleasure you, as she squeezes and releases her yoni and thighs around you. Or as she wriggles provocatively against your pubic bone and presses her breasts hard into your chest. When she's in control this way she may feel more secure, playful, and loving.

Clasping Sideways (Jewel Case—Samputa)

From Clasping Supine move into Clasping Sideways with a gentle roll of your hips. Pressing your body in tight to hers and holding her close to you with

your right arm, roll over on to your left side. Pull her with you so that she's on her right side, your bodies still stretched out full, every inch of sensitive skin touching. Your lingam remains happily nestled inside her warm yoni.

Whenever you lie together in any face-to-face sideways pose, Vatsyayana suggested that the man should always be on his left side and the woman on her right, according to practices of yogic solar lunar breathing. Solar breath is linked to the right side of the body and equated with masculine energy, lunar breath to the left side and feminine energy. Your aim is to bring both into harmony. When you lie on your left side, you naturally breathe through your right nostril, and vice versa. Powerful desire awakens between a couple who intentionally breathe together in this way: inhaling and exhaling each other's breath, man through his right nostril, woman through her left. Match your breath to hers in a sensual rhythm of awakening passion.

Clasping Sideways

Milk and Water

in love with each other, and not thinking of any pain or hurt, embrace each other as if they were entering into each other's bodies, while the woman is sitting on the lap of the man … it is called an embrace like a 'mixture of milk and water.'" (II-2)

As he sits up, you lower yourself onto his lap, gently and tenderly coaxing his penis inside you. You wrap your arms around him and revel in the closeness of his heart beating next to yours. Because you're atop him, most of the action is up to you. You can rock your pelvis back and forth or brace your legs to help you move up and down. Shift the angle of entry by grasping his shoulders, pulling in close to him, and then letting go and leaning your upper body back and away. Generally, movement is slow and relaxed, a heart-connecting build-up to more vigorous activity. Although you're technically on top, there really isn't much dominance in this pose. It's more a union of loving equals.

Al's Outlook

Because you aren't necessarily moving much in a sitting position, your erection can start to go. I've found that squeezing my PC muscles a lot in this pose will help maintain it.

Vary how and where you're sitting. If he's very flexible, he might sit on the floor with his legs crossed beneath him, as you snuggle down into his lap. On the bed, he can stretch his legs straight out in front. For maximum comfort he can lean back against the headboard or a stack of firm pillows. Chairs, particularly straight-backed chairs without armrests, are a great location for Milk and Water. His back is supported and his feet rest comfortably on the floor. You can wrap your legs eagerly around him as your hands hold onto the back of the chair for leverage while you sway. Begin with loving eye contact as you slowly rock back and forth. Now, move in for kisses, first a tentative Nominal Kiss, then a tender Throbbing Kiss, and on into the passion of a Pressed Kiss.

If you're interested in exploring Tantric sex, Milk and Water is an ideal pose for consciously circulating your sexual energies. Because you're in an upright position, a sexy version of the basic

Milk and Water (Kshiraniraka)

Strictly speaking, Vatsyayana described Milk and Water as an embrace that takes place at the time of sexual union. But it's such a loving and intimate pose that we've included it here as an intercourse posture, not just as an embrace leading up to intercourse. "When a man and a woman are very much meditation posture, it'll be easier to send your hot energy up from your genitals to your heart, to your head, to each other. Appendix C gives you a basic introduction to Tantra and its ritualized sexual practices.

Sesame Seed with Rice (Tila-Tandulaka)

The Mixture of Sesame Seed with Rice is another loving embrace that's perfect for slow, sensual sex. When you're lying together on the bed and "embrace each other so closely that the arms and thighs of one are encircled by the arms and thighs of the other" (II-2), you've melded into sesame and rice magic. This is an especially intimate position for cuddling, perhaps even lying still, and feeling

the slow heat of your connection through genitals, hearts, mouths, and eyes.

She's lying on her back. You're lying on your left side next to her and partially curled over her. Both of you turn your hips to each other for subtle penetration, as your thighs entwine in a tangle of love. Your arms cradle each other with exquisite empathy. Feel her quiver with delight, as you trace your fingertips in beguiling waves up and down the sensitive skin along her ribcage. A mix of very deliberate, very measured Moving Forward and Pressing strokes add the final touch. Wrap yourselves completely around each other, creating a safe and loving cocoon, both outside and inside. Combine your seeds and rice sideways, and in man and woman on top, for delicious diversity.

Mixture of Sesame Seed With Rice

Pressed

Pressed
(High Squeeze—Utpiditaka)

In the Pressed position, you squat or kneel in front of her, as she lies on her back with her knees bent and her feet pressed flat against your chest. A good degree of flexibility is needed to hold this pose comfortably for any length of time. Neither of you has much range of movement, but she's especially confined, particularly if you're leaning the weight of your upper body heavily against her feet.

Some women are really turned on by the sense of containment the Pressed position brings. They love the feeling of utter surrender to their masterful lover. But for many others, that thrill of captivity needs to be tempered with the knowledge that they're safe and respected. So, focus your attention on your feelings for her, not just your physical sensations, and let your reverence show in your eyes. Softly speak her name and tell her how magnificent she is.

As you squat in front of her, grasp each other by the arms and use them for leverage as you move together in gentle thrusting rhythm—your pelvises rocking together, your chest and her feet pushing in time to love's music. Let her have some control—she can set the pace and use the strength of her legs to push you back to just the right distance.

Experiment, too, with this variation: you kneel in front of her, spreading your legs wide, and as she draws her knees toward her breasts, you grasp her buttocks and raise them to nestle against your thighs. You'll be able to penetrate her more deeply. Holding her hips, you move tantalizingly in and out with the Blow of a Boar. Reach down with one hand to tickle her inner thighs, her groin creases, and, of course, her tingling clitoris. When done with skill and affection, the Pressed pose awakens an amazing connection between captor and captive.

The Crab (Karkata)

It's easy to move from the Pressed into the Crab position—a pose that's usually more comfortable for her. You back off a little, enabling her to relax her leg muscles and drop her lower legs and feet. Her legs are still bent back toward her torso. The tops of her thighs may touch her tummy. You kneel between her legs for thrusting fully into her tightened yoni. Drawing her legs back and up this way deliciously constricts her vaginal canal—you'll both love the intense sensation you can get with simple Moving Forward thrusts. Penetration can become very deep in the Crab, so take it slow and easy at first. Grasp her legs firmly to give her support so she can stay comfortably relaxed.

Another extraordinarily satisfying thrust for this pose is Churning. To begin, put a thin pillow under her hips to support her back and curve her yoni and buttocks up slightly toward you. Kneel in front of her and take a long look at the beauty she's presenting for your pleasure. Hold your lingam in one hand and, before you enter her, tease her with gentle strokes and taps of your penis all over her genitals—around her anus, over her perineum, along her vaginal lips and clitoris. Then, slowly, slowly slide inside and, still holding your lingam, churn him all around. When she lets you know she wants you deeper, switch to the hip-swiveling motions of Blow of a Bull.

Move your upper body down toward her so she can reach you with soft, caressing hands, on your heart, your nipples, your entire chest. Bring your face close to whisper words of wonder and endearment. Dissolve her heart with your sighs.

The Elephant (Aibha)

You're lying flat on your tummy, arms and legs stretched out, relaxed, in effortless anticipation. He lies down atop you, covering your whole body with his, and enters you from behind. For the most part, rear-entry positions aren't noted for their emotional-connection capacity, but the Elephant is a prominent exception. As he lies over you, supporting his weight on bent arms, you feel surrounded by love. Head-to-foot, full-body touch feeds your skin hunger. Pressure on your tailbone, as he snuggles in close, stimulates your sacral acupoints—fingers of fire spread to your yoni. His declarations of desire, murmured delicately into your ears, entrance you. And, if he moves into this posture by starting at

The Crab

The Elephant

your feet and enticingly kissing, nipping, and licking his way up over your legs, buttocks, and back, only entering when your entire body is aquiver, you'll cherish him forever.

Stop in the Name of Love

In the Elephant, be careful how much weight you lean on your lover. You want to surround her with tenderness, not squash her with it.

Even though it may seem like he's in control, you exert a definite influence over the outcome, too. You can greatly alter sensation for both of you by squeezing your thighs tight, then opening them wide, and by raising and lowering your feet. If you want to give him the thrill of deep penetration, put a small pillow under your belly to tilt and open your yoni. Electrify him by pushing your buttocks up to meet his thrust. Inclining your hips will thrill you, too, because it's the perfect angle for G-spot strumming, especially if he uses the Rubbing thrust.

For a lightweight variety, shift into a sideways Elephant. Simply roll to your right; he'll stay pressed in tight behind you. This is particularly appealing if he's much bigger than you are. Plus, your hands, and his, are freed up for extra attention to your clitoris and breasts.

Twining (Veshtita)

Perhaps you've begun intercourse in the Clasping position and, as desire swells, your bodies want to be even closer. The Twining position is a natural progression. As you're lying full-length against her, she spreads her legs, so that now you're lying nestled between her thighs. She raises one leg, wraps it around your thigh or buttock, and pulls you in tight. The higher up your body she raises her leg, the deeper your penetration will be.

With subtle or powerful leg pressure on your butt, she can direct the speed, depth, and power of your thrusting. She can press her heel into the hollows at the bottom of your tailbone, activating the sacral acupoints and sending delicious waves of pleasure cascading into your genitals. Or she can use her heel to move in deep circles around your butt cheek,

Twining

massaging and relaxing your gluteus maximus muscles.

It doesn't matter which leg she wraps around you. We encourage you to experiment with both, one at a time, to see if you notice any differences in sensation or if one's more comfortable than the other. Explore Blow of a Boar strokes while Twining, first stroking the vaginal wall on the side of her lifted leg, and then on the opposite side. Which makes her moan most? You can also add variety by raising and lowering your upper body—coming in close for a bewitching kiss, pushing up and away with your arms to look at her with lusty love and to gain more leverage for thrusting.

The Lotus (Padmasana)

The *Lotus*, based on the yoga posture of the same name, is one of the most difficult positions in the *Kama Sutra*, particularly for women. You must be extremely pliant throughout your lower body—hips, groin, knees, and even ankles. If you'd like to try the Lotus, practice it as a yoga posture first. Sitting on the floor, bend your right leg and tuck the heel of your right foot into the groin crease of your left leg. Then bend your left leg and tuck that foot into your right groin crease, or rest it as far up your right thigh as you can. Place your hands on your knees, settle your gaze on the tip of your nose, and breathe slowly and evenly. Practicing this posture frequently, even for short periods, will noticeably amplify your elasticity, not only for this pose, but also for all the others that require you to hold your thighs wide. You'll also begin to develop the inner balance and focus that comes from contemplative practices.

Love Bites

The lotus, national flower of India, is a powerful symbol for both Hindus and Buddhists. It signifies the spiritual journey of humanity, from muddled material duality to pure, enlightened oneness.

When you're ready to bring these meditative qualities to your lovemaking with the Lotus, you have two options. First, you can sit down and arrange yourself in the lotus yoga pose, and then roll over onto your back. You might want a pillow under your head to cradle your neck and shoulders and prevent any strain. Invite your lover to stand back and watch as you offer yourself to him so enchantingly. Then entice him to kneel in front of your beautiful blossom and make his way slowly inside. The second option, if you've become very lithe with your exercise, is to fold your legs up into the lotus posture while you're already lying down. You can move quite handily from positions like the Crab for instance, without really having to break your genital connection. The change in sensation as you widen and rotate your hips outward is powerful and unique.

If you'd like to experience some of the delights of the Lotus, but can't bend quite so far (which will probably be the case with most women), try this less-stressful alternative. Raise your legs, bend them at the knees—just like with the Crab—and instead of leaving your feet pointing forward, cross your ankles. Your lover kneels astride your hips and leans over you for penetration. Your crossed ankles press against his belly.

Penetration in the Lotus is relatively shallow. The farther he leans over you, the closer he brings his face to you, the shallower penetration will be, the farther back he leans, the more depth you'll get. Unless he's very supple as well, leaning in all the way for a kiss is pretty difficult to do.

Peaks and Valleys

Most of the positions, movements, and touches in this guide are geared toward building to Peak Orgasm during your lovemaking. Peak Orgasm comes to you via friction sex—two bodies rubbing together, swiftly or leisurely, creating a crescendo of excitement, accompanied by intense sensations of pleasure, often, but not always, localized in the genitals. Peak Orgasms are intensely physical. You don't need an emotional or energetic connection, although such bonds immeasurably enhance your experience. Peak orgasm can arrive through a quickie, as a rapid release of physical, sexual tension. Or, if you've been making love for a long time and built a high level of arousal, such orgasms may leave you utterly satiated, spent, and deliriously giddy.

For a man, Peak Orgasms generally include ejaculation, a great shuddering, climactic culmination. But, if he's learned how to delay this process and to move his intense sensation away from his genitals and up through his body, he may have one without ejaculating. (See Chapter 13.) During more extended periods of lovemaking, a woman may well have two, three, or more Peak Orgasms of varying intensity and in different parts of her body. (See Chapter 9.)

A Valley Orgasm is a completely different animal, more a sexual meditation than a sexual activity. While physical sensations are an extraordinarily pleasurable part of it, the essential experience is energetic and emotional. Although you have genital connection, there's no thrusting. In fact, you don't move at all. Rather than animatedly building sexual excitement to a climactic release, you rest together in stillness and allow the orgasm to come to you. You are not "doing" anything; rather, you are "being"—here, now, in the present moment.

Pala's Perspective

I've found Clasping Sideways and Sesame and Rice to be excellent positions for this erotic, emotional experiment.

Lie together, with penetration, in a position that is comfortable to maintain for a relatively long period of time (an hour or more). An hour may seem a long time, but, hey, it's a matter of perspective. Think of all the other ways you commonly fritter an hour away. Do yourselves a favor one night: skip the nightly newscast or sitcom reruns, and go to bed early for an information session of a completely different kind. Use the following practices to help you surrender into the experience:

- Relax your entire body; let it be loose, liquid, sinking into the bed.

- Focus your attention on your genital connection; feel every sensation, every nuance of magnificent lingam enveloped by welcoming yoni.

- Breathe in rhythm together—deep, slow abdominal breaths.

- Make intermittent eye contact, allowing your lover into your heart, through your eyes.

- Visualize energy (as a beam of light, a wave of water, a ripple of rhythm) moving up through your body, from your genitals, and out through the crown of your head.

- Mostly you are silent; if you do speak, only use words of love, endearment, and adoration.

- Be fully present and observe what is happening physically, emotionally, and energetically from one moment to the next. If your attention wanders, gently bring it back.

- If he loses his erection (which is quite likely to happen after a while), simply stay still, maintaining as much genital contact as possible.

- Let go of any desire or determination to "make" a Valley Orgasm happen. You can't; you must simply surrender to what may come to you.

While you are "waiting" for something to happen, time may seem to move very slowly. You may find yourself becoming quite impatient for a result that you imagine you would like to happen. But when you truly let go into this meditation, and the energetic movement of Valley Orgasm comes over you, you'll move into a state that makes ordinary time and space irrelevant, a timeless state of vast space—infinity. As the *Kundalini* energy awakens and rises up through you, it can bring powerful physical, emotional, and psychic experiences. You may feel sensations of heat or electrical currents moving through your body. Bright colors and multifaceted shapes might appear. Intense happiness could consume you in a feast of affection and adoration. You may even leave your individual self to merge with the divine mystery.

Pillow Talk

Kundalini is a concentrated force of life energy that rests, coiled like a snake, at the base of your spine. When it is awakened, through meditation, yoga disciplines, or even focused sexuality, it can lead to profound spiritual awakening.

If these feelings seem too overwhelming or unacceptably scary, try to remain completely relaxed, keep your breathing slow and deep, and ground your energy by imagining it falling into the center of the earth. If necessary, stop your practice. Try again later. Remember, any demons you may encounter in your consciousness are only aspects of your self, disguised to look scary. These inner dragons can be tamed if you face them rather than run away and hide.

Even with repeated tries, the Valley Orgasm may elude you. If you find yourself becoming frustrated, bored, or feeling like a failure, know that such responses are only part of the learning curve. Valley Orgasm is an advanced lovemaking practice worthy of disciplined perseverance. Relax and enjoy the time of being so totally connected to each other and away from the world. Learning to let go, to surrender, to allow, and to be fully present in the moment, won't just bring you orgasmic pleasure, it'll also open your heart to untold joys of love.

The Least You Need to Know

* Lots of skin contact, eye gazing, and breathing in harmony with your lover strengthens your emotional connection during intercourse.

* Words of endearment and sensuous sounds create intimate bonds.

* Slowness—slow movement, slow thrusts, slow caresses—is a key for soulful union.

* In sideways positions Vatsyayana suggested the man should always lie on his left side, the woman on her right.

* Peak Orgasms are powerful releases that come about through intense activity and sexual excitement.

* Valley Orgasms are the outcome of sexual meditation through stillness, surrender, and focus.

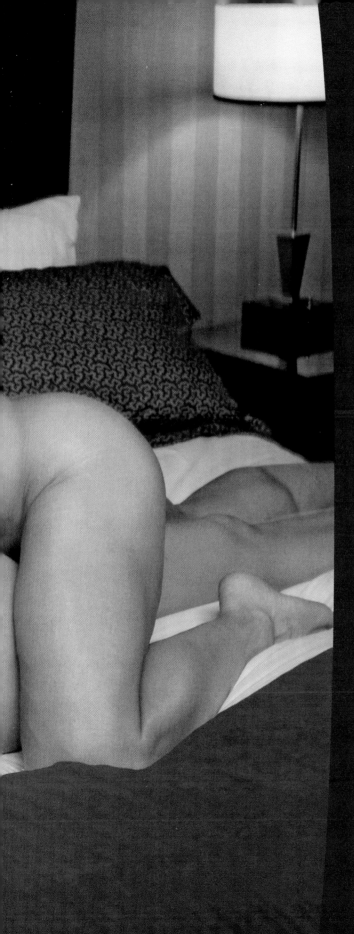

"G" Marks the Spot

In This Chapter

- ❧ The many types of orgasm women can experience
- ❧ The complexities of the G-spot
- ❧ How to include her clitoris during intercourse
- ❧ Eight amazing *Kama Sutra* positions that enhance clitoral and G-spot pleasure

Women and their orgasms. It's a hot topic that has ignited debate for just about as long as people have been making love and talking about it. What are a woman's orgasms like? What parts of her body are involved? Can she have more than one?

Vatsyayana and his cronies had very differing views on women's orgasmic response. They disagreed about what a feminine version of the "little death" would feel like, how it would happen, when it would happen, how long it would last, or even if it would happen at all. You can understand their dilemma. When a man has an ejaculatory orgasm, it's pretty obvious. But women are different; they're much more complicated. Even though sexual explorers, scientists, and therapists have come a long way since Vatsyayana's day, they're still probing the great mystery of female sexual satisfaction.

Vatsyayana himself was quite certain that women are indeed orgasmic. And, he was most adamant that a cultured man would learn the proper way to help his ladylove find bliss. The *Kama Sutra* positions we introduce you to here are especially potent for pushing two of her orgasm-awakening buttons—her clitoris and her G-spot.

A Cornucopia of Orgasms

Before we go on to those delicious poses, let's talk a bit about women's orgasmic potential. Women have a remarkable capacity for sexual pleasure. You can learn to experience any number of many types of orgasm: clitoral orgasms, vaginal orgasms, ejaculatory orgasms, whole body orgasms, energy orgasms. Orgasms come in varying degrees of intensity, physical focus, and duration. They can be a pleasurable little tingle or a body/mind/soul explosion. Some last for seconds, others minutes or even hours. Each woman's orgasmic experience can shift from day to day, depending on a host of factors—physical, mental, and emotional. Although they most often stem from genital stimulation, orgasms need not be confined to the genitals alone. Indeed, as the following list of some types of orgasm shows, orgasms are available all over.

Clitoral Orgasms

There are disagreements about describing or classifying other types of female orgasm, but just about everyone agrees that women can climax from direct manipulation of the clitoris. Indeed, for many women, this is the easiest way to come. Not all love-button orgasms are the same—some are tiny ripples of pleasure, others are a major climax. They can arrive one at a time, in a spaced-out series, or in a continual flowing from one to the next. See Chapters 4, 6, and 13 for exciting ways to make her clitoris happy other than during intercourse.

Stop in the Name of Love

More than 50 percent of women admit to having faked an orgasm at some time in their life.

Vaginal Orgasms

Your vagina is a powerful pleasure place—a truly sacred cave. Although some parts may be more easily sensitive to satisfying stimulation, every part of your yoni, from its wondrous mouth all the way back to your cervix, can be taught to respond orgasmically. The effects you'll feel will vary from subtle to earth shattering. Your yoni is home to that hearty thrill-giver, your G-spot.

Ejaculatory Orgasms

During an ejaculatory orgasm, fluid is expelled through your urethra. This expulsion may be accompanied by intensely pleasing sensations or by a very minor little ruckus. And you thought only guys did this!

Love Bites

ABC's *Primetime* poll confirmed that women who regularly have orgasms are more likely to enjoy sex a lot, think about it frequently, and to consider their sex lives not only fulfilling, but very exciting.

Energy Orgasms

By working with your energetic body as well as your physical body, you can experience energy orgasms. Focused breathing, PC squeezing, visualizing, and undulating your body during lovemaking all help to build a high energy charge that you can direct from your genitals up through your entire body in a Kundalini wave. Tantra and Taoist masters share this energy with their sexual partners, and through it connect to the Divine or cosmic consciousness. Energy orgasms are quite powerful and can be enormously healing. Appendix C gives you more detail about Tantric practice. Energy orgasms can come in two forms: Peak and Valley. See Chapter 8 for more discussion.

Anal Orgasms

Your anus is packed with nerve-endings and, if you can relax and get past the cultural taboos associated with this sensitive part of your genitals, the right type of provocation may lead to intense orgasm. Vatsyayana didn't go into much detail about anal play, except to note that "people in the Southern countries have also a congress in the anus, that is called the 'lower congress.'" (II-6)

Mini-Orgasms

Not all orgasms are body-shaking climaxes that come from deliberate genital stimulation. Women can experience mini-orgasms through thinking erotic thoughts, or focusing intently on the pulse of their bodies, or tensing and relaxing their genital muscles, or by eroticizing other pleasurable physical sensations—gentle caresses, the sun's warmth, soft breezes. Mini-orgasms are waiting inside you to wiggle their way out—let them!

Pala's Perspective

Based on my personal experience and that of the many women I've worked with, I believe most women can become multi-orgasmic. We only need permission from ourselves to embrace our sexuality, and time to set our fires raging.

Blended Orgasms

You may be conscious of very separate and distinct types of orgasm. You may be thoroughly aware of how and where each delicious release of feeling begins and ends. However, you are just as likely to have blended orgasms, where pleasure plows

through you from clitoris and vagina and breasts in a delightful mix of sensation—a limitless orgasmic sea.

Super-Sex Orgasms

Super-sex orgasms are mind-blowing, body-shaking, and heart-opening. They usually occur through extended, intense physical sex accompanied by deep emotional vulnerability and fearless opening to the flow of energy. Sex-goddess and educator Annie Sprinkle calls them "megagasms." Their power is enormous: you may scream, laugh, cry, sob as your whole body explodes with pleasure that lasts and lasts and lasts, fed by euphoria, visions, and even other-life memories.

The Goddess-Spot

In 1905 medical doctor and psychiatrist Sigmund Freud first postulated the existence of two kinds of female orgasm, clitoral and vaginal. Western medical science had previously believed that all female orgasms were clitoral. In spite of Freud's "discovery," debate continued to rage as late as the 1940s over whether women were capable of having orgasms at all. The G-spot was unknown in the West at the time—or, more correctly, no one had given it a name. Even more surprising is that as late as 1990 the sex research pioneer Kinsey Institute was continuing to claim that there was insufficient evidence to prove there was a G-spot, or, if there was, whether it did anything. According to sexuality researcher John Perry, Kinsey was so set against the idea of a vaginal orgasm that he ignored evidence of vaginal sensitivity. Both Kinsey and later Masters and Johnson denied the existence of the G-spot.

The original research identifying what is now commonly called the G-spot was conducted in the 1940s by two gynecologists, Ernst Gräfenberg (German), and Robert Dickinson (perhaps the first American sexologist). Thanks to their research, some of which appeared in Gräfenberg's article, "The Role of Urethra in Female Orgasm," this sensitive area is now well known. In 1981, sexuality researchers Beverly Whipple and John Perry first used the term G-spot in honor of Dr. Gräfenberg. However, many modern sexual explorers are now calling this famous spot the "goddess-spot" in honor of the fact that it belongs to women after all. Besides that, goddess-spot sounds so much sexier than G-spot.

Love Bites

Studies of twins have suggested that female orgasmic capacity might be genetically influenced.

If you're having difficulty finding your G-spot, be sure you're looking in the right place, at the right time. It's on the anterior wall (the inside upper wall) near the front of the vaginal canal. Look at your yoni as if it were a clock, with the clitoris at 12:00. The G-spot is 1 or 2 inches inside (3-4.5 cm), somewhere between 11:00 and 1:00. There you'll find a collection of spongy tissue that becomes sensitized as your sexual arousal increases. Before you're sexually excited, it'll be difficult, if not impossible, to differentiate this spongy tissue. Also, if you're like most women, touching your goddess-spot prematurely doesn't feel too good. Rather than turning you on, it may well turn you off.

However, once you're sufficiently sexually aroused, your G-spot can be a source of great pleasure if your lover strokes it with the proper motion, speed, and pressure. Even after you're all fired up, he might still not be able to feel any noticeable difference in texture. But, he'll know he's on the money, because your responses will show your enjoyment, whether it's a sweet, mild buzz or an off-the-charts sizzle. Some women who've become numbed to vaginal stimulation, perhaps through sexual trauma or a variety of physical ailments, won't respond to G-spot touching. But most do, or can learn to, especially if they remain open and relaxed, and feel safe and loved.

Wet and Wild

When your lover strokes your G-spot, don't be surprised if there's a forceful expulsion of fluid from your urethra, which may or may not be accompanied by orgasm. Studies have shown that lots of women experience this. Just before their ejaculation, some women feel like they have to urinate, and so they tense up and hold back out of embarrassment. But rest assured, this clear watery liquid isn't pee—it's much more like the fluid from a man's prostate gland. In fact, Slovakian medical pathologist Milan Zaviacic, who's been researching this phenomenon for 25 years, refers to the G-spot as the female prostate. Until recently, most authorities have denied the existence of a female prostate, and many still do.

Love Bites

In 2001, the Federative International Committee on Anatomical Terminology officially accepted the term "female prostate" for use in its specialist publications.

Confusion results because the shape and structure of the G-spot is quite different from the shape and structure of the male prostate gland. In men, the prostate is a single gland, about the size of a large grape, which drains into the urethra through two ducts. By contrast, the female prostate is actually a collection of perhaps 30 or more *paraurethral glands*. They surround the urethra on all sides and empty into it through many small ducts. Think "function" rather than shape or structure and it's easy to get the similarity.

Pillow Talk

Paraurethral refers to glands that are *near the urethra*. They're also called *Skene's Glands*.

In addition to these glands, a woman's urethra is surrounded by erectile tissue very similar to that found in a man's penis. Refer to Chapter 10 for an inside peek into the ups and downs of erection. You may not know it, because it's mostly hidden inside, but a woman's vagina has as much erectile tissue as a man's genitals. With arousal, this tissue fills with blood, reaching an engorgement peak at the time of orgasm.

G-Whiz!

Once you've sufficiently strengthened your PC muscles (see our discussion in Chapter 7), you can squeeze his penis along your goddess-spot in lots of intercourse positions. But some poses naturally align the penis and vagina for maximum G-spot stimulation:

* Rear-entry positions, especially when you're on all fours, with your head down and your buttocks raised high
* Woman-on-top poses, because you can determine the right angle of penetration
* Woman on her back with hips and buttocks raised into the air, and with her legs over the man's shoulders

Some researchers speculate that Darwinian evolution was at play in the development of the G-spot. Our early ancestors most certainly copulated like other animals, in a rear-entry mount. Pleasure from G-spot stimulation might make a woman more receptive to mating, improving the odds of survival of the human race. Others disagree, saying that female orgasm, unlike male ejaculation, has no purpose other than fun; after all, lots of women get pregnant without having an orgasm.

Love Bites

In her book *The Case of the Female Orgasm*, Dr. Elisabeth A. Lloyd points out that only 25 percent of women experience orgasm during intercourse without additional clitoral stimulation.

Clitoris Conundrums

Lots of positions will stimulate your G-spot, but your clitoris isn't quite so lucky. Because of her location, your precious pearl doesn't get the rubbing she longs for during the usual in/out motions of intercourse. She wants up and down to make her happy. You can arrange for it in woman-on-top versions of poses that include full-body contact, like Clasping and Twining, which we saw in Chapter 8, and Pressing, which we'll tell you about in this chapter.

Lying atop your lover, press your groin and pubic bone very tightly to his and slide down and then up a little as you move against him. This action adds plenty of contact with your clitoris. You can get the same scintillating pressure in man-on-top positions

when he uses the Piercing thrust. If you arch your back or put a pillow under the small of your back, your vulva and clitoris will be more exposed to fabulous friction.

Love Bites

If you want more intensity, topical creams that sensitize the clitoris are now available. Many of them contain the natural amino acid L-Arginine, which excites nerve endings and increases blood flow, thereby boosting clitoral responsiveness.

Your best bet, however, for making sure your clitoris gets the attention she wants is for one of you to give it to her directly with those amazing appendages, your fingers. If, like the majority of women, you need lots of clitoral excitation to reach orgasm during intercourse, adopt positions in which at least one partner has a free hand. Vatsyayana suggested a particular hand stroke, mimicking the way an "elephant rubs anything with his trunk." (II-8) Form a curved tripod with your index, middle, and ring fingers. Cup your hand over her pubic bone. Your index and ring fingers press on either side of her clitoris, bringing her jewel out more into the open, where your middle finger can pet it perfectly—up and down, soft or firm, depending on her preference.

Positions for Her Pleasure

You'll notice that the eight *Kama Sutra* positions presented here run the gamut of possibilities. There's man on top, woman on top, face to face, standing, sitting, and rear entry. That's because many poses can be adapted to grant ease of G-spot stimulation. A lot of what counts is angle of penetration. And, much of that is dependent on thrusting techniques. Plus, for guaranteeing reliable clitoral pleasure, all you really need is one hand clapping. Give her all the satisfaction she can imagine with these *Kama Sutra* postures of love:

* Half Pressed (Half Squeeze—*Ardhapiditaka*)
* The Mare's Position (*Vadavaka*)

- Packed (the Squeeze—*Piditaka*)
- Pressing (*Pidita*)
- Splitting Bamboo (*Venudaritaka*)
- The Cat (*Marjara*)
- The Horse (*Ashva*)
- The Swing (*Prenkholita*)

Half Pressed (Half Squeeze—Ardhapiditaka)

As she lies fetchingly on her back, kneel in front of her with your legs spread wide. Keep your torso upright. You'll be well balanced and able to nestle your groin comfortably into hers. She presses one foot firmly into your chest. Her other leg stretches out in sweet anticipation.

The Half Pressed pose gives you opportunity for the double whammy of both G-spot and clitoral incitement. In your upright stance, you've got hands free to tickle her clitoris, and, of course, to stroke other spots as well—nipples, inner thighs, belly, groin creases. With one of her legs stretched out, there's more space in her yoni and, because she's flat on her back, penetration isn't too deep, so it's a good pose for investigating her G-spot sensitivity. The side of her goddess-spot corresponding to her stretched-out leg gets more contact with your penis. Add to the intensity with Blow of a Boar thrusts.

She can vary her sensation, and yours, by switching legs. Shifting her pressed foot to different parts of your torso, belly, chest, or shoulder, will also change the angle of penetration. If you'd like to give her an extra thrill, play with the Churning thrust. Pull back from her a little and wave your magic wand all over her vulva before you enter.

Mare's Position (Vadavaka)

This intensely pleasurable pose is a variation on the third position of the Top, which we cover in detail in Chapter 10. The Top is a complex maneuver that not everyone may feel confident enough to attempt. But this individual part of it is very easy and richly

Half Pressed

rewarding, so we've included it here, especially for her satisfaction.

He can lie down or sit up with his legs extended straight out in front of him. With your back to him, you snuggle down onto his groin. Use the strength in your thighs to bob gleefully up and down. He can fondle your beautiful butt as you bounce. You're in complete control—speed, depth, and angle are all up to you. If you arch your back somewhat, your pelvis will tilt for better G-spot access.

If he's sitting up, he can lean back on his arms or wrap them fervently around you. He's in a good spot to spur your frenzy with Bites of a Boar on your shuddering shoulders. You've got both hands available. One can stroke your clitoris *exactly* the way

Mare's Position

you like. The other can titillate any erogenous zone that's calling out to you. Go ahead and have it all.

Stop in the Name of Love

Sigmund Freud believed a real woman's primary pleasure center had to be her vagina. Any woman dependent on clitoral excitation for satisfaction was infantile, immature, neurotic, or dysfunctional. He knew a lot, but obviously not everything!

Vary your pleasure with a thrusting mélange of speedy Sporting of a Sparrow to build your excitement. Then open to spasms of rapture as you glide your goddess-spot ever so slowly past his penis with steady Moving Forward. Double your fun with repetitive PC squeezing. The Mare's Trick and the Mare's Position make a dynamic duo. Let your love goddess out for a ride on her bronco with artistry as well as abandon. As you race for the finish line, keep part of you tuned to his escalating excitement.

Remember, Sparrow thrusts are really, really arousing for him, too.

Even though he can stay fairly relaxed in this pose, you don't want to send him over the precipice without you. If you don't want to have to gauge his response, ask him beforehand to let you know when the ride's getting a little too wild. For instance, he can simply grasp your hips and hold you still until he's calmed his raging passions. You can continue to stroke your clitoris, maintaining your excitement level, as you wait for him to ease up on the reins.

Packed (the Squeeze—Piditaka)

The Packed position is one of those intense but fairly still postures where a lot of the thrill comes from the erotic connection between you. It's definitely a male-dominant pose; she really can't move much at all. Essentially the pleasure play is up to the man.

Packed

Lying flat on her back, she raises her legs up in the air, squeezes her thighs tightly together, and crosses her ankles. You kneel in front of her on one knee and extend your other leg out behind, to give you stability while you thrust. Holding her hips firmly, you pull her in close for total surrender. She can hold her legs up in the air, or rest them against your shoulder. You can also hold them by her ankles, straight up in front of you. Use them as an anchor to pull against as you swivel your hips in Blow of a Bull, thrilling every part of her yoni, including her juicy G-spot. The tighter she squeezes her thighs together, the cheerier her clitoris will be.

Love Bites

As you grasp her ankles, press on the hollow between her anklebone and Achilles tendon. You're activating Bigger Stream, an acupoint that energizes her sexual system.

Pressing (Pidita)

Pressing is one of the few poses that offers direct stimulation of your clitoris. You're stretched out on your back, your thighs spread just wide enough for him to fit snugly between them. He reclines above you, spurring you on to ecstasy with Pressed and Clasping kisses. You push your groins, pubic bones, and thighs hard into each other. As you grind together the forceful pressure propels you toward climax. Modify your movements by contracting or loosening your thighs' hold on him.

Penetration isn't deep, but he can maximize your gratification with the Piercing thrust. Starting his slide about 4 inches (10 cm) farther up your body than usual, he glides past your clitoris on his way down and in. You'll never want him to stop.

Love Bites

Pharmaceutical researchers, determined to develop a drug that will do for women what Viagra's done for men, are keenly investigating women's arousal responses. There's even suggestion of a neurobio-feedback machine that would assist women to become superorgasmic.

Be bold and take command in Pressing by staking your claim on top. Spread his arms, entwine his hands in yours, and hold him firmly down with your arms and upper body. Polish your pearl against his pubic bone as you slide up and back along his length. Provoke his passion with Broken Cloud bites along his chest to his nipples.

Pressing

Splitting Bamboo (Venudaritaka)

Splitting Bamboo is an action pose in more ways than one. There's not only the expected movement of intercourse thrusts, but there's also an added motion with your limber legs. You start this position, like so many others, on your back. He kneels in front of you with his knees spread wide on either side of your hips.

You slowly lift your right leg and drape it over his shoulder. Your left stretches out. Now, in a pulsating rhythm of love, you switch legs, lowering your right leg and lifting your left. This up-and-down cycling motion of your legs continually changes the angle of his penis, bringing subtle shifts that ripple along your G-spot.

By changing the timing of your leg shifts, you can build your excitement bit by bit—slow it down and speed it up, according to your desire. Sitting up straighter to free his hands, he keeps his body still while you rotate against him in the Blow of a Bull thrusts. Moving only his arms and hands, he assists

Splitting Bamboo: Second Position

your climb to bliss by fingering your clitoris or helping you to raise and lower your legs. For a delightful difference, he can take charge of penetration. If you tilt your pelvis up a little as you cycle your legs, he'll be able to galvanize your goddess-spot with the Rubbing thrust. If you're extremely bendable, he can lean over and fire you higher with a Kiss of the Upper Lip.

Splitting Bamboo: First Position

The Cat

The Cat (Marjara)

The Cat's a difficult pose. It requires her to be as flexible as her feline counterpart. It doesn't hurt for you to have some tomcat resilience, either. This time she's on her belly. As she opens her thighs invitingly wide, you slide in between them. She wraps her legs around yours and brings her feet together, trapping you. With her hands at her shoulders, she pushes her palms hard into the bed and arches her head and neck up toward the ceiling. The alignment of her arms gives support for her bowed back. You reach up with one hand and tenderly cradle her chin. Your other hand reaches back to grasp her ankles.

Stop in the Name of Love

The Cat is one of those poses that you want to steer clear of if you've got back problems. Even if you've got a strong and limber back, you might want to warm up with a few stretches before you attempt this.

You nuzzle in exquisitely close with steady Forward thrusts. Then, tease her to agonizing anticipation with the stillness of Pressing. Put a small pillow under her pelvis. Rock her back and forth across it as you thrust, to further titillate her tingling clitoris. Nip or lick her shoulders, neck, and ears, and she'll wriggle till dawn.

The Horse (Ashva)

Here's a standing position that you might like to try sometime when you're actually out at the OK Corral. It's one of those that thrills with or without clothes, so it's great for an outdoors quickie. The Horse is a handy, multi-purpose position:

❋ It gets you both hot, fast.

❋ It offers manageably deep penetration.

❋ There's a good angle for G-spot strokes.

❋ Her breasts are within reach of your eager hands.

❋ It's easy on both your bodies.

The Horse

She stands facing a wall, or fence, or high counter-top. Leaning over from the waist, she bends just far enough so that her torso is parallel to the floor. Her arms stretch straight out in front, as her hands push against the wall, giving her leverage to grind against you. You're behind her, between her legs, with your groin pushed in snugly to her buttocks. You can grab her shoulders and hold on tight, as you move your hips in and away, again and again.

Stroking slowly by her goddess-spot on your way out will drive her wild. Switch your hold to her hips and besot her with the daring Giving a Blow thrusts. Your hands are perfect passion pushers. Move them lightly and incessantly over her body—stopping only briefly to tweak a nipple or tingle her clitoris. Or if she's in the ready-to-pop zone, wildly out of control, a few taps of Prasritaka may make her buck her way to bliss.

The Swing (Prenkholita)

The Swing is a proudly female power position—one that's likely to be easier if you do it on the floor, rather than the bed. You'll have better balance that way. You can always put a thin mat down if you're concerned about rug burn or splinters. He's on his back for a change, welcoming the opportunity to let you have your fill of him. His knees are bent, and his feet are flat on the floor. Raising his hips in a pelvic lift, his shoulders and upper back remain on the floor. He can use his hands to support his hips. Firm pillows will do the trick just as well, and enable him to relax more.

Stop in the Name of Love

Flexible young men in Vatsyayana's time performed this position in a full back bend—hands and feet flat on the floor, arms and legs extended, back arched. We don't suggest you try it unless your middle name is "gymnast."

You squat over him, your legs on either side of his hips as you lower yourself onto his enthusiastic lingam. You'll need strong thighs and flexible hips to really work this pose for all it's worth. Churn your body over him, moving your hips and waist in

The Swing

The Least You Need to Know

* Women can learn to have many types of orgasm.

* The intensity of female orgasms ranges from very mild to off the scale.

* For G-spot excitement, when you touch is as important as where you touch.

* At least 75 percent of women don't reach orgasm during intercourse without additional clitoral stimulation.

* The Piercing thrust works best for exciting her clitoris during intercourse.

* Many *Kama Sutra* intercourse positions can facilitate G-spot stroking, because mostly it depends on the angle of penetration.

elegant figure eights. Imagine that you're an exotic temple dancer being pleasured by her raja. Tilt your pelvis forward to graze your clitoris along his pubic bone. Squeeze and relax your PC muscles to sensitize both of you. Cup your breasts or raise your arms in graceful circles as you sway to life's oldest and sweetest music.

A Hard Man Is Good to Find

In This Chapter

- ❧ The ups and downs of erections
- ❧ How erections involve your mind as well as your body
- ❧ Four *Kama Sutra* positions that are erection arousers
- ❧ Four intercourse poses that help a man last during sex

The male erection is a marvel to behold. The transformation from limp to looming seems a minor miracle, each and every time. Men are entranced by the mystery of their erections, and no wonder. One minute he's relaxed, just hanging around, the next he's on red alert and aching to act. Sometimes it seems he has a mind of his own. He can wake up without warning when you'd prefer he be napping. Or he can desert you just when you were counting on him to stand fast, front and center.

As in most matters sexual, Vatsyayana provided assistance for taming your tiger, or at least making him a little more manageable. Particular *Kama Sutra* positions can excite him, while others can help him stand at attention a while. Here you'll find both.

The Anatomy of an Erection

Despite appearances to the contrary, your penis has no *baculum* (erectile bone). It relies entirely on engorgement with blood to reach its erect state. Inside your penis are three chambers. The *corpus spongiosum* contains the urethra, through which urine and ejaculate leave your body. The other two are the *corpora cavernosa*, which are a combination of smooth muscles, spongy erectile tissues, veins, and arteries.

Pillow Talk

A **baculum**, from the Latin for "staff" or "stick," is a bone found in the penis of most mammals.

Nothing happens until something stimulates your brain to send electrical and chemical messages to your genitals, signaling sexual arousal. As you're well aware, the stimulus can be just about anything, from the sight of your lady's breasts straining against her sweater to the scent of her perfume or the sound of her voice; from a casual word overheard to an image that just pops into your mind.

When your penis receives an erotically charged message, the *smooth muscles* there relax, dilating arteries and allowing blood to flow into the spongy erectile tissues. Ninety percent of the blood goes into the corpora cavernosa chambers. The corpus spongiosum gets the other 10. As more and more blood enters, your penis can double, triple, or quadruple in size. Penises that are smallest when flaccid grow the most during erection.

Pillow Talk

Another name for **smooth muscle** is involuntary muscle. They're muscles that do their thing without your conscious direction, like your intestinal tract.

When the inflow of blood creates enough pressure, the veins surrounding the chambers are squeezed so tight that they can't drain blood back out, and your penis becomes fully erect. As long as more blood flows in through the arteries than leaves through the veins, the pressure will be high enough to maintain your erection. If too much blood leaves, it's bye-bye, baby.

By the way, it's a good idea to let your erection subside every 35 to 40 minutes. The blood trapped in your penis carries with it oxygen and hormones that are consumed and transformed over time. You need fresh blood to keep him virile. So let him soften up a little from time to time.

Healthy Life, Healthy Erection

Because erections are cardiovascular events, the steps for maintaining a healthy hard-on are the same as for a healthy heart.

* Stay physically fit, with aerobic, strength, and flexibility exercise. Uphold your sexual fitness with PC squeezes.

* Pay attention to what you eat: lots of fiber, fresh fruits and vegetables, and balanced meals combining all food groups.

* Practice substance intelligence. Use recreational drugs—alcohol, caffeine, tobacco—in moderation, if at all.

* Deal effectively with stress. Make decisions and take action to solve problems with a positive outlook.

Stop in the Name of Love

Even two cigarettes prior to sex can affect erection capacity. And too much alcohol is a total downer in more ways than one.

Some men have physical reasons for inability to get and maintain erections. Diabetes, multiple sclerosis, hardening of the arteries, and hormone imbalances can all contribute to what used to be called impotence, but now goes by the less ominous term erectile dysfunction (ED). See Appendix B for information about dealing with this sensitive topic.

Love Bites

According to the Harvard Medical School about 1 man in 10 suffers from ED. In the United States, that's about 30 million men.

Performance Anxiety

One reason healthy men may have difficulty getting an erection is psychological distress caused by insecurity, shame, and guilt, all of which can add up to an immobilizing performance anxiety. Men may fear they won't be able to please their partners, and then feel ashamed when that turns out to be the case—perhaps a self-fulfilling prophecy. If you throw in a bit of guilt because of how horny they usually feel, how frequently they think about sex, or how much they masturbate, you have a sure prescription for impotence.

If you can't achieve or sustain an erection, your penis may be forcing you to confront something you're reluctant to acknowledge. For instance, you may not have any true feelings for your sexual partner; you may not find her attractive, or you may be harboring deeply buried feelings of anger or resentment toward her or toward all women. Perhaps you feel sexual intercourse is something you have to do, but that you secretly don't want to. Be honest with your feelings and explore them with your lover in a way that's respectful of the truth for both of you.

No matter how well your equipment's working, your head and heart need to be aboard, too. Men who easily get and keep erections, also:

- Have sexual intelligence. Sexual mastery is a learning process.
- Have emotional intelligence. Dare to be real, open, and available to feelings.
- Focus their attention on what they do want, rather than worrying about what they don't want. They think about keeping an erection and completely satisfying their partner. They don't waste time worrying about how humiliating it will be if there is no erection.
- Are able to be fully present in whatever they're doing. During lovemaking they're not distracted by thoughts of outside responsibilities, work commitments, and so on.

Stand Up for Your Partner

Just as a man's loving attention plays a big role in your arousal, so does your response affect his. Tell him with words and gestures that you think he's sexy, handsome, and powerful, and that you want to make love with him. Let him know that you don't hold him responsible for your orgasmic pleasure. He's surely not irrelevant, but no matter how good a lover he is, you're ultimately responsible for your sexual satisfaction.

Men get really turned on by a woman who's really turned on. Revel in your feminine sexuality. Give yourself permission to let go, join with him, and open to the great mystery.

One of the best ways you can help your man get an erection and keep it is to give him a massage at the outset of lovemaking. See Chapter 4 for massage tips. During intercourse, be aware of his arousal level. If you keep pumping while he's right at the edge, it's not all his fault if he drops off the mountain before you're ready to go with him.

Turn Me On—Positions to Arouse Him

You'll notice that, of the four intercourse positions in this section, three are rear entry and one is woman on top. That's because men rank these two variations highest in turn-on value. With rear-entry poses, especially if a woman is daring enough to initiate them and offer herself with brazen abandon, that basic animal instinct, a "me Tarzan, you Jane" response kicks in. Nothing can lust-glaze his eyes more quickly than a woman on her hands and knees, with hips raised and wriggling, juicy vulva exposed, and bare breasts bobbling.

Experiment with these *Kama Sutra* high-octane positions when you want to turn him on tout-suite:

- The Ass (*Gardabha*)
- The Boar (*Varaha*)
- The Dog (*Svanaka*)
- The Top (The Bee—*Bhramara*)

The Ass (Gardabha)

The Ass is a user-friendly pose, with little demand on either of your bodies. You don't have to be strong or agile to thoroughly enjoy it. And, as an added benefit, it's one of those postures you can do just about anywhere, indoors or out.

You stand with your feet shoulder-width apart and your knees slightly bent, so that your weight is evenly distributed. Lean forward slightly, just far enough to rest your hands on your thighs or knees. Standing this way, you'll be well balanced and primed for your eager partner, as he approaches you from behind. Depending on your respective heights, he may have to crouch somewhat to make sure buttocks and groin make the perfect fit.

The Ass

Because you're not bent over very far, penetration won't be really deep. But because he has lots of room to maneuver, most thrusting techniques match well with the Ass. For maximum excitement, he can experiment with this combo: Churning—holding his lingam in his hand, watching as he wiggles it all over your vulva before he dips inside, is sure to get his blood flowing. When he's firmly swollen, a series of Giving a Blow will blast you both. Switch to Pressing, so that you can ride the passion wave for a while, surfing along its crest rather than dropping down too quickly into the trough.

His hands are available to roam busily over your body, in ways you like the best—a Samatala slap to your butt, a gentle cradling of your breasts, a persistent pull on your hips, a trail of fiery fingers up your spine. He can even reach around to caress your clitoris. If you want to hear your man bray long and loud, reach one hand between his legs and tantalize his testicles as he thrusts.

Al's Outlook

Women often worry that the on-all-fours positions don't show their bodies to the best advantage. But we men love that view, especially if you'll let go of shyness and let us look, so relax, wriggle, and writhe … please.

The Boar (Varaha)

The Boar's a position guaranteed to bring out your fierceness. As soon as she settles into this position, your ancient caveman will drag himself out into the light of day. She's on her knees, bending forward with her forearms on the bed. Her pelvis is tilted up, with her vulva presented in that most ancient of animal offerings. Her head hangs down, free and loose, her hair flowing. You kneel behind her and make your way home.

Penetration is very deep, so you may be tempted to ride her hard, ferociously feeding your frenzy. Rubbing is a great stroke for this, and her G-spot will love you for it. Once again, your hands are free. Even if you want to maintain balance with one hand on her hip, shoulder, or waist, you've still got

The Boar

The Dog

another, so use it to her ultimate advantage. She can't move her arms, but she can bring her wild woman out through her yoni. As you strike deep, she meets your thrust with a forceful bearing down of her genital muscles. She'll swallow you whole.

The Dog (Svanaka)

Everyone loves man's, and woman's, best friend. The Dog is a playful position, simple, adaptable, and lusty. You kneel on all fours. He mounts you from behind. Situating himself fairly high up on your buttocks, and wrapping his arms around you, he devours you with his passion. Penetration is medium to deep, so Sporting of a Sparrow thrusts are especially arousing.

The Dog lends itself to a wide range of variations. He can lean back away from your body, freeing up his hands for carnal exploration. He can use them to grab your hips and pull you in and push away to emphasize his thrusts. If you want more depth, bend your arms at the elbows, and lower your upper body. Do this in a controlled fashion, raising and lowering in a fluid, nonstop motion, and you'll get the welcome side-effect of built-up biceps—it's the doggy-style push-up.

If you're feeling like you just have to move more, switch into the humping action of the Deer pose. If you want more rest and lots more depth, drop down into the Boar. You can also experiment with raising and lowering your legs, stretching them out to the side or behind you. Each move will bring a delightfully different sensation to you both.

The Top (The Bee—Bhramara)

The Top is a playful pose, requiring dexterity and perseverance. A woman-dominant position, in the Top you sit astride your lover and turn completely around on his penis. You're a sexy, spinning wheel of love. You need well-developed vaginal muscles to grip him as you revolve. It also helps to have strong thighs to support some of your weight rather than resting entirely on your partner. Vatsyayana warned that this position takes practice, but with enough repetitions you'll be able to make a smooth circuit without his penis slipping out. You'll get different angles of penetration and a variety of sensations for both partners.

Your balance will likely be best if you do this on a firm surface. If your bed mattress is very soft, try it on the floor or a mat. You can move in a continuous circle all around him or you can pause at each station for some passionate play.

Stop in the Name of Love

When you first try the Top, it's best to move very slowly, just inch by inch, because you don't want to bend his penis awkwardly. He needs to trust that you'll be careful with his precious scepter.

Starting Position: He lies down on his back, with his legs stretched straight out. You sit astride him with your feet flat on the bed on either side of his hips. Holding his hands will give you something to push against as you bob up and down on his lingam. Use a few quick Sporting of a Sparrow thrusts to make his penis hard and happy. The harder he is, the easier it will be to keep him inside you.

Second Position: Squeezing him very tight with your yummy yoni, swivel your hips to the right. Lift your left leg over top of his body and place your left foot on the bed beside your right foot. Place your hand on his chest, or thigh, for better balance. He can also use his hands to assist you.

You're now at a 90-degree angle to his body. You can pause here and wiggle gently back and forth, circle your hips around, or push up and down, to appreciate the differences in sensation. Or you can simply continue on your merry way.

The Top: Starting Position

The Top: Second Position

The Top: Third Position

The Top: Fourth Position

Third Position: Turn your hips again to the right, lift your right leg over his body, and place your right foot on the bed by his upper thigh. You're facing his feet.

Feeling more adventurous? Bend over, put your hands on the bed beside his legs, and push up and down along his penis. Or, shift your leg position so that you're kneeling rather than squatting, and bend way over to play with his feet.

As you bend forward, you're presenting him with a spectacular view of your buttocks and vulva. If you slide up and down on his lingam he'll be able to watch himself disappear inside you—it'll drive him crazy. He can look and knead and squeeze to his heart's content. If you're tall enough to suck on his toes while you press on the acupoints in his feet, grip his penis with your yoni, and thrust gently up

and down, you'll set his pulse pounding. Stop short of giving him a heart attack.

Fourth Position: Continue your circle of love by again swiveling your hips to your right and lifting and turning your legs as you go. Remember to use your arms to help maintain your balance. You can rest here in this cross-wise pose, giving him a lovely profile view, with a few wild wiggles thrown in. Or you can sail smoothly through to end up back where you started—atop your beloved, looking into his astonished, excited, and very impressed eyes.

Love Bites

If you can bend far enough to reach his feet, you can give him an all-over energy boost by pressing on the Bubbling Spring acupoint. It's on the sole of his foot, in the middle, between the two pads at the base of the ball of his foot.

Stay with Me— Positions for Maximum Staying Power

Your erection can disappear for any number of reasons, but the main one is that you've ejaculated. A lot of men ejaculate prematurely, before they or their partners wanted. In Chapter 13, we give you detailed, specific techniques for becoming an ejaculation master, but here are a few key pointers:

* Change position
* Focus your mind
* Relax your body
* Slow your pace

Fixing a Nail

Love Bites

According to Sir Burton, Hindu men would drink, chew betel, and even smoke during intercourse to preoccupy their minds and thus delay ejaculation.

Each of the following positions incorporate all or most of those key elements. Play with them if you want to make sweet lovin' all night long.

* Fixing a Nail (Spit-roast—*Shulachita*)
* Pair of Tongs (*Samdamsha*)
* The Goat (*Aja*)
* The Turning Position (*Paravrittaka*)

Fixing a Nail (Spit-roast—Shulachita)

Fixing a Nail is a position of subtlety and focus, although it may seem downright odd when you first look at the photo or attempt it yourself. She's lying on her back, legs stretched out. You kneel facing her, and settle back on your heels. Gracefully she raises one leg and rests the heel of her foot on your forehead. Obviously, she needs a fair bit of flexibility to enjoy this pose. As you slide inside her, she can grasp your hips to pull you even closer.

Now you begin the rhythm of love. There's little room for you to thrust, and she can hardly move at all, so work with a very slow, deliberate Moving Forward. She matches your stroke with hers. As you slide inside, she gently taps your forehead with her foot. She's the hammer and she's fixing a nail to awaken your sixth chakra center. The power of your sex flows into her, and resonates through her willing body, through her foot, into your third eye. Here is the center of intuition and psychic connection. You might place one hand on her heart center, between her breasts, the other on yours. Thus joining lust with love with all-seeing mind.

This position is an example of Vatsyayana's astute awareness of the intricacies of lovemaking; so much pleasure can be in the details. You try such positions for the range of experience they offer, the exquisite skill of combining male and female bodies in myriads of couplings. Each position isn't just a means to an end. The means has merit and enjoyment and artistry in and of itself.

Pair of Tongs

Pair of Tongs (Samdamsha)

Pair of Tongs is the simplest and easiest of woman-on-top positions, and one that can bring you both great pleasure. It's also a position in which a woman can show her true artistry as a love goddess. By tuning in totally to her partner's level of arousal and timing her moves accordingly, she can help him stay at a peak of pleasure for quite some time. Tongs can squeeze him back and forth from excitement to staying-power over and over again.

He lies flat on his back (for a well-deserved rest) as you kneel astride him. A pillow under his head and shoulders will enable him to see you and your enticing action better. Vatsyayana suggested that you grip his lingam firmly with the juicy vice of your vagina, squeezing and relaxing your PC muscles in time to the beating of your heart. As you become very adept at the Mare's Trick, you can vary your yoni enchantments, with speed, pressure, and special spots you focus on. If your thighs are quite strong and your hips pretty limber, you can get him even deeper, by crouching over him rather than kneeling.

Pala's Perspective

This is one of my favorite yoni dances: start by squeezing at the entrance of your vagina and, keeping those muscles tight, contract each muscle slowly all the way back to your cervix. When you have his whole length in your firm grip, relax all the muscles at once and bear down—you'll swallow him deep inside.

Intersperse periods of relative stillness (you're only moving on the inside so far) with some active rock and roll. Rock your pelvis back and forth to get some fabulous friction on your clitoris. Throw in some up and down by raising and lowering your body over his with the power of your thighs. Feel your full female power as you sway wildly above him (think Sharon Stone in *Basic Instinct*). Ever watchful, you bring him to the brink then stop until he subsides enough for you to recommence his exquisite torment with more gentle flutterings.

To spread his heat up from his loins so that it doesn't want to erupt into you so quickly, run your hands up his torso from his pubic bone to his heart

The Goat

center. He'll last longer, plus his heart will open in warm love. You can also lean back and with one hand press firmly on his perineum to give that hot energy a little push.

With your torso upright, lots of your delicious bits are available for handling, too. He can excite your passion with the Jump of the Hare on your breasts. Depending on how far back or forward you lean, he'll be able to caress your clitoris with his talented fingers. You might want to bring yourself to orgasm with your own clitoral stimulation as he watches. But remember, you want to keep him hot, not send him up in flames.

The Goat (Aja)

The Goat is another pose that speaks to the creativity of lovemaking. While it's randy like its name suggests, it's also noted for its intensity and relative

stillness. It's about power and penetration. It's a restrictive pose for her: she's essentially offering herself to you for your pleasure. She curls up on her right side, and then stretches out her right leg beneath her, as her left leg remains bent. You kneel behind and between her thighs and straddle her right leg. Bend your legs backward so that your calves are doubled up under your thighs; in effect, you're almost sitting on your calves. Move in close to plunge inside her. Then, lift her left leg up and around you so that it rests across your lower back.

Although she can't move much, if she's fairly lithe she can twist her upper body a little to look back at you, letting you know with her eyes that you're all man. Pressing, Blow of a Bull, Moving Forward, and Blow of a Boar are all excellent thrusting patterns for this position, because they don't require a lot of range of movement.

The Turning Position (Paravrittaka)

The Turning position is a moveable feast. You not only move in and out, you also move around, for as you can see, Turning is a combination of four poses. Like the Top, it's not for the faint of heart, the easily embarrassed, or those without a sense of humor. Lovers who want variety, challenge, and an opportunity to show off their skills will love it. Because it requires a great deal of mental focus on the man's part, it's a good position for helping him last longer. The intense concentration you need to complete the circuit without slipping out of your lover's yoni distracts you from the intensity of sensation building in your genitals. But you're still very involved in your lovemaking, very tuned in to your partner and what's happening between you.

Love Bites

Cosmo magazine's "His Frisky Wish List" survey revealed that for 45 percent of men, the best way to "last longer in the sack" was to change positions, followed by 28 percent who liked the stop-start method.

Essentially, you start out facing your lover's head and end up facing her feet. The various moves you make in your transit will stretch her vagina in different ways, creating new sensations for you both. The descriptions below might make Turning seem more complicated than it is—we just want to give you a thorough understanding so that you'll be tempted to try it. The main thing to remember is to move very, very slowly as you shift position. And, don't fret if you slip out; just slip back in again.

The Turning Position: Starting Pose

The Turning Position: Second Pose

Begin Turning from a basic man-on-top pose. She's lying on her back, thighs spread wide, legs bent comfortably so there's lots of room for you to wiggle your way in between. Warm each other up with some deep strong kisses, like Upper Lip and Clasping, with a little Fighting of the Tongue thrown in for good measure. You may also want to spend a few moments in very active thrusting, a vigorous Moving Forward or Sporting of a Sparrow. Carry on only until you're really hot and your

lingam is thick as a brick. Then become very still; use Pressing to push deep inside. Whisper into your beloved's ear that you've got a unique treat in store for her. Other than a few helpful leg movements and perhaps some PC squeezes, she can pretty well lie back and enjoy the novelty.

Slowly raise your head and torso, supporting your body with your arms, hands pressing into the floor alongside her head or shoulders. Give her a bliss-ful blast with your eyes. Now, leaving your arms in

The Turning Position: Third Pose

The Turning Position: Finishing Pose

place, turn your upper body to your left. She can also help support your weight by pushing against your chest with her hands, maybe teasing your nipples, too. At the same time, lift your right leg slightly to move it over her left leg. Your left leg slips in between her legs. It'll be easier for you if she drops her left leg so that it's flat. Be sure to keep your groin pressed in tight, so you've less chance of slipping out as you move. She can hold you in with the loving clamp of her powerful yoni.

Continuing your turn, move your arms and legs so that you're now lying completely across her. Your bodies are at right angles to each other. Both her legs are flat on the bed. Your legs stretch straight out behind you. Because you're using your arms to move your upper body and support your weight, your hands aren't available for anything else, but hers are. She can stroke and squeeze and pet along your thighs, across your butt, and up your spine.

To complete your turn, continue moving your upper body to your left until you're facing her feet. Carefully lift your right leg over her head; she can help guide your feet with her hands. Now her head's between your legs and your head's between hers.

In this pose, she has a view of you she doesn't see too often. She can please you in lots of ways, like:

- Kneading, scratching, or slapping your butt cheeks.

- Pressing on your tailbone with both hands, one over the other, to stimulate your sacral acupoints.
- Tickling your anus and testicles.

You can nibble on her tasty toes.

Grind your pelvises together in a kind of inverted Pressing position. Or, you can rock your hips from side to side or up and down. If you like, you can continue your circuit until you end up face to face again. Where, no doubt, she'll reward your dexterity with a hearty kiss of accomplishment.

The Least You Need to Know

- Erections are cardiovascular events.
- Your mental state is just as important as your physical state for getting and maintaining erections.
- Your partner's response affects your erection capacity.
- You can last longer during intercourse by changing positions fairly often.
- Relax your body and slow your pace for extra stamina.

Fast and Deep

In This Chapter

- Five intense *Kama Sutra* postures that rapidly build excitement for both men and women
- Four powerful positions that provide deepest penetration during intercourse
- Position variations that accommodate differences in flexibility and strength
- Vatsyayana touches that work best with these postures to raise excitement and intensify sensation
- A new level of understanding about a woman's cervix

In lovemaking, you reach those moments when it's time to turn the passion up to a fever pitch, to flame higher and burn brighter than your daily mind thought possible. Throughout the *Kama Sutra*, Vatsyayana extolled the power of love that consumes you. And as always, he thoughtfully provided positions that will propel you both into a fiery frenzy. At that intense peak, you become absorbed in a longing to devour each other, to merge your bodies so intensely that they become one.

Helpful as ever, Vatsyayana gave precise instructions for postures that connect your bodies so deeply you'll erupt in an explosion of utter satiation. In this final chapter on lovemaking positions, you'll learn those spectacular poses, as well as how to combine them with touches and thrusts that will inflame you even more.

Building Excitement Rapidly for Both Partners

Sometimes you want to fire up your furnace of love very quickly. Maybe you've only got a short time to connect. Perhaps you're aching to add some spice back into lovemaking that's become routine, boring, and predictable. You might be recently reunited after a separation, or one of you has recovered from an illness, and you can't wait to get right down to it.

Well, these five *Kama Sutra* positions will ignite your fire faster than you can scratch a match. They're excellent as rousing preludes to longer loving, as wild intervals between slower, more tender poses, and as remarkably rewarding quickies. Because they build excitement so rapidly, men who have a tendency to ejaculate before they'd like must entertain some caution with these postures, or you may be finished before she's even started.

You'll notice that the following five positions fall into the standing and rear-entry categories. That's because, as mentioned in Chapter 7, these types of postures have qualities that help stimulate sexual passion most swiftly.

Rear entry brings out the animal, not just in men, but in women as well. Although there's a degree of passivity for women in all come-from-behind postures due to restricted range of movement, you're not just meekly lying there and taking it. You choose to let this magnificent male animal dominate you so you can experience the pure carnal delight of erotic surrender. It takes trust, and trust is a big turn-on. And, even though he may be in control for some of these positions, others enable you to move more freely and take charge of thrusting.

As the two of you play in animal postures, don't just make their moves, make their sounds, too. Grunt, howl, snarl, hiss, bellow—let loose. If you're shy, consider that making sounds brings big benefits. For a woman, making sound encourages you to abandon control, to get into the joy of your body and out of the distractions of your mind. Because sound carries energy, each roar men release moves that hot excitement up from your genitals, helping you last longer.

Love Bites

Ancient Tantric lovers believed that because everything is one, when you mimic animals' postures, movements, and sounds during lovemaking, you assimilate their inherent qualities, too. You'll absorb the deer's agility, the tiger's ferocity, and the bull's stamina.

Use these positions when you want to build excitement for both lovers very quickly:

- Standing Suspended (*Sthita*)
- Standing Supported (*Avalambitaka*)
- The Cow (*Dhenuka*)
- The Deer (*Harina*)
- The Tiger (*Vyaghra*)

Standing Supported (Sthita)

An essential requirement for this standing pose is a vertical surface to support and balance you. Either of you can be leaning against the wall, with your back or your sides against it. Wrapping her arms around your waist, shoulders, or neck, she stands on one leg and curls the other around you to bring you in tight. If your back is to the wall, then she'll simply hold her leg out at a right angle. When you're leaning with your sides against the wall, she lifts the leg that's away from it. You can help her maintain balance by holding her leg up, cradling her thigh in your hand. Depending on your respective heights, one of you may have to squat down a bit so the yoni and lingam are at the same level.

Standing Supported

Standing Suspended

Penetration will be relatively shallow, but will deepen the higher she can hold her leg. Moving Forward and Blow of the Boar thrusts are excellent maneuvers in this pose. With Blow of the Boar, concentrate your strokes on the side of her yoni that corresponds with her lifted leg.

Standing Supported is most fun when you're both flexible and have good balance. It's a classic quickie position that builds excitement fast. In fact, you can do it while almost fully dressed if you're so hot that you just can't wait another instant. It's perfectly suited for lovemaking in the shower, but be sure to have a handhold for additional support, as a wet, soapy shower can be dangerously slippery.

Standing Suspended (Avalambitaka)

While you're leaning your back against the wall in the Standing Suspended pose, holding her rounded bottom in your happy hands, she can be in charge of thrusting. Her arms cling to your shoulders or neck, her thighs grip your waist, and her feet rest against the wall behind you. With the power in her legs, she pushes back and forth in Sporting of a Sparrow, making your heart race and your lingam pulse.

For an interesting variation, make love within an open doorframe. In this case, her back is against one side of the opening and her feet are against the other. It gives her good leverage for pushing and adds more support so that you don't have to bear her full weight.

In the most challenging variation, you're standing in open space, holding her up, no wall behind you. Both lovers need exceptional balance and you need great upper-body strength. Just this display of your physical power can be a real turn-on for her. Unless you're extraordinarily strong and can pull her body back and forth along your lingam, there's very little range for thrusting, so Pressing or a little Moving Forward work best. Consider using this position as a sexy way to move from one place in a room to another, or from one room to another, without disrupting your connection.

Standing Free

When you tire in any of these variations, you can move to sit on a chair or the edge of a bed or you can slide to the floor. With a little practice, no interruption of penetration is necessary. You'll end up with her sitting on your lap in the Milk and Water position (see Chapter 8), her thighs wrapped around your waist, her feet crossed, her arms holding your back, shoulders, or neck.

The Cow (Dhenuka)

The Cow is basically a standing, rear-entry position. You bend at the waist, touching your palms to the floor or grasping your ankles. Keep your legs straight or slightly bend your knees, whatever feels most comfortable. Bent over this way, your derrière is proudly presented, with your engorged vulva fully exposed to plunder by your lover. The sight is extremely arousing for him. Standing behind you, he seizes your shoulders or hips and pulls you in for intense penetration. In this tremendously vulnerable position, you have little influence over penetration and thrusting; you simply offer yourself for his pleasure, and yours.

His hands play a big part in your excitement, fondling your breasts, tickling your clitoris, slapping your thighs, or stroking your back. If he tries this pattern of thrusting and caressing, passion will build rapidly for both of you: grasping your hips, he places his thumbs on your butt halfway between the top of your hip bone and the bottom of your buttocks, an inch or so out from your tailbone. Firmly bearing down here for a minute or more stimulates your sacral nerves, intensifying your sexual pleasure significantly. As he is pushing on these spots, he thrills you with the thrusts of Giving a Blow. Because continued thrusting in this way could quickly drive him over the edge, he keeps his own passion in check, while continuing to build yours, by switching to the Pressing thrust. Standing still

The Cow

and deep inside you, he lightly slaps your thighs and buttocks with the rhythmic palm beats of Samatala. Then, he inflames you even more by spreading fire up your back with the featherlike nail strokes of Ripping Silk.

Unless you're quite flexible in the back and hips and are used to inverted poses, the Cow may be difficult to sustain for long. If you aren't used to being upside down, beware of a possible blood rush to your head, which can bring pressure, light-headedness, and constricted breathing. You may want to try a simpler version, keeping your legs straight, but leaning your upper body over a slightly elevated surface such as a low table, chair seat, or ottoman. The angle of penetration won't be quite so deep, but you'll have support for your weight and more influence on thrusting.

Because women get turned on by words, he can ignite your auditory responses by bending over you and murmuring sweet endearments or wild, dirty talk into your ears. While holding your hip with one hand, he can titillate you by tweaking your nipple or rubbing your clitoris with the other. You can use the Cow as an excitement builder during a longer love-making session, but this position also lends itself to quickies in almost any location, inside or outside. You don't even have to take off your clothes!

Love Bites

If you can maintain full upside-down poses like the Cow for a while, you'll get the added benefit of stimulating your pituitary and pineal glands. Located in your head, they're very important for regulating your body's hormone production.

The Deer (Harina)

The Deer pose lets loose your natural, playful sexiness and sets your sexual energy surging. You're down on your hands and knees on the bed or the floor, undulating your spine in wild abandon. These rhythmic movements send the sexual excitement and energy you feel in your genitals up your back and throughout your body. If you're also employing the Mare's Trick (see Chapter 7), your sensations will be significantly multiplied.

With his torso upright, he kneels behind you, grasps your hips and pulls you eagerly toward him. To bring your excitement to a fever pitch, he can rotate bouts of the Churning thrust with Pressing. As he presses in deep and still, he uses his thumbs to stimulate the acupoints high in your buttocks.

He can also push the palm of one hand slowly and firmly down on your tailbone. Holding these

acupressure points for a minute or more blasts luscious waves of sexual pleasure throughout your genitals. For variety, he can alternately lift your right or left leg, extending it out behind his body. This changes the angle of penetration and contact with the G-spot. Sensations may be deliciously different, depending on which leg is lifted.

The Deer

The Tiger

The Tiger (Vyaghra)

The Tiger is definitely a male-dominant, power position. She lies face down, her head on the bed, her knees drawn up under her, and her rump raised invitingly. You kneel and mount her gleefully from behind. She can't move much, especially if you lean heavily on her, grab her hair, or push her head into the bed. But remember, her surrender doesn't mean submission—a tigress is no pussycat. She's willingly offering herself to your fierceness so that it will spur hers to awaken. She may relax her body, remaining relatively motionless, quivering slightly in anticipation of each splendid thrust. Or she can move with you, wildly pushing her hips back to meet yours, angling her yoni just so for maximum G-spot strikes.

Lean over her, with your chest against her back. Playfully bite at her ears, neck, and shoulders, marking the Line of Points on her tender skin. Reach beneath her with one hand to pet her breasts and raise her nipples into peaks. Rumble throaty growls into her ear. Listen, as her responding purrs escalate into sexy snarls. Pillows beneath her belly and hips will support her body if you want to play big cat for any length of time. Otherwise, she may tire quickly if you rest all your weight on her. Because the angle can be extreme for her lower back, pillows are a good addition if she's resting her chest on the bed for long.

The Tiger builds arousal quickly for both lovers, but it can be so exciting that men must be careful to avoid ejaculating too soon. If there's any danger of doing so, only hold this position for a short time, or your tigress may really bite. On the other hand, if you have difficulty ejaculating, this position ought to help you come easily. Blow of the Bull thrusts are especially suited for the Tiger pose.

Deep Penetration

While the best lovemaking is much more than physical, there's no denying the primal satisfaction of being utterly fulfilled on a physical level, a satisfaction that leaves the body completely spent and undone, with nothing left over. Perhaps no other aspect of lovemaking delivers this satisfaction as successfully as thrusts that reach to the depths of the yoni, all the way back to the extreme end of the vaginal canal. These fierce, deep, powerful thrusts are synonymous with abandonment of all restraint, of complete and unconditional surrender.

When you feel an overwhelming desire to claim each other, to become one, to merge in absolute physical closeness, experiment with the four positions introduced here. Because these postures open the yoni very wide, Vatsyayana particularly recommended them for smaller yoni, larger lingam combos. Be sure to use them later in lovemaking when your vagina is fully lubricated, engorged, and enlarged. That only happens once you are totally ripe with sexual arousal. These poses are perfect, too, when you're ready to bring your lovemaking to a mutual climax.

Love Bites

A QueenDom.com survey of 25,000 people revealed that women like it deepest when they're on top. Next favorite for really intense penetration is doggy style. Men preferred it the other way around—rear entry, and then woman on top.

Expanding your yoni also often means opening your thighs wide, stretching your legs, and/or lifting your pelvis, all of which require a certain degree of elasticity. To become flexible enough so that you and your man are comfortable in any *Kama Sutra* pose, make yoga part of your fitness routine. Yoga stretches and tones your muscles and helps build stamina and balance, as well as flexibility. Like love postures, many yoga *asanas* take their inspiration from nature and animal life. You'll find that some yoga poses are directly transferable to your lovemaking, such as the pelvic lift for Widely Open, the cat pose for the Deer position, the downward dog for the Cow, and the tree for Standing Supported.

Pillow Talk

Hatha Yoga includes hundreds of **asanas,** or body positions, from the Sanskrit word for "seat." While practiced with the physical body, they also enable you to focus the power of the mind and tune into the energy of the spirit.

Your Cervix: Unknown Erogenous Zone

Really deep penetration can lead a woman to a profoundly intense orgasm. It's a climax due to stimulation of the nerve endings that enclose the *cervix* and connect to the upper reaches of the vaginal canal. When the lingam presses repeatedly against the cervix, it causes the uterus to move. As everything starts moving—muscles, ligaments, membranes—fantastic feelings spread deep inside you.

Pillow Talk

The **cervix** is the lower, tapered end of a woman's uterus, the opening into the vaginal canal.

In their work on women and orgasm, Masters and Johnson described a process called tenting. At times of peak arousal, a woman's uterus lifts up and the penis can reach the depths of the vaginal canal, into the small area behind the cervix. Sexologist Barbara Keesling named this area the cul-de-sac. In her book *Super Sexual Orgasm*, she instructs women how to strengthen their PC muscles enough so that by squeezing them in a particular manner, they can make this space accessible to their lover's penis. The resulting sensations are beyond anything you've experienced before—all-encompassing, ecstatic pleasure.

Not all women enjoy pressure on their cervix. If you'd like to experiment, you might like to start with extremely slow penetration—take a full minute or more to make it all the way in. Use the Pressing thrust and, when his lingam has reached your depths, just hold very still and feel the power. Then move on to try more active motion.

Love Bites

Women's genitals contain more than one special site. In addition to the G-spot, now there's the X-spot (the cervix), and the U-spot (the highly sensitized urethral opening).

These sexual intercourse positions allow for the deepest penetration of the yoni by the lingam:

* Widely Opened (Flower in Bloom—*Utphallaka*)
* Yawning (Widely Yawning—*Vijrimbhitaka*)
* Rising (*Bhugnaka*)
* Position of Indrani (*Indranika*)

Widely Opened (Flower in Bloom—Utphallaka)

As you can see, you make your beautiful flower bloom by raising your vulva. Lifting your yoni higher than your head helps it open wide for deep penetration. To experience the delights of Widely Opened, you lie on your back with your knees bent, your feet flat on the bed and comfortably apart, shoulder width or more, and then raise your yoni into the air. Your eager lover kneels between your legs. You pull him deliciously close by grasping his hips.

The most comfortable way to explore this wide-open position is to place a pillow or two beneath your back and buttocks. They will support your lower back so that you can relax and thoroughly enjoy

Widely Opened: Easiest

Widely Opened: More Challenging

yourself as he plunges deep inside you. You'll enjoy this pose even more if he includes Rubbing as part of his thrusting maneuvers. Sliding up from beneath you, his lingam will rub tantalizingly past your G-spot on its path home.

If you've been working out with your yogic pelvic lifts and are feeling fairly strong and supple, you can push your feet against the bed and raise your pelvis up to meet his. Balance there, unmoving, as he slides in and out. Or he can remain still as you thrust, pushing up ardently to take him deep inside and then sliding slowly, exquisitely back down,

until only the tip of his lingam rests inside you. Even a few strokes this way will thrill him. Your hands are free for delicious additions wherever you'd like.

Add a little fierceness with this variation. He helps support your weight by encircling your buttocks with his arms as he pulls you forcefully to him. In time to the rhythm of his thrusts, you strike the center of his chest with Apahasta, the backhand slap, boosting his excitement and opening his heart chakra.

Yawning: Easiest

Yawning (Widely Yawning—Vijrimbhitaka)

You can understand how the yawning position got its name when you picture a woman's part in it. She lies on her back with her hips firmly on the bed, her beautiful legs stretched high in the air, and her thighs spread wide in a V-shape. This opens the vagina tremendously. Lots of men really enjoy this position because it gives them deep penetration and a powerful feeling of dominance. It's a good one to switch into when her passion is at a peak. Her yoni will be relaxed, expanded, and ready. To maintain an expanded V-spread for more than a minute or two, she needs good flexibility in her hips

and strength in her thighs so she can keep her legs spread wide. You can also offer her a helping hand.

Pala's Perspective

I've found that holding a position like this (stretching my legs wide, pointing my toes up to the sky) really does help keep legs looking great. Relaxing into the pose, holding my body wide open for my lover, is an amazingly pleasurable mini-fitness practice.

By changing the position of her legs, for instance, lowering them, and increasing or decreasing the V-spread, she can noticeably alter the pleasurable sensations both lovers feel. In a most easy-on-the-body variation, she lifts her legs to the height of your waist, as you lie between her widespread thighs. You

Yawning: More Challenging

need a strong upper body to support your weight above her and a flexible lower back and hips for ultimate thrusting.

Kneeling between her legs, you can hold your body upright or bend over her for passionate kisses or erotic nipple sucking. Drive her wild with light Stormcloud nips on her breasts. Alternate Moving Forward thrusting with Pressing—keeping your body erect, set a sensuous in and out rhythm, and then become still and hold your lingam inside her as far as it will comfortably go. Grasp her hips and press your thumbs slowly and firmly against the ropy band in her groin crease, halfway between her hip bone and the tip of her pubic bone. Delightful sensations will flood her entire genitals as you hold these sexy acupressure spots. You can also spice

this position up with the Piercing thrust. Instead of kneeling, lie between her legs. Bend over her and start your movement with your body a little higher on hers. Slide down past her pubic bone and clitoris, and then push in deep.

Edge-of-the-bed or table-top lovemaking suits Yawning to a tee—it's quite comfortable for both of you so you can stay in this position for some time, especially if you support her legs with your arms or she rests them on your shoulders. She lies with her hips at the extreme edge of the surface you've chosen. You stand, or crouch, or kneel between her legs at whatever height works best. Your thrusting range will be considerable and you'll be able to mix and match your strokes for prolonging your pleasure and hers.

Rising (Bhugnaka)

Rising is a very simple position, but one that can give you both lots of genital thrills. He's kneeling in front of you. You're flat on your back (yet again!) with your legs straight up in the air, but this time you press your thighs tightly together. Your squeezing makes your clitoris happy and creates more friction for his penis inside you. This is a good posture if you haven't perfected the art of the Mare's Trick. He grasps your legs and uses them to give leverage for his thrusts. You'll both notice a delicious difference in genital sensations. You can instigate changes in sensation by moving your legs from the upright position to one side or the other. For a relaxing breather, you can rest your legs on one of his shoulders.

Because of the angle of presentation, this is a very good position for Giving a Blow thrusts. He can also boost your charge by rhythmically thrusting in Moving Forward as he twirls your nipples. There's a direct connection between nipples and genitals, so you'll get double the pleasure. Remember, you don't have to wait for him to play with your nipples; you can do it, too, and he'll love to watch.

Position of Indrani (Indranika)

In the ancient Indian *Vedas*, Indra was king of the gods and Indrani was his queen. Vedic legend has it that she created this position to better please her randy royal husband. If you're looking for a really deep connection, then Indrani is for you. As Vatsyayana said, it takes practice to master the flexibility of this posture, but you'll both agree it's worth every minute she spends stretching and bending in preparation.

With her legs drawn back as far as they'll go, her knees bent, and her thighs spread wide, her yoni is as open as it will ever be. This is *the* position for maximum penetration.

You can kneel between her legs as she bends them, spreads them, and pulls her knees back alongside her breasts. The farther over her you lean, the deeper your penetration will be. Or you can sit up in front of her, your legs extended along the bed, your feet toward her head. In this version your range of movement is more limited, so thrusting is greatly enhanced if you grasp her hips and pull her toward you and away with each plunge.

Position of Indrani

Experiment with all the tools in your thrusting arsenal—a mixture of slow Moving Forward, sensuous Blow of a Bull, rapid Sporting of a Sparrow, and the deep immobility of Pressing is particularly amazing. If you want to last a while longer, keep the Moving Forward quite slow and bring it and Pressing into play most. If you want to build to a mind-blowing climax, go for it with lots of Sparrow thrusts. For added thrills, bend over her far enough to kiss her and mimic your penis moves in her vagina with your tongue moves in her mouth, in the passionate Fighting of the Tongue.

Some considerations to remember as you explore Indrani: she may feel restrictively boxed in if you lean heavily over her; she may even have difficulty breathing. Because it does require extraordinary suppleness, don't stay in this pose very long the first few times you try it. Finally, although this is a fabulous posture when your lingam is larger than, or matched to, her yoni, it's not that great if your penis is smaller. With her yoni opened so wide, sensations for you will be limited.

The Least You Need to Know

* Excitement comes not just from a particular position or angle of penetration, but also from the kisses, caresses, and sounds that you add.

* Tilting the pelvis up and spreading thighs wide opens the yoni for maximum penetration.

* In very wide-open postures, take care with the depth of thrusts to ensure it's good for both of you.

* Yoga practice can help you prepare for love postures that require flexibility, strength, and focus.

* The cervix can be a surprising seat of intense pleasure for a woman during deep intercourse.

PART
FOUR

In the Afterglow

After the Big O arrives, do you roll over and snooze? Do you feel like the finale's a little too abrupt? Although your previous experience might not agree, sex doesn't end when intercourse is over. In Vatsyayana's view, what occurs afterward is as important as what happened before. Maintaining your connection now helps you build a desire to reconnect another time.

The *Kama Sutra* suggests simple ways to continue your playtime—either to wind it down, or crank it back up for another whirl. From talking to touching, from sharing food to sipping wine, it's easy to please one another.

Sensual Nutrition

In This Chapter

- Maintaining your connection after intercourse
- Why men drop into a post-coital trough—and how to climb out of it
- The power of now
- How to make your love words last
- Exotic food and drink

Vatsyayana knew that for truly supercharged sex, what comes after intercourse packs as much punch as what happens before. Even though things may seem to have come to their satisfactory conclusion after a rousing climax, it's only the untutored who abruptly end there. A cultivated connoisseur of the sexual arts savors a love feast's dessert just as much as the appetizers and main course.

As important as the 64 arts are to lure your lover into bed, they're equally invaluable for enticing your beloved to come back again. Now's the time to show your expertise, for every sublime sexual encounter "must include embraces and other signs of affection that continue afterward … in order to create a bond." (Daniélou II-10, P.197) The *Kama Sutra* gives definite directions about what those signs are, and we're delighted to share them with you.

The Afterplay Challenge

Afterplay can be quite a challenge, particularly for men, whose bodies, now that the sexual need's been fulfilled, turn their attention to something else: sleep. It's not because men are insensitive. It's because they are sensitive—to their internal hormonal levels. The testosterone that drove him to reach for satisfaction drops significantly after ejaculation. Oxytocin and prolactin rise up to take testosterone's place. While oxytocin may motivate him to cuddle, it's usually overwhelmed by prolactin, which can decrease sex drive, sensation, and mental sharpness. Prolactin determines his refractory period, the time between his ejaculation and his next erection.

Al's Outlook

Tantric and Taoist sexual masters often cease lovemaking while they still have desire, meaning that the man hasn't ejaculated. Although supremely satisfied, they don't experience any post-coital let-down—on the contrary, they're full of energy. See Chapter 13 for tips.

Although it's understandable that a man may want to immediately roll over and go to sleep, or jump up and get busy at something else, doing so is purely a self-indulgent reaction. As Vatsyayana repeated over and over again, master lovers pay utmost attention to their partner's needs, as well as their own. And even though a man may not quite feel like being loving right after intercourse, he'll benefit greatly if he does. By acting in an affectionate manner, his drowsiness can disappear and his awareness can revive.

A woman, on the other hand, is usually quite keen on afterplay. With her body satiated and her heart happy, she wants to bask in that exquisite afterglow. She's still feeling the effects of oxytocin and estrogen, which have been boosted by intercourse. She wants more touch and more connection. Loving interaction after sex also reassures her on emotional levels—her man values her in all ways, not just as a sexual release valve.

Immediately Afterward

Immediately after intercourse is the time to appreciate, affirm, and celebrate your union. Your actions may be relaxed or energetic, simple or elaborate, depending on your inclination. Very simply, you do the same kinds of things you did before lovemaking. Only now they're a gentle wind-down rather than a stirring build-up. Kind of like a runner who stretches to warm up before the race, and then stretches to cool down afterward. Both are equally important for the quality of the overall experience. To spark your own inventiveness, we're offering you some of Vatsyayana's suggestions for elegant afterplay.

Cuddle Up

You can maintain your loving connection in a number of "touching" ways. If you come to the conclusion of intercourse in a position that's quite comfortable for both of you, try to stay joined for as long as possible, even when your erection fades. As you lie together this way, your bodies absorb each other's vital fluids and your energies intermingle, prolonging the harmony you've created throughout your loving session. And the effects will last long after you've gone on to life's other business.

Love Bites

One study of American women indicated that semen absorbed through the vagina might have anti-depressant effects.

You certainly don't have to maintain a genital connection in your embrace. Many types of affectionate touch will keep your magic moving. You can "remain clasped in each other's arms, one against the other, like sesame seeds." (Daniélou II-10, p.200) You might hold hands, interlace legs, or nestle into each other like spoons. If you match the rhythm of your breaths, you'll feel even closer.

Loving Embraces

Being in the Now

As with so much of lovemaking, you'll enjoy this time of intimacy even more if you can be fully engaged in the present, rather than going through the motions. If your body's snuggled up, but your mind's gone to the office or waiting impatiently to shut down, you'll miss the wonder of this instant. Being completely in the now is of such extraordinary value—to both men and women—that once you learn how to do it, you'll want to be present every minute of every day, and definitely throughout your lovemaking—before, during, and after intercourse.

One of the simplest ways to move into the now is to shift your attention to sensory input—what you see, hear, taste, smell, and touch. The trick is to receive sensory information without trying to identify what it is and without going off on a tangent of thought about it. Simply take in the experience directly. For example, as you smell a scent, let it waft through your nose and into your body. Enjoy the aroma, but don't jump to the thought, "Oh, what a great smell; I bet it's that Chanel No.5 I got her for our anniversary. Yikes, is that coming up soon?" Or, as your lover's hand slowly sweeps your hip, feel the smoothness of skin on skin, feel the warmth spreading, notice sensation coming into your body and out of your body. Don't let your mind distract you from experiencing it with ideas like, "Gee, that feels so good. I love it when he pets me that way. I hope he likes it, too. I wonder if my skin's soft enough. I hope there aren't any cellulite bumps. Maybe I need to work out more."

When you're able to be present, you'll find that you feel naturally high and happy. Your consciousness will be expanded and your awareness acute. Your physical tiredness will drop away, but you won't be trying to get somewhere else. Right now, just as it is, is complete and whole, with nothing lacking, nothing to be added, nothing to be changed.

After ecstatic intercourse, not only is your body at ease, but your mind can be, too. You may be amazed at the clarity and insight that come upon you, if you allow yourself to stay in a relaxed—not lethargic—here-and-now state.

Scrub My Back

Vatsyayana's lovers went off by themselves to do their tidying up after intercourse, but you don't have to follow their example precisely. If you feel like you need to shower after lovemaking, why not do it together? Lovingly wash the body that's given you so much pleasure. Show your appreciation in your touch. If you're fortunate enough to have a hot tub, now would be a perfect time to soak together. Ease any body parts you may have pushed to the limit in your sexual adventure.

TLC for Those Tender Spots

The *Kama Sutra* suggests ministering to a beloved's well-used body with "pure sandalwood ointment, or ointment of some other kind." (II-10) You can perform the same service for your sweetie. Help those love-worn muscles relax even further with a wondrous rubdown. Oils and ointments containing eucalyptus and citrus are both soothing and invigorating—ideal in this instance.

If you're feeling a little lazy and thinking, "I don't have the energy to give my lover a massage now," understand that this isn't a huge undertaking. You can complete a full-body mini-massage in 5 to 7 minutes. And your entire system will thank you. See Chapter 4 for more massage tips.

Words of Love

Talk, talk, and talk some more—all about love, and romance, and ideas that inspire. After intercourse is a time that's ripe for conversation, about each other and how absolutely amazing you are. Vatsyayana suggested that satisfied lovers should retire to their private terrace. There, with her head cradled in his lap, they would "enjoy the moonlight and carry on agreeable conversation." (II-10) The artful gentleman would impress his lady with his knowledge of the starry heavens above, pointing out the myriad constellations and telling her of their meaning. Or, he could penetrate her heart even more deeply with pleasant love stories.

Perhaps you're a silver-tongued lover, comfortable expressing your innermost thoughts and feelings, knowing that such words are the stuff bonds are built on. If you're like most, and many men in particular, such revealing conversation may not come easily to you. So here's a top-10 list of things to talk about after intercourse. They reinforce that you're a great lover and a sensitive and caring person.

To make it easier for you when the moment arises, picture yourself speaking this way ahead of time. You could even practice. Build your confidence by saying sexy things to your lover—without your lover being present. Perhaps record your voice and listen to yourself, and then work on changing your tone and timing to create a sensual, sexy sound. If this seems weird, consider how much time you might spend preparing for a business meeting or a special presentation. For most people, in the grand scheme of life, successful relationships carry more weight than career accomplishments. Act to support that understanding.

1. Say, "Thank you," and mean it.

2. Shower her with compliments about her beauty, elegance, ability, intelligence, and desirability. Praise him for his maleness, sensitivity, personal power, intellect, and strength.

3. Reaffirm that your affection, respect, and love for her have increased, not diminished, now that she's surrendered to your seduction.

4. Talk to him about the lovemaking experience

you just had together. Tell him what thrilled you about it. If there are things that you didn't like that much, talk about them later, when you're in a nonlovemaking situation.

5. Share some of your positive feelings—express your affection, adoration, gratitude, and excitement.

6. Find out how to say words of love in another language. The romance languages, Italian, Spanish, and French, are particularly sexy. Whisper them in soft, sultry tones.

7. Converse about subjects and ideas you're both passionate about. Ask each other about daily life and share some of your personal dreams for the future.

8. Reminisce about outstanding experiences from your past together—when you first met, your first date, a memorable trip.

9. Talk about things that will make you both laugh. Tell each other jokes and funny tales.

10. Read love poetry or romantic stories aloud to each other.

Expand on your compliments and statements of affection to make them meaningful. Simply saying, "I love you" can lose its power after many repetitions, especially if there's no eye contact, physical touch, or vocal empathy when you speak those words. But a comment like, "I didn't know it was possible to love someone as much as I love you," adds emphasis to your emotion. And, "You look splendid. You make that nightgown come alive," has much more oomph than, "You look nice."

To help you prepare for afterplay conversation, here are some pillow talk examples. Fill in the blanks for intimate and inspiring post-coital conversations. Make your rapport reach beneath your words, by matching your body movements and gestures to your lover's, as you speak. Mirror the tilt of a head, the cross of a leg, the lift of a hand.

* "One of your most amazing qualities is …"

* "I love the way you …"

* "It was absolutely fabulous just now in our lovemaking when you …"

* "It makes me so happy to remember when we …"

* "Something I've always admired about you is …"

* "Something about you that really turns me on is …"

* "I can't wait until we …"

* "You're so beautiful (handsome) when …"

* "You make me feel so much like a man (woman) when you …"

* "The emotions I feel for you after we make love are so strong that …"

* "You're such a sexy goddess, and such a wonderful mother, and such a successful …"

* "You're such a vibrant man, smart, sexy, a great dad, and …"

* "What are your dreams for the future?"

* "I heard a great joke today …"

* "Which story do you want me to read to you?"

* "May I read a few of my favorite poems to show you how much I care about you?"

* "This quiet time after our lovemaking is so important to me because …"

* "When I think about you, I smile because …"

* "Please tell me about your day."

* "What's exciting in your life right now?"

* "You touched my heart with your kindness (thoughtfulness, generosity) when you …"

* "I really felt your love for me when you …"

* "When you smile like that it makes me feel …"

Alternatively, as you embrace, share the silence. Be in that space together in which nothing needs to happen, nothing needs to be said. Gaze deeply into each other's souls as you gaze into each other's eyes. Or, with eyes closed, simply breathe together in the rhythm of love. Maintain your emotional, energetic, and spiritual intimacy without any words at all. It will be a profound encounter.

Share the Breath, Share the Silence

Nibbles and Sips

In Chapter 3, we talked about incorporating a sensual approach to food for your love sessions. Now we'll make some mouth-watering suggestions about intriguing food and drinks to include during those happy hours. No matter which foods you choose to use, whether they're plain or elaborate, partake of them with style. Serve snacks in bed, have a picnic on the patio, or eat an elegant dinner in the dining room.

The right kinds of food do more than taste good and keep your bodies strong. They can add to your sexual capacity, too. Almost any edible can become an *aphrodisiac* if you think of it that way. A particular food can have aphrodisiac properties because of its nutritional makeup or chemical compounds, but mostly it's related to what you're thinking and how you're eating. For inspiration, watch the film *Tom Jones*, famous for its erotic scene in which a meal acts as both a prelude to, and an analogy for, sexual intercourse.

Pillow Talk

An **aphrodisiac** is a food or a drug that arouses and intensifies sexual desire. See more about aphrodisiacs in Appendix B.

Food becomes sexy when you pay attention to the astonishing array of colors, shapes, textures, and aromas it presents to your hungry senses. With food, as with lovemaking, taking your time is better, and taking time together is best.

Vatsyayana suggested that, after intercourse and while "conversing sweetly and gently," lovers should "take a pleasant meal, a clear soup tasting of mulberries, appetizing grilled meats, drinks of ripe fruit juice, dried meat, lemons, and tamarind fruits …. Then, at their ease, they drink sweet liquors, while chewing from time to time on sweet things." (Daniélou II-10, p.200) Here are some singular foods for modern lovers to enjoy.

Charming Chocolate

Chocolate wasn't known in India in Vatsyayana's day or you can bet your booty he would have recommended it. The cacao tree, theobroma cacao, from which chocolate is made, was named by Linnaeus, a seventeenth-century Swedish naturalist. Theobroma is a Greek term meaning "food of the gods." And no wonder, for chocolate enhances mental alertness, boosts energy and strength, increases longevity, and might even reduce the risk of heart disease. Plus it tastes sooo good. Among its most interesting properties: chocolate has noticeable aphrodisiac effects for quite a few people.

Love Bites

Italian sexuality research concluded that women who eat chocolate every day have higher levels of desire than those who don't.

The psychoactive ingredients in chocolate that contribute to its known aphrodisiac effects, as well as other health benefits, include caffeine, theobromine, phenyethylamine, tetrahydro-beta-carbolines, and phenols. The first three stimulate your central nervous system and increase your heart rate. You feel energized. Your heart's beating faster, just as it does when you're attracted to someone. You could even feel slightly giddy or high.

Phenyethylamine (PEA), also called the "love drug," is a naturally occurring chemical related to amphetamines. Besides mimicking the sensations your body feels when you fall in love—alertness, contentment, attraction, excitement, and euphoria—PEA also stimulates the release of dopamine. Dopamine is your ultimate feel-good chemical. During sexual orgasm, dopamine release is at its peak. Tetrahydro-beta-carbolines, also known as neuroactive alkaloids, inhibit dopamine metabolism. A good thing, because the longer dopamine lasts in your brain, the happier camper you'll be. The darker the chocolate, the more neuroactive alkaloids it contains. Eat chocolate after you've had an orgasm to maintain your euphoric high longer.

Phenols are *antioxidants* that, among other things, protect against heart disease by preventing hardening of the arteries. Red wine is high in phenols and is well known for its heart protecting properties, but a piece of milk chocolate has almost as many as a glass of red wine, and dark chocolate has even more.

Other foods contain healthy amounts of PEA, including cheesecake, yellow cheeses, citrus fruit, berries, apples, and almonds. Include them in your post-amorous eats. Strawberries dipped in chocolate are sensational. Prepare them ahead of time and arrange them artfully on a serving dish, or make a chocolate fondue and dip each succulent berry before feeding your beloved.

An Array of Aphrodisiac Eats

All sorts of foods have been promoted as aphrodisiacs at some time, in some culture. Appearance seems to have been a big factor in connecting foods to sex. If a food resembled male or female genitals it must have been good for them. Men who consumed asparagus, bananas, ginseng root, or rhino horn, watched for their penis to get longer and harder.

Eating the penises or testicles of bulls, goats, or rabbits, was supposed to give a man that animal's strength, endurance, and virility. One *Kama Sutra* recipe advised that gentlemen who wanted to increase their vigor should drink a concoction of sweetened milk in which a ram's testicles had been boiled.

Flavor and scent were also part of the aphrodisiac selection. When women ate oysters, avocados, figs, pomegranate, or vanilla, they expected their yonis to be sweet, fragrant, and juicy. At the very least these foods stirred the imagination and aroused the senses. And, in true folk-wisdom fashion, oftentimes they contain elements that promote sexual health and sexual desire.

The Aztecs adored avocados—their Aztec name meant "testicle." Look at the lovely oval shape of this luscious fruit, which, it turns out, is high in PEA. Cut one in half to reveal its exotic green flesh, with the bulging dark brown seed at its center. What a visual titillation for lovers. Mix and mash it into a guacamole snack to set your sensual juices flowing with a PEA mood boost.

Bananas were magical fruits in Africa and Asia, and they're saucy symbols for today's lovers, too. They're high in potassium, which is necessary for proper performance of your muscles and nerves. For a post-coital sweet treat, melt 2 ounces of butter, 2 tablespoons of brown sugar, and the juice of half a lemon in a frying pan. Stir until melted and add quartered bananas. Sprinkle them with cinnamon and ginger and cook for 2 minutes on each side. Serve as is or on ice cream. Or, for a fiery finale, add 2 ounces of rum and set them aflame.

Fresh figs are undeniably sweet and lavishly luscious. They also contain cancer-fighting chemicals and are high in calcium, magnesium, and potassium. Magnesium is an essential element that aids with the proper functioning of about 300 of your body's enzymes. For the *Kama Sutra* Hindus, figs stood for both the lingam and the yoni. They're especially appealing when lightly grilled and topped with chopped pecans and honey.

Another unadulterated love food, honey is rich in the lore of lust all over the world. Its golden beauty is complemented by its formidable flavor and wonderfully thick consistency. Not only does honey contain essential minerals, but it's also digested easily and absorbed almost instantly into your system, providing a high-charge energy source. In ancient India, honey was used liberally in intoxicating drinks as well as in snacks, main courses, and desserts.

Love Bites

Giacomo Casanova, the famous eighteenth-century seducer, was as much a lover of fine food as he was of women. He made a habit of consuming chocolate before lovemaking and solicitously served his conquests oysters.

Oysters have the randiest reputation. They're also bisexual—closed, they imitate male testicles; open they're reminiscent of women's genitalia. Ever wonder why lovers the world over have sworn by oysters as a sex food extraordinaire? That's because they're loaded with zinc, which is essential for testosterone production. So they're good for boosting both men's and women's sex drives. For visual appreciation and juicy delight, eat them raw on the half shell. If raw food's more of a libido depressor for you than an arouser, then grill them lightly.

Drink Up

Kama Sutra lovers enjoyed their fine drinks just as much as they liked their fancy foods—from juices made of the freshest fruits to all manner of alcoholic beverages. Wine, liquors, and mead, a honey-based drink, were served at dinner parties, country outings, and from the beginning to the end of romantic one-on-one interludes. Drinks were thought to impart "strength, courage, audaciousness, spirit, and stimulated the gentlemen's eroticism." (Daniélou I-4, p.68)

Al's Outlook

According to the Alzheimer's Association, one of the best ways to care for your brain and prevent dementia is to eat chocolate and nuts and drink red wine. Who could argue with that? Who'd want to? These foods are good for your head, your heart, and your private parts.

Modern views are pretty similar. In moderation, alcohol helps some lovers relax, let go of inhibitions, and open up to the experience of sexual bliss. Another name for alcohol is spirits, because it does raise them. But with alcohol, more isn't better. After you've passed your tolerance level, further consumption will interfere with your sexual functioning.

It can hinder a man's ability to get and keep an erection and affect both lovers' potential to reach orgasm. That's because, although you feel stimulated when you first drink it, alcohol is actually a depressant that decreases the responses of your central nervous system.

Stop in the Name of Love

If you've had too much to drink, as the porter in Shakespeare's *Macbeth* observed, it "provokes the desire, but it takes away the performance."

As long as you're aware of your limit and stay below it, alcohol can enhance your sexual encounter. It, too, contains that love potion, PEA, and those dopamine prolongers, neuroactive alkaloids. Be sure to intersperse your alcoholic drinks with juices and lots of water—you need to keep yourself hydrated. Bring some of these scintillating beverages to your bedside:

- **Champagne:** Those thousands of tiny bubbles feel like silk as they slide down your throat. They're a celebration of romance.

- **Wine:** Good wine is truly a lover's drink, before, during, and after a meal. Sharing a bottle of wine will leave you with a rosy glow on your cheeks and a gleam in your eye.

- **Brandy:** Distilled wine, brandy improves greatly with age. Its taste is mouthwateringly mellow, full of luscious richness and complexity. Cognac is brandy produced from grapes grown in the Cognac region of France.

- **Tequila and mescal:** The best tequila is always distilled 100 percent blue agave, while mescal is made from a variety of other agave plants. The type of high from both drinks is somewhat similar, although mescal's a little rougher round the edges. Both hit you with a noticeably different effect than other alcoholic beverages and can be quite sexually enhancing.

Keep the Torch Burning

You'd like to keep your love sparks sizzling between encounters as well. Wondrous afterplay aims not only to fully round out your rendezvous, but also to instill desire in you for another ecstatic episode. With some forethought and a little effort, you can ensure that you're both eager to start back up where you left off—whether it's tomorrow morning or a week or two away.

It's All in Your Mind

Between your bouts of love play, turn your thoughts to your lover and your passionate times together. Brand-new sweethearts do this quite naturally, but longtime lovers can cultivate that same eager attraction with conscious thought. It's an interesting life lesson that you get a lot more of what you pay attention to. So if you want your love life to carry on passionately, think about it that way. Nobody else is going to come along and do it for you.

Fantasize about your partner and all the amazing activities you might do together—in bed and out. Let your ideas wander to unusual places and unique situations. Use this guide to help you begin picturing some new moves.

It's often easier for men to ramble through fantasyland. In fact, sexy thoughts just pop into their heads without even asking—that testosterone thing again. If you're a woman who finds it difficult to fantasize, you may find it easier to just reminisce. Call up a scene, a scent, a sensation of your lovemaking. Roll

around in it, revel in it. You're setting free your good old pal PEA, those molecules of love, with this process. Fantasies do the same favor.

If your darling left you a love label with a bite, or scratch, or bruise, every time you see or touch that spot, recall how much fun and excitement you had. Use those tender places as anchors that hold you fast to your passion. "The love of a woman who sees the marks of nails on the private parts of her body, even though they are old and almost worn out, becomes again fresh and new." (II-4)

When You Live Together

Couples who live together, married or not, can carry their connection throughout their days, so that when nighttime rolls around, or you have an opportunity for an afternoon delight, you're in the mood. Remember also to set a regular time, at least once a week, to focus on just the two of you. On a daily basis, respect, affection, and attention are imperative if you want to make marvelous body music with each other for the rest of your lives.

Vatsyayana went into considerable detail about the roles of husbands and wives in his time, and how they should conduct themselves to create harmony and cultivate passion. You know what your own relationship position is: live up to it.

When You Live Apart

The *Kama Sutra* is full of delightful bits of advice on how those long-ago lovers made use of all sorts of messengers to keep their love link strong. You've got it much easier today—with cell phones, instant messaging, and web cams. Phone romance and phone sex will boost your love barometer and your imagination. Don't forget that old standby, the written word. A love note or card, sealed with a kiss, will make your darling's day. Oh yeah, if you're living in the same house, it's still fine to send each other love letters, too.

The Least You Need to Know

* Supercharged sex doesn't end when intercourse is over.

* After sex, tender embraces and affectionate conversation create a lovers' bond.

* Focusing on your senses helps you be fully present.

* Post-coital conversation should be positive, playful, and focused on each other.

* Sharing food and drink intensifies your playful connection.

* You can use fantasy and fond reminiscences to keep your passion afloat.

The Second Fire

In This Chapter

- Discover how to recover after an ejaculation
- Learn three hands-on revival skills
- Understand the importance of attitude for reawakening desire
- Find out how women can experience orgasms all in a row
- Learn about male multiple orgasms

Sometimes once is not enough. You want more. A little more, a lot more—it isn't really important. You simply don't want to end your active loving yet, no matter how rewarding your post-coital connection may be.

Whatever your motivation for another assault on the mountain of love, here you'll find some firm steps to set you in motion. Whether you're climbing back up from his ejaculatory letdown, or continuing your orgasmic ascent after a nonejaculatory rest near the summit, our guideposts will help you find your way.

Relighting His Wick

In most cases when you're thinking of starting a second fire, it's after a man's had an ejaculatory orgasm. Instead of flowing into the sensuous afterglow, or nodding off with Mr. Sandman, you're willing, if not yet eager, to rekindle your pilot light. There's any number of reasons you might want to carry on creating your frenzied fireworks, such as these:

- Your first love bout was a short one.
- You don't have to be at work for seven more hours.
- One partner or the other is feeling less than complete.
- He wants to see how quickly he can once again become a member in good standing.
- She wants to know just how many orgasms she can wriggle into.
- You're both randy as rhinos.

Depending on a whole host of factors—your age, your physical fitness, your overall energy, your frequency of ejaculation, your skill, and the talents of your partner—this may take mere minutes or much, much longer.

Love Bites

Age and Manhood: Between 16 and 30: tri-weekly; between 31 and 50: try weekly; over 50: try weakly.

Unless you've got an unbreakable appointment in an hour, don't *worry* about how long it will take to revive you. If you start down that road, you may as well keep driving, because you likely won't be rising up at all. Instead, let go of your expectations. Call on laughter and simplicity. Focus on your senses so you'll be present, just as you would if you were gliding off into afterplay. Turn your attention to your partner and her pleasure. Then carry on and see where you end up.

Don't, Don't, Don't Stop

A simple practice, and one that usually works best with younger men, or older ones who are in amazing physical condition, is to keep on pumping. After you ejaculate during intercourse, don't stop your thrusting action. Keep your hips moving and push in fast and hard as you can—a Sporting of the Sparrow on steroids. Whatever you do, make sure you stay inside her. If you slip out you'll need to explore another method. That's perfectly fine, because it's your willingness to resume that's important, not the exact manner or precise moment of your resurrection.

Your lingam might start to become soft at first, but with enough friction you can work him back up again. Vigorous, vigorous motion is the key. Once your erection is reawakened, you can slow down and employ less-aggressive plunges. This technique is often most effective if your first go-around didn't last that long to begin with. For those of you whose genitals become so sensitive after ejaculation that continued stimulation is actually painful, this course of action is not an option.

The Pause That Refreshes

A half hour of other activity—not watching the ballgame; you *do* want to keep your focus on sex—will often be enough for many men to start back up the sexy slope. This might be a good time to exchange mini-massages, fix a superb snack, talk sex fantasy, watch a little bit of erotica, or just hold each other close. You can also win major points in the game of love by giving your lady some selfless sexual attention. Her pleasure can spark your pleasure and, before you know it, you're both back at it. We'll talk about exactly what to do for her later in this chapter.

Give Him a Hand

After his brief time-out, the best revival technique is talented handwork. Any of these three hands-on maneuvers will help him perk right up.

Stop in the Name of Love

Don't try these moves with dry hands. You'll get some friction happening all right, but it won't be the pleasurable sort. Remember to use a lubricant so you'll slide smoothly.

* **The Palm Roll:** Placing his penis between the palms of your hands, firmly and briskly rub your hands back and forth along his shaft. Move up and down as well as back and forth. It's the same motion you've seen in movies where the stranded hero tries to start a fire using a stick, a stone, and some moss. Here, rapid friction will make the kind of fire you both can enjoy.

* **The O Ring:** With one hand pressing securely at the base of his lingam, wrap the other around his shaft. Make an O with your thumb and forefinger or curl your whole hand around him. Slide up and down, up and down, up and down. Switch hands occasionally and vary your speed and pressure. Intersperse pressing at the base with gentle tugging or tickling of his testicles.

* **The Two-Hand Glide:** Starting at the base of his penis, grasp his shaft and slide your hand up toward the tip. Place your other hand by the base. Just before your first hand slides off the end, start the other hand moving up. As it's gliding up, put your first hand back down on the base. Maintain this steady rhythm, gradually increasing your pace. Add a little thrill with the Corkscrew—twist your wrist a little as you slide past the glans and off his head.

Love Bites

Most men agree that the secrets to superlative handwork are mixing up your stroking technique and paying some attention to testicles.

Helpful handwork

Restoking his fire

More Pointers

You can continue pleasuring him with your hands all the way through to orgasm, if that's what you both want. When that's the case, take your time. Pay close attention to his responses and his level of arousal; back off when he's near the edge, and turn it on when he's calmer. Change things up—rhythms, pressures, spots you focus on—so he experiences a range of sensations. Learn to keep him in exquisite torment and you can add "handjob *artiste*" to your lovemaking resumé.

Besides your hands, you've also got your lips. Oral sex doesn't have to be restricted to foreplay. Now's a great time to reintroduce some of those ingenious *Kama Sutra* mouth moves you learned about in Chapter 6.

Your attitude is crucial for his awakening. Approach your revitalizing with respect, patience, playfulness, lustiness, and appreciation. Such perspectives are always important, but especially when you're helping him to make a comeback so that you can go on to more intercourse for your pleasure. If you're demanding and impatient you could end up with nothing but a sore arm. He'd like to get back in the game, but he'll resent being used as a sex object just as much as you would.

If her attentions with mouth and hands haven't gotten you riled up and rigid, there's no reason why you can't take matters into your own hands. Through masturbatory practice, most men know just how and where to touch for the most immediate results.

Al's Outlook

For a new take on an old theme, show her how you stroke yourself; then ask her to do it like that. Of course, her touch won't be quite the same as yours and you'll feel an exhilarating balance between familiarity and newness.

When your desire's there, but your lingam won't quite cooperate, you can commence intercourse even with a semi-erection. Both of you lie on your sides, in a semi-spoon version of the Elephant position, and, using your hands, insert your lingam into her yoni from behind. A little pleasurable thrusting will usually inspire him to stand up and be counted.

You'll probably be a little more evenly matched time-wise in a second spell of intercourse. You'll be able to last longer and her responses will often be more immediate. For as Vatsyayana noted, "At the first time of sexual union the passion of the male is intense, and his time is short, but in subsequent unions on the same day the reverse of this is the case. With the female, however, the first time her passion is weak, and her time long, but on subsequent occasions on the same day, her passion is intense and her time short, until her passion is satisfied." (II-1)

Her Turn

Especially while you're learning to become masters of the erotic arts, it can and often does happen that his fire's been extinguished while yours is still flaming brightly, or just starting to catch. If there hasn't been enough foreplay so that you've had an orgasm before intercourse, and you didn't reach one during, you'd probably like some loving assistance to blow your top. Even if you've experienced an explosion or two, but feel like you've been left simmering, don't suffer in silence. Such "noble" self-sacrifices can thoroughly douse your enthusiasm for future lovemaking.

Love Bites

The morning after their honeymoon the new bride says, "You know, you're really a lousy lover." Her husband replies, "How can you tell after only 30 seconds?"

Satisfaction

We aren't suggesting that you have to have a peak orgasm to have satisfying sex. You can get lots and lots of pleasure from the physical, emotional, and energetic connection, whether you've had a climax or not. In fact, if coming to orgasm is your only reason for making love, you'll be missing out on a lot. And, ironically, it can be more difficult to reach

Satisfy her desire.

one when you're entirely focused on the big bang. However, we do advise you to be honest with your feelings about your sex life. If you're truly content, that's wonderful; if you're not, don't pretend to be and just let it slide.

Love Bites

Statistics vary but, on average, about one in three women reach orgasm every time they have sex.

When you're in the throes of passion, it can be extremely aggravating to be left on the edge. But we recommend that you do not emulate this unsatisfied lady from the *Kama Sutra.* "She shakes her hands, she does not let the man get up, feels dejected, bites

the man, [and] kicks him." (II-8) If he's already wandering off, you may be justified in such a display, but you won't get what you're looking for. He's likely to go into a pout, too. Instead, gracefully let him know that you'd like some more, and take charge to ensure that you get it. You can wait for a while as we've indicated and then use your talents to help recharge him. But if you're aching for satisfaction right now, then why not have it?

Pala's Perspective

I used to hope my lover would make it happen for me. I finally understood that, although he's certainly not irrelevant, whether I had an orgasm or not was up to me. Then my satisfaction level and my orgasmic frequency jumped big time.

Don't try to reason with him; you want him to stay in his body, not go off into his head—which, right after ejaculation, is probably a little fuzzy anyway. Action is your best plan. If he's sensitive to your needs and eager to become an artist of love, he'll initiate some of the following ideas himself. But don't vaguely wait for something to happen. While your partner's important, ultimately you are responsible for your sexual satisfaction. He wants you to be happy, so help him help you.

* Ask him to stimulate you manually—show him exactly how you like it. There's a good *Kama Sutra* technique in Chapter 9. Vatsyayana wanted women to get as much pleasure as their men, and when they hadn't, "in such cases the man should rub the yoni of the woman with his hand and fingers." (II-8)

* Suggest he practice his oral exercises from Chapter 6. If he's ejaculated inside you and isn't keen on tasting his own cum, you can excuse yourself for a quick refresher.

* Playfully present him with a vibrator or dildo and show him how to wield it. See Appendix B for more on toys.

* Boldly pleasure yourself while he watches. It's perfectly okay for you to give yourself satisfaction, as long as you do it with gusto, not resentment. If you make him feel like a loser for coming too soon, he may well turn into one. But watching you excitedly going about your orgasmic business can be enough to get him off the bench and back on the field.

Love Bites

Well over half of the men who participate in *Cosmo* surveys say they're comfortable both with their lover stimulating herself to orgasm and bringing a vibrator to bed.

How One Becomes Two or Three or …

You know that, for most women, clitoral stimulation with hands or mouth is the surest way to orgasmic bliss. For many though, after they've had one orgasm, their clitoris feels overly sensitive and they need a considerable break before further stroking is at all pleasant. You can break through the long pause barrier with this simple technique.

* You've been exciting her manually or orally and now she's floating onto the waves of orgasm. Stop all stimulation, but do not break your contact with her clitoris.

* Wait, with your tongue or finger resting ever so lightly against her skin, for a little while—15 or 30 seconds—then delicately and slowly begin to stroke her again.

* You'll know instantly by her reaction if you've moved too soon. If you have, wait a little longer then try again. When she's receptive, keep on going.

With practice, she can learn to go on to a number of orgasms all in a row. As the woman receiving this gift, you can gain its full benefits if you relax your body. Its natural inclination might be to tense up, which constricts the orgasmic flow. Instead, let your limbs be loose. And slow down your breathing. You can also experiment with this process during masturbation, to give yourself multiple delights.

Masculine Mastery, Multiple Orgasms, and Maximum Pleasure

For a lot of lovemaking, intercourse is the highlight in the middle of the process. You progress in a lovely linear pattern, from foreplay to intercourse, to orgasm and ejaculation, to afterplay. Occasionally you'll add to this sequence with more foreplay, more intercourse, and another ejaculation. But there's also a different kind of cycle for you to explore. That's when you interrupt intercourse before a man has had an ejaculation. You take a break in the action and then come back for more.

Surfing high on the wave of pleasure that intercourse brings, and not slipping off into its trough, requires a great degree of sexual mastery. In Chapter 10, we presented a few basic steps for learning to make your ejaculation reflex voluntary. Here we'll give you more details so that eventually you'll be able to choose exactly when to ejaculate, rather than having it come before you want to.

It's also possible to take this skill to an even higher level. You can actually learn to separate your orgasm from your ejaculation. Then you'll experience the intense high of orgasm without the accompanying low that follows ejaculation. When you become adept at it, you can have multiple orgasms during the same session of lovemaking. That's right, multiple orgasms for men.

Al's Outlook

An ejaculation feels great—all eight seconds of it. But I don't like the letdown that follows. A series of nonejaculatory orgasms is incomparably better.

How's That Possible and Can I Do It?

It's possible to separate your orgasm from your ejaculation because, even though we often use the words interchangeably when referring to male sexual climax, they are two distinct parts of the whole exciting event.

An orgasm is a complex physical and psychological process that includes your whole body. After a certain amount of sexual stimulation, your heart rate speeds up, your breathing quickens, your blood pressure rises, and your genital muscles pulse rhythmically. There's a build-up of tension and then a pleasurable release that can be genitally focused or spread throughout your body.

Love Bites

Every man experiences orgasms in slightly different ways. Some feel sensations in different parts of the genitals, and some in various areas of the body as well. Their experiences can be extremely intense or very mild and a whole range of in between.

Ejaculation is simply a muscle contraction that causes semen to be expelled from your testicles through your prostate gland and out through your penis. Because the onset of orgasmic response is so quickly followed by ejaculation, you've probably come to think of them as the same thing. However, by paying careful attention during sexual arousal, you can learn to influence this seemingly inevitable sequence, so that you can experience one without the other.

Body Signals

Your first step in learning to master your ejaculation response is to pay close attention to the signals your body gives you as you're getting close to orgasm and ejaculation. Some signals are these:

- The stage of your erection: there are four. In stage one, you're thinking sexy thoughts and feeling a tingle or two in your genitals, but nothing's showing on the radar screen. Stage two is a "semi": your penis is starting to come alive, and anyone seeing you naked would know it. In stage three, he's standing tall, straight out and straining. By stage four, he's at full attention—bursting with blood, hot, hard, and deeply colored. For most men, stage four means ejaculation is unpredictable. You could last another 10 minutes or be gone in 10 seconds.

Love Bites

It's important for your partner to know what your signals are, too, so that she can work with you to help you delay your ejaculation. It'll be to her benefit as well as yours.

- **Breath and sound:** As you approach orgasm, your breathing becomes ragged and gasping.

You may hyperventilate. Your sound level will likely increase—with moans, growls, grunts, even howls.

* **Tension:** Your body tenses up pretty much everywhere, outside and inside. You may clench your fists, squeeze your lover very tight, flex your stomach muscles, and contract your buttocks.

* **Testicles:** Your testicles will pull up close to your body just prior to ejaculation.

Pala's Perspective

Testicles shrink up so immediately close to ejaculation that it doesn't give you much time to react. But you can assist him to delay by gently pulling them away from his body during your loveplay. Remember, the key word is gently.

* **That "certain feeling":** If you're paying very close attention, you'll identify a sensation—a tingling, a vibration—in your genitals, particularly around your prostate gland. It's the onset of orgasm, the *point of no return*. If you don't back off now, forget it.

Delaying Your Ejaculation

Once you've identified your close-to-ejaculation signals, you'll need to make some changes. That's the harder part, because your body wants to keep on going to release. Rather than continuing to build to orgasm and ejaculation, however, you can fly along at the heights of pleasure for quite some time if you:

* Change your breathing. Take slow deep breaths, preferably through your nose.

* Allow your erection to subside a little from stage four to stage three, or two, or even one. Slowing down your movement or stopping it entirely for a minute or two can help with this.

* Relax your whole body. Body relaxation is something you've learned to do in many other life situations, such as when you're engaged in

sports activities, for instance. It's hard to imagine you'd make it through life if you couldn't relax your body under challenging, stressful, or even dangerous situations. But it probably hasn't occurred to you to relax during lovemaking. In fact, the automatic response is to tense up as you approach orgasm. However, this tension hastens your ejaculation.

With enough experience of feeling what it's like to be really relaxed, you can eventually learn to keep your smooth muscles in your genitals relaxed as well. These are the muscles that contract during orgasm, causing your prostate to spasm and sending your ejaculate out through your penis. When they're relaxed, your system can experience orgasmic pleasure without the ejaculation. In Appendix B, we tell you how the nutritional supplement arginine can help you learn to keep those internal smooth muscles relaxed.

Nonejaculatory Orgasm

Are you ready to move on to nonejaculatory orgasm? The next step is to send your hot sexual energy up from your genitals, to spread sensation throughout your body. You can do this with some or all of the following techniques:

* PC squeezes—they're fully described in Chapter 7.

* Make sound—sound carries energy.

* Run your hands up your body, front or back, touching your skin or not—you can do this or your partner can.

* Touch your tongue to the roof of your mouth.

* Turn your eyes up toward the top of your head.

* Visualize your sexual energy moving up from your genitals to your head—picture a golden flame, a neon light, a flowing river.

Stop in the Name of Love

Don't focus on "not ejaculating"—that's paying attention to what you don't want. Remember, you get more of what you pay attention to, so think about staying relaxed and moving your energy.

The two easiest ways to learn about separating orgasm from ejaculation are:

1. Masturbation.
2. Being the receptive partner.

Rather than approaching masturbation as a quick tension release or a second-best alternative to "real sex," consider it a way to improve your sexual skill. When you're self-pleasuring, you have complete control, an instantaneous understanding of right where you're at, and a much easier time of shifting your actions. You can build yourself up to several peaks, to that point of no return, and then back off and begin again, and again, and again.

When you're with your lover, ask her if she'll help you practice, like this:

* You lie back on the bed.
* Sitting beside you, she stimulates you manually, until you're highly aroused.
* You're focusing on keeping your body relaxed, breathing slowly, squeezing your PC muscles, and visualizing a beam of energy going up your body.
* She's paying very careful attention to your excitement level. When you're getting close to orgasm, she stops or slows her stimulation. When you've relaxed enough, she starts again.
* Make eye contact and match your breathing rhythms to make a deep connection.
* Run your hands up your body, or she can.
* Build to several peaks of arousal, concentrating on internal sensations. If you get too close to ejaculatory orgasm, either one of you can stop it by pressing strongly at the base of your penis and slowly and firmly grasping the head. Hold like this until the urgency to ejaculate subsides.

Stop in the Name of Love

Never try the grasp-and-press technique when he's already started to ejaculate—even if it's just a little start of a spurt. It won't work and it will hurt.

Eventually, if you've been making love long enough to build a high level of sexual charge, if you're maintaining that excitement at a manageable level with relaxation and breath, and if you're spreading that energy up through your body, then you'll experience an orgasm without ejaculation. You won't have quite the same intensity of feeling in your penis as when you have an orgasm with ejaculation. You'll feel sensation in your genitals, but also throughout your body. Waves of electric pleasure will run through you and they'll probably carry on for a lot longer than the spasms of ejaculatory orgasm. Another big bonus is that orgasms without ejaculation leave you relaxed but not tired. You'll still have desire. You'll still have your erection.

This is a very high level of sexual mastery, so give yourself some time and some slack. Don't expect to be able to do it tomorrow just because you've read about it today. After all, Vatsyayana told you that supercharged sex is an art requiring extensive study and practice. But, hey, it's not like you're being forced to practice the violin. You're going to love the homework.

How Long Does This Go On?

When we suggest that you experiment with delaying ejaculation, we don't mean only for a particular session of lovemaking. While it's true that the longer you delay your ejaculation while making love, the stronger it will be when you do have it, there are also some interesting benefits from delaying ejaculation over a period of days or weeks. Over time, repeated ejaculation weakens most men and diminishes their ability to get erections. If instead you delay ejaculation for relatively longer periods, you'll notice certain benefits.

Love Bites

Because Taoist sexual masters believed that ejaculation drains your life force, they suggested various rates of ejaculation according to your age, physical health, and the season of the year. For instance, one manual suggested that a 20-year-old ejaculate every 4 days, a 30-year-old every 8, a 50-year-old every 20; in the winter, less often, and in the spring and summer, more often.

* You can last as long as you want in active love-making, including during intercourse.

* You can give your partner complete sexual satisfaction because you'll be there as long as she wants.

* Your relationship with your lover can be immeasurably enhanced and strengthened. She will adore you!

* You'll experience more physical pleasure than you've ever imagined.

* You can become a multi-orgasmic man, having any number of orgasms in a single session of lovemaking.

* Each orgasm can last longer and be more intense than an ordinary ejaculation.

* You can super-boost your immune system.

* You can experience a tremendous increase in available energy throughout each day.

We aren't suggesting that there's anything wrong with ejaculation, just that there's something else as well. And as a supercharged lover, wouldn't you like to experience everything that the world of sexual adventure has to offer?

Delaying Ejaculation and Prostate Health

There's a common misconception that regular ejaculation is essential for a healthy prostate. That's despite the fact that the practice of delaying ejaculation dates back thousands of years in India and China, with beneficial, not harmful, effects when practiced properly. Naturally, if you don't ejaculate and you don't move your hot sexual energy away from your genitals, you'll get a little sore—what you might have called "blue balls" as a teen. Until you learn to successfully circulate your sexual energy, all you have to do is ejaculate to relieve any discomfort.

You can also help keep your prostate relaxed and healthy with prostate massage. You can do that externally through the perineum or internally through the anus.

Massaging the prostate through the perineum is one of the surest ways to move excess sexual energy away from the area. Press into the perineum with two or three fingertips, at about the halfway point—slightly closer to the anus than the scrotum—until you feel a firm lump, which is the prostate. Rotate your fingers clockwise and counterclockwise alternately for 2 to 3 minutes. Experiment with various pressures and speed until you discover the right combination for best results. This will vary over time.

Prostate massage through anal penetration is one of the quickest ways for men to learn surrender in the art of love. If your lover is skilled, an internal prostate massage can also be a source of extraordinary pleasure. See Appendix F for instructional videos.

A short prostate massage before lovemaking relaxes those smooth muscles and helps you delay ejaculation. Afterward it helps disperse any excess energy. We highly recommend it—whether you've ejaculated or not.

The Least You Need to Know

* Sometimes continued thrusting after ejaculation is enough to maintain erection.

* Really good hand action is one of the surest penis revivers.

* Women should take action for their satisfaction.

* With the "stop but don't break the connection" technique, women can experience a series of orgasms.

* Orgasm and ejaculation are not the same thing.

* Men can have orgasms without ejaculation and become multi-orgasmic.

WANT TO KNOW MORE?

Glossary

acupoint   A location on your body where muscular tension collects, often in the spots where bones join and ligaments, tendons, and muscles connect. There are 365 acupoints on your body.

acupressure   The application of pressure to the acupoints on your body, using the fingers, thumbs, and palms. It helps relax the tissues, release blocked energy, and promote blood circulation.

adaptogen   Plant substances that stimulate your body to produce energy on demand without depleting your stored energy reserves.

alkaloids   Organic compounds in plants with biologically active ingredients, many of which have medicinal (and sometimes poisonous) properties.

antioxidant   Chemical compounds that can protect body cells from the damaging effects of oxidation.

anus   The muscular ring at the entrance to the rectum.

aphrodisiac   Food, drink, or drugs that stimulate your sexual desire and/or improve your ability to get an erection and have an orgasm.

apocrine glands   One type of sweat glands that also secretes pheromones.

arginine   An amino acid. Proteins are constructed from combinations of amino acids. In its form as L-arginine, it acts as a precursor to nitric oxide (NO), which is essential for relaxing smooth muscles and allowing erectile tissues to engorge with blood. In its pro-sexual applications, as a nutritional supplement it helps a man gain erections, and as a topical cream it sensitizes a woman's clitoris.

Artha   Refers to the material world of possessions, property, money, and commerce, for example, earning an income, acquiring wealth, and increasing one's standard of living. The second of the four aims of Hindu life.

Arts, 64   A list of 64 categories of knowledge and skill that, according to the Kama Sutra, men and women in the higher castes were expected to master.

asana   Sanskrit for seat. A physical posture or position, such as a yoga posture or sexual intercourse position.

ascetic   The fourth stage of life in which one leaves behind every worldly responsibility to focus exclusively on spiritual liberation. Ascetic refers both to the stage of life and to the one who is engaged in it.

Ayurveda   Sanskrit meaning knowledge of longevity. A comprehensive system of holistic medicine originating in India early in the Common Era, with roots in the Artharva Veda.

baculum   Erectile bone found in the penis of many mammals, but not in humans.

BDSM   The letters stand for bondage, domination, sadism, and masochism. It includes forms of sexuality and lovemaking in which the line between pleasure and pain is finely drawn. BDSM sexuality includes the consensual inflicting of pain, physical restraint, and servitude. The emphasis on informed consent is sometimes referred to as SSC: safe, sane, and consensual.

cardiovascular   Relating to and involving the heart and the blood vessels.

caste   Hierarchical class structure in India. There are four castes including Brahmin, Kshatriya, Vaishya, and Shudra. The Brahmin caste is the highest caste and includes priests, religious officials, spiritual guides, and intellectual leaders. Next is the Kshatriya caste, which includes warriors and rulers, such as emperors. Next is the Vaishya caste, which includes merchants, craftsmen, and farmers. The lowest caste is Shudra including servants, laborers, and peasants.

cervix   The cervix is the lower, tapered end of a woman's uterus. It opens into the vaginal canal.

chakra   From Sanskrit for wheel. One of the seven spiral centers of your energy body, with corresponding points in your physical body aligned along your spine from your tailbone to the top of your head. The degree to which energy can move easily through them exerts a powerful influence on a person's physical, mental, emotional, and spiritual well-being.

clitoral hood   See prepuce.

clitoris   A woman's supersensitive elongated erectile organ whose tip appears externally above her vaginal opening and whose two roots surround the vaginal canal. It has no other function but pleasure. Stimulating the clitoris is the easiest way for many women to reach orgasm.

congress   The act of sexual intercourse. In the Kama Sutra, congress is further classified according to the sizes of the genitals in men and women. Low congress means the penis is one size smaller than the vagina. Lowest congress means the penis is two sizes smaller than the vagina. High congress means the penis is one size larger than the vagina. Highest congress means the penis is two sizes larger than the vagina. Congress may also refer to oral sex.

copulation   The act of sexual intercourse.

copulins   Female pheromones produced in the vagina.

corona   The ridge of skin near the tip of the penis where the glans joins the shaft of the penis.

corpus cavernosum/corpora cavernosa   The corpora cavernosa are a pair of chambers of spongy erectile tissue in the penis that engorge with blood during erection. They are located on the top side of the penis. Approximately 90 percent of the blood in a full erection goes into these two chambers.

corpus spongiosum   A single chamber of spongy erectile tissue in the penis that engorges with blood during erection. This chamber is located on the underside of the penis, and the urethra passes through it leading out of the body. Approximately 10 percent of the blood in a full erection goes into this chamber.

courtesan   A prostitute, usually well educated, refined, and attractive. In India during the time of the Kama Sutra, courtesans were accorded a great deal of freedom and respect.

crure/crura   Two roots of the clitoris that extend around both sides of the vagina ending in two vestibular bulbs. The clitoral shaft is approximately 2 to 4 centimeters (0.79 to 1.57 inches) long. The crura are 5 to 9 centimeters (1.97 to 3.54 inches) long. The vestibular bulbs are 3 to 7 centimeters (1.18 to 2.76 inches) long.

cunnilingus   Oral sex by contact of the mouth with the vulva. Cunnilingus is often abbreviated as cunni or cunny.

dental dam   A small square of material resembling saran wrap that is placed between the mouth and vagina or mouth and anus during oral sex. Part of safer sex practice.

deva   Sanskrit term for god or masculine deity. Term used when referring to the Hindu god Shiva.

devi   Sanskrit term for goddess or feminine deity. The Divine Mother in Hinduism. Term used when referring to Shakti who was Shiva's wife, consort, and lover.

Dharma   A life-code. Bringing truth, spiritual truth, religious practice, virtue, morality, and duty into all of one's actions. The first of the four aims of Indian life.

dopamine   A neurotransmitter produced in the hypothalamus of the brain that is closely associated with sensations of pleasure throughout the body.

endorphins   Peptide hormones, neuropeptides, produced by the pituitary gland and the hypothalamus. They bind to opiate receptors concentrated in the brain but also throughout the body. Their effect is like opiates such as morphine, resulting in feelings of well-being and reduction of pain. Sexual pleasure stimulates the release of endorphins.

enlightenment   To light within. The spiritual experience of awakening to god-consciousness or cosmic consciousness.

erectile dysfunction (ED)   The condition in which a man is unable to get and keep an erection long enough for successful sexual intercourse.

erectile tissue   Tissues that enlarge as they fill with blood.

estrogen   Group of female steroid hormones influencing sexuality and reproduction, responsible for the development of female secondary sex characteristics. Strongest in women (produced in the ovaries), but also important in men.

fellatio   Oral sex performed by taking the man's penis into the mouth.

frenulum A layer of loose, bunched flesh on the underside of the penis at the point just below the corona that connects the glans and the shaft of the penis.

gandharva An unorthodox form of Indian marriage based solely on love and personal choice.

glans In males the glans is known as the glans penis, while in females the glans is known as the glans clitoris. It is the head of the penis and the tip of the clitoris.

gluteus maximus Muscles of the buttocks.

G-spot Collection of spongy erectile tissue on the front wall of the vaginal canal. A highly sensitive spot that when stimulated can result in vaginal and ejaculatory orgasms. Named after Ernst Gräfenberg, M.D.

Goddess-spot Alternative name for the G-spot, in honor of the fact that it is a woman's body part, one that can bring her powerful pleasure.

guru Spiritual guide or teacher. One who can counsel you and guide you toward enlightenment.

impotence *See* erectile dysfunction.

involuntary muscle *See* smooth muscle.

jati Name given to sub-castes within the four-caste system of Indian social structure.

Kama Refers to love, but also generally relates to the body and the senses: affection, romance, sex, emotional relationships, and the power of desire. It confirms the importance of appreciating and exploring the great gifts of sensory pleasure and the erotic impulse. The third of the four aims of life.

Kama Shastra Record of a divine transmission about the rules of erotic love, probably more than 3,000 years old. Kama Shastra may be translated as Science of Love. It was the first erotic text from India, and the precursor to the Kama Sutra.

karma Sanskrit term for action. Religious term in Hinduism that suggests how you live your present life influences what your next life will be like. Presupposes the existence of reincarnation. Often used as a synonym for fate or destiny.

Kegels An exercise in which you squeeze the pubococcygeous muscles, for instance, when you try to stop the flow of urine. Strengthening these muscles prevents incontinence, aids in childbirth, strengthens the female orgasmic response, stimulates the man's prostate, and can assist men in learning to delay ejaculation. Named for Dr. Arnold Kegel.

kundalini Yogic term for energy that lies dormant at the base of the spine until it is activated and channeled upward through the chakras in a process of spiritual perfection. Yoga, meditation, and ritualized sex can all awaken this energy, which is often pictured as a coiled snake.

labia majora *See* labium.

labia minora *See* labium.

labium/labia Labium from the Latin means lip, and labia is the plural of labium. Labia majora are the two lip-like bulges of tissue on both sides of the opening to the vagina, and they are typically covered with pubic hair after puberty. When these are spread apart, the labia minora are revealed. They are the two lip-like folds of tissue on both sides of the opening of the vagina lying inside the labia majora. They are typically hairless.

liberation Spiritual term referring to awakening to god-consciousness or cosmic consciousness, and escape from the cycle of births and deaths.

libido Sexual desire.

linga, lingam Sanskrit term for the penis.

lotus Yogic posture in which you sit with legs crossed in front of you and your back straight. National flower of India and a symbol of spiritual transformation.

mantra Special sounds (syllables, words, or phrases) that, when spoken in a particular way, have the ability to awaken a higher consciousness.

Mare's Trick *See* Kegels.

meatus Opening of the urethra at the tip of the penis.

meditation Practices that assist you to bring your thought to a quiet stillness, your attention to a focused point, and all of your awareness to be completely present in the now moment.

Moksha The final of the four aims of Indian life. Also, spiritual term referring to ultimate liberation, or freedom from the cycle of births and deaths.

mons pubis The soft mound of fatty flesh that pads the pubic bone. It is generally covered with hair after puberty. Mons pubis is the generic term for both men and women, but mons veneris ("mound of Venus") usually refers to women.

mons veneris *See* mons pubis.

mudra Ritualized body movements that have the ability to awaken a higher consciousness.

mystery religion A religion with a core of secret beliefs, teachings, and rituals, only revealed through a ritual initiation to those who meet special qualifications for membership. By this definition, Tantra could properly be included as a mystery religion.

nirvana Term in Hinduism and Buddhism referring to the experience of awakening to god-consciousness or cosmic consciousness.

Orphism Ancient Greek mystery religion dating from the sixth century B.C.E. postulating death and resurrection, and belief in a sacred afterlife. They also believed that future lives lived well could redeem the evil from previous lives.

outcaste A person excommunicated from his or her caste. See also untouchables.

oxytocin A hormone that acts as a neurotransmitter in the brain. It is released in both men and women during orgasm. Sometimes referred to as the monogamous bonding hormone, because it makes people want to touch and cuddle with the same person again. When you have that strong falling-in-love feeling, you have lots of oxytocin in your system.

paraurethral glands Also called Skene's glands, located on the front wall of the vaginal canal, an inch or two inside. These glands are often referred to as the G-spot and, with the correct stimulation, are the source of female ejaculation. The fluid they produce is similar to that made by the male prostate gland.

Parvati *See* Shakti.

PC squeezes *See* Kegels.

peak orgasm An orgasmic climax which occurs from the delightful friction of rubbing your bodies together, particularly your genitals.

penis The bone of contentment.

perineal sponge A pad of erectile tissue just beneath the female perineum.

perineum The part of the body between the scrotum and the anus in men, and between the vagina and anus in women.

pheromones Chemicals produced by males and females (and other animals) to attract the opposite sex for mating. In humans, pheromones are primarily produced in the armpits and the genitals. They are registered by the vomeronasal organ (VNO) located in the nose.

prepuce Layer of skin covering the glans clitoris in women and the glans penis in men. The prepuce, or foreskin, is often removed in men during the surgical procedure known as circumcision.

prolactin A hormone primarily produced in the pituitary gland. It is responsible for stimulating the mammary glands to produce milk in women, and in men it is responsible for the refractory period after an ejaculation. Prolactin makes both men and women feel sated after orgasm and ejaculation.

prostate, male and female The male prostate gland is approximately the size of a small walnut or large grape. It surrounds the urethra at the base of the bladder. It controls the release of urine and is important in male ejaculation, contributing approximately one third of the ejaculate fluid. It may be reached through the anus with a finger. See paraurethral glands for females. The paraurethral glands (Skene's glands) are also called the female prostate.

pubococcygeus A group of muscles stretching from the pubic bone to the coccyx and forming the pelvic floor. It helps control the flow of urine and is involved in the orgasmic response.

Pythagoreanism Philosophy of Pythagoras with its description of reality in terms of arithmetical relationships.

refractory period The time it takes for a man to regain an erection after an ejaculation.

reincarnation The idea that human beings experience an almost endless cycle of births and deaths. It is possible, through enlightenment, to escape from this cycle.

sacrum The sacrum is constructed from five fused bones lying at the base of the spine just above the tailbone (coccyx), and between the two hip bones.

samadhi *See* enlightenment.

samsara Sanskrit term for the recurring cycle of births and deaths, including the ideas that what seems like reality is only an illusion, and that life in a body is primarily suffering.

sannyasin Sannyasins lived simply as traveling holy men, renouncing all aspects of the world in order to reach the fourth aim, Moksha.

Sanskrit The ancient Indian language used mostly by priests and scholars. The Kama Sutra was written in Sanskrit.

sensual nutrition A term we have created to suggest the life-enhancing and health-promoting properties of sensual stimulation, particularly physical touching, hugging, and kissing.

sexual magic The practice of visualizing results you wish to manifest in your life at the peak of sexual arousal or orgasmic climax.

Shakti Shiva and Shakti are considered to be masculine and feminine aspects of a single indivisible divinity. Shakti is the feminine creative aspect of this consciousness. She is the Divine Mother out of which is born all of life or creation. She is wife, consort, and lover of Shiva. She is also called Parvati or Devi.

shastra Sanskrit term referring to knowledge or information, which may be of a scientific, religious, or spiritual nature.

Shiva   Shiva and Shakti are considered to be masculine and feminine aspects of a single indivisible divinity. Shiva is the masculine fundamental principle of essential, unchanging consciousness.

Skene's glands   *See* paraurethral glands.

smooth muscle   Smooth muscle is a type of involuntary muscle that operates without nerve stimulation. This muscle, found in many of the internal organs of the body, such as blood vessels, bladder, uterus, prostate, gastrointestinal tract, is capable of sustaining contractions indefinitely. In its normal state, smooth muscle is contracted. Smooth muscle must relax in order for a man to get an erection.

soma semá   Greek phrase denoting the idea that the body is a tomb or prison from which human beings must escape in order to experience spiritual liberation.

standardized extract   Plant extracts guaranteed to contain a stated percentage of the plant's biologically active ingredient.

sutra   Form of writing in verses that are short and succinct, or in point form. A brief statement of a general rule, maxim, or aphorism. Often used in countries in which the oral transmission of information is important.

Tantra   A spiritual tradition and practice that originated in the Indian sub-continent as many as 6,000 years ago. The word Tantra may refer to the spiritual practices (leading to enlightenment), or to the spiritual texts that document those practices. In the West, the term Tantra

is now commonly associated with a collection of ritualized sacred sexuality practices.

Tantric   Adjective form of Tantra.

Tantrika   Practitioner of Tantra.

testosterone   A male (androgen) steroid hormone that is primarily produced in the testes in men. It is responsible for the development of male secondary sex characteristics. It is found in both men and women and strongly influences their sex drives.

Trimurti   The Hindu trinity of three gods: Brahma (creator), Vishnu (preserver), and Shiva (destroyer).

union   An experience in which you understand, not just mentally but with your entire being, that you are connected to all, and you're not a separate soul.

untouchables   An underclass outside of the traditional caste system of India, including the lowest of the low in terms of the social structure and the types of work they were expected to perform. *See also* outcaste.

Upanishads   Indian sacred texts originating between 800-400 B.C.E.

urethra   Duct through which urine leaves the body.

urethral sponge   *See* G-spot.

vagina   An elastic muscular tube, the internal part of the vulva, extending from the cervix to the opening out of the body. This is where the penis is inserted during sexual intercourse.

valley orgasm   An orgasm you allow to happen by moving and circulating sexual energy throughout your body and up to the chakra at the crown of the head, while keeping the body still, and without any friction of rubbing bodies together.

varna   Another term for caste.

vasodilator   Any substance that causes blood vessels to become wider, usually by relaxing smooth muscles in the vessel walls.

Veda   Sacred texts of Hinduism dating from 3,000-6,000 years ago. There are four Vedas: Rig Veda, Yajur Veda, Sama Veda, and Artharva Veda.

visualization   Using your imagination to create internal images or experiences, which may involve any of the five senses, including seeing, hearing, smelling, tasting, or sensations (tactile or emotional).

vomeronasal organ (VNO)   An organ located in the nose that detects pheromone chemicals, typically triggering a signal from the brain to the genitals, of sexual arousal.

vulva   The external genitals of a female, the vagina being the internal portion.

yantra   Special visual images of geometric shapes that have the ability to awaken a higher consciousness.

yoni   Sanskrit term for female genitals—the vulva and vagina.

B
Tools & Toys

Lovers like variety. New sensations and different situations add excitement to sexual play. Technique, ambience, and attitude are all elements of variety, but you can also employ other exotics, such as sex toys and aphrodisiacs. As well, lovers occasionally need some assistance to arouse desire and achieve satisfaction. Aphrodisiacs and sex aids can help out there, too. Vatsyayana provided important advice on both subjects.

Toys for Boys … and Girls

According to the *Kama Sutra*, "if a man is unable to satisfy … a woman, he should have recourse to various means to excite her passion …. He may make use of certain Apadravyas"—an apparatus, or dildo. (VII-2). An artfully wielded dildo can extend a woman's orgasmic response. You can pleasure her with one:

* As part of your foreplay.
* Between bouts of intercourse while you take a break so that you can delay ejaculation.
* After you've ejaculated, if she'd like a little more activity.

Dildos

Vatsyayana was of the opinion that dildos could be made of anything that appealed to you. Other sages had suggested they should be made from "gold, silver, copper, iron, ivory, buffalo's horn, various kinds of wood, tin, or lead [yikes!], and should be soft, cool, provocative of sexual vigour." (VII-2)

Today, dildos are made primarily of rubber, silicone, metal, and glass. They may include small vibrating motors. Rubber dildos, usually black or beige, sometimes have wires inside so you can bend them to your preferred shape. Jelly cocks are soft, slippery, and smooth, and come in every possible color. Silicone, manufactured by a vacuum process that increases the density of the atoms in the rubber, has a special silky texture. If you're feeling creative, you can make your own silicone cocks from mold kits. Silicone dildos last much longer than rubber or jelly. With proper care, cocks made from Pyrex glass or metal, usually gold or silver plated, could last for hundreds of years—long after *you'll* be needing them! There's also a fairly recent synthetic "cyberskin" material with the look and feel of a real penis. It simulates the softness of skin and the rigidity of erectile tissue.

With modern technology there's a vast array of dildo design and function. You'll find dildos that:

* Are specifically designed to reach the G-spot. They have a crook in the end, shaped just like the come-hither motion you make with your fingers. It can be turned to exactly the right angle to sweetly stroke her goddess spot.

* Stimulate both the clitoris and G-spot at the same time.

* Have two probes, one for the vagina and the other for the anus.

* You can fill with hot water or put into a microwave oven to warm up before use.

* Glow in the dark.

* Inflate.

* Plug into the cigarette lighter of your car for sex on the road.

* Ejaculate on demand!

Penis Extenders

Besides dildos for use with hands, Vatsyayana suggested penis extenders and strap-ons, "things which are put on or around the lingam to supplement its length or thickness." (VII-2) There was the Kantuka or Jalaka, an open-ended tube that a gentleman tied to his waist. Specially made to fit the size of his lady's yoni, it had a rough surface that was "studded with soft globules." (VII-2) He could also tie on dildos made of natural materials, like gourds, reeds, and pieces of wood that had been softened with plant oils. For increasing girth and adding stimulation, a wire bracelet was wrapped around the lingam. For adding length and more sensation, "armlets" or sheaths with textured surfaces were placed over the penis. You could add one, two, or more depending on whom you wanted to impress.

Modern counterparts include rubber, cyberskin, and remote wireless penis extensions. An interesting variation is the French Tickler—small, textured additions that you slip on the head of your penis. They're colorful, sexy, and fun for all lovers. Penis extenders also come with an array of harnesses.

Harnesses are made from leather (most expensive and longest lasting), rubber, and nylon (least expensive), and can hold a wide range of regular or vibrating attachments. There are attachments for both erect and flaccid penises. Many of the cyberskin and jelly realistic dildos are harness-compatible. And picture this if you will—the strap-on dildo for your chin!

Size Matters

Vatsyayana's advice was to use an instrument that fit the size of the woman it was intended for. We agree and generally recommend average-size dildos, approximately 6 inches in length, just like your average guy. At least start out with smaller models and work your way up if you want to. Huge size isn't an advantage unless the woman is very big and much larger than her partner. An elephant woman with a hare man would definitely be a candidate for larger models. In any case, your skill and your connection with your lover are more important than the size of the dildo, same as when you're wielding your own wand of light.

Vibrators, Massagers, and Stimulators

Because we live in an electronic world, our sex toys are electronic, too. Vibrators, massagers, and stimulators come in an extraordinary array of shapes, sizes, colors, and materials. Vibrating bullets, 2 to 4 inches (5 to 10 centimeters) long, are easily transportable and can be used internally or externally. Eggs, with or without vibrators, are the shape and size of a small hen's egg. Besides giving pleasure, they're also popular as vaginal exercise aids to help women gain strength and control with their vaginal muscles. It's adding another degree of difficulty to the Mare's Trick. You may become adept enough to add weights to your eggs. Vaginal weight lifting—the next Olympic event? Some stimulators are strictly for external use—primarily clitoral excitement. There are even remote-control versions that are inconspicuous under your clothing. Your sweetie can send you special thrills when you're out together.

When purchasing a vibrator, think about whether you want battery or plug-in. Electric vibrators last longer—they even come with warrantees. Generally of higher quality, their vibrations are stronger. Battery-powered vibrators tend to be more versatile, more portable, offer softer vibrations, and are much less expensive. But they can break down much faster, too.

Penis Piercings and Cock Rings

Today's pierced penises seem tame compared to those of the young men in the "southern countries" during Vatsyayana's day. They believed that "true sexual pleasure cannot be obtained without perforating the lingam." (VII-2) Penises were pierced at the glans. The hole was gradually enlarged to accommodate Apadravyas of various forms, for the wearer's pleasure and his lover's—"a rounded stick, a curved stick in the shape of a mortar, an object shaped like a flower bud, heron's bone, elephant's trunk, octagonal, shaped like a bracelet, shaped like a horn … or other accessories that are of use in many erotic activities." (Daniélou VII-2, p.513)

Some men also wound a rosary of small wooden balls around their penises. They were similar in form and function to modern cockrings. If you have plenty of equipment but sometimes ejaculate sooner than you want, cockrings can help. Placed at the base of the penis after erection, they keep it hard by stopping blood flow. Some varieties also stimulate the woman's clitoris and anus. A strip of Velcro called Control for Men wraps around your entire scrotum above the testicles. It prevents your testicles from rising and thus delays ejaculation. When you want to ejaculate, pull the release tab. Up they rise and off you go.

Anal Play

Anal climax beads are available in small, medium, and large—small ones are about the size of cranberries. Inserted into the anus of either a man or woman during lovemaking, they're withdrawn at the exact moment of orgasm, prolonging it and increasing its intensity.

Anal plugs are as varied as dildos—with or without vibrators; rubber or silicone material; all possible colors, sizes, and prices; and even inflatable models. The Recto Prostate and G-Spot Stimulator is excellent for stimulating the prostate gland.

Hygiene and Safety

Because rubber and jelly rubber are porous, it's impossible to keep them properly sterilized. The risk is obvious if you're sharing your toys or using them for both the vagina and anus. The only way to be safe with rubber and jelly rubber toys is to use them with condoms.

Silicone, on the other hand, is nonporous, so it can be easily cleaned—boiled for sterilization or run through the dishwasher. Because of their many advantages, silicone toys are worth the extra cost.

Here are some silicone properties:

* Hypoallergenic—many people are allergic to latex and other forms of rubber
* Warm to the touch—responds quickly to temperature, will match and retain your body heat, can be quickly warmed under hot water
* Sterile, does not retain bacteria like rubber and soft vinyl
* Cleans easily with soap and water
* Can be boiled—four minutes kills anything
* Suitable for dual use in anus and vagina or for sharing between partners, if cleaned properly
* Odor free—does not retain smell like rubber and soft vinyl
* Nonporous—does not absorb fluids
* Does not flake or break apart like rubber and soft vinyl, and can last a lifetime
* Does not leak toxins into your body like rubber and soft vinyl

Many people are allergic to latex. A lot of sex toys are made from nonlatex rubber, but even supposedly nonlatex products may contain a little bit of latex. If you're concerned about a latex allergy, then select hard plastic, silicone, metal, or glass toys only.

Aphrodisiacs: Better Sex Through Chemistry

An aphrodisiac, named for Aphrodite, the Greek goddess of sensuality, eroticism, and sexuality, is something that increases your desire to have sex and may even improve your sexual ability. Under the right circumstances, almost anything could have aphrodisiac qualities. Traditionally, aphrodisiacs were foods and plant extracts. Now they're also human-made substances. Some aphrodisiacs work because they feed your body what it needs to produce your own natural sexy chemicals.

Some of the aphrodisiacs mentioned here fall into the category referred to as *adaptogens*. These substances work with your central nervous system (CNS) to deliver more energy and endurance when you need them. But unlike other CNS stimulants, such as caffeine or amphetamines, they don't give you that extra boost and then follow it with a big letdown. They don't deplete your body's reserves; instead, they build them.

Aphrodisiacs can be helpful and lots of fun, but they're never an alternative to:

* A positive attitude toward sexuality.
* A positive attitude toward members of the opposite sex.
* Doing your inner work to remove psychological barriers to sexual intimacy.
* Taking positive steps to solve relationship challenges.
* Dealing effectively with stress-producing circumstances in your life.
* Sexual skill mastery.
* A healthy diet.
* A healthy lifestyle.

In Chapter 12, we talked about food as an aphrodisiac. Here we'll introduce you to some other aphrodisiacs, particularly herbal and natural supplements. They affect the organs of your body, stimulating libido, or making orgasms and erections stronger, easier to get, and longer lasting. Some are from the days of the *Kama Sutra*, while others are modern mixtures.

There are thousands of aphrodisiac products on the market, but in this short guide we present only a few selections of some of the best. You're invited to try some of these items, but be cautious. *Like all drugs, these aphrodisiacs could have side effects, even serious side effects, for some users. Consult your physician before consuming any of these substances.* We're providing you with information about aphrodisiacs, not medical advice.

Why Try Aphrodisiacs?

Many lovers choose to experiment with aphrodisiacs out of simple curiosity and to add the spice of diversity to their lovemaking. Others explore the world of aphrodisiacs because they want a solution to a sexual problem. Women may want assistance with lack of desire, deficiency of lubrication and sensation, or difficulty with orgasms. Men may struggle with low sexual desire, premature ejaculation or difficulty ejaculating, or inability to get and/or sustain an erection.

Some of these difficulties may have psychological and emotional causes. Others are the results of physical ailments and diseases. Still others are the simple effects of aging. Aphrodisiacs can offer assistance in some of these instances. You might find the aphrodisiacs we mention below on their own in capsule, powder, tablet, or tincture form, or as part of a pro-sexual mixture.

Aphrodisiacs from the Kama Sutra

According to the *Kama Sutra,* the use of sex toys and aphrodisiacs was considered a last resort. "Good looks, good qualities, youth, and liberality are the chief and most natural means of making a person agreeable in the eyes of others. But in the absence of these a man or a woman must have resort to artificial means, or to art, and the following are some recipes that may be found useful." (VII-1) Vatsyayana recommended the use of traditional Ayurvedic herbs and formulas "to prevent the power of enjoyment from declining and to maintain it." (VII-1) All the aphrodisiacs listed in this section are from his recipes for love success.

Valerian (Valeriana wallichi)

Name used in the *Kama Sutra*: Tagara
Part used: root and rhizome
Habitat: India, Himalayas, Bhutan, Afghanistan
Action: sedative, antispasmodic, relieve symptoms of PMS and menopause, reduce blood pressure

"Physical attractions are improved by anointing the body with a product made of Tagara, Kushtha, and Talisha patra …. This ointment increases sexual attraction." (Daniélou VII-1, p.490) It supposedly had more power if you prepared the potion in a human skull! Valerian roots and rhizomes yield an aromatic oil, which was applied to the body as an anti-aging and cosmetic preparation. It was also traditionally used to prepare perfumes and incense, and for hair treatments. As an antispasmodic, it helps relax smooth muscles, thereby aiding erection in men and orgasmic response in women. It's also helpful for menstrual cramps. Another variation, Valeriana officinalis, is used as a sedative and aid to sleep, because it relaxes the central nervous system without leaving you feeling hungover the next morning.

Costas (Saussurea lappa)

Name used in the *Kama Sutra*: Kushtha
Part used: root
Habitat: India, Himalayas, Kashmir Valley
Action: antispasmodic, aphrodisiac, anti-inflammatory

This plant has a narcotic effect when smoked. According to the *Kama Sutra* it was used to anoint the body for anti-aging and cosmetic purposes. One of the hymns in the *Atharva Veda* (XIX, 39) appeals to the god of the Kushtha plant to protect women from various ills. In another verse (V, 4) Kushtha is referred to as "the visible manifestation of amrita (ambrosia)."

Sarsaparilla (Hemidismus indica)

Name used in the *Kama Sutra*: Sariva
Part used: root, milk, stalk, leaves
Habitat: India, Himalayas, South and Central America
Action: strengthen erection, strengthen reproductive organs, anti-inflammatory, blood purification, boost memory

Roots from the sarsaparilla vine have been used for centuries by the indigenous peoples of Central and South America for sexual impotence. It was also used as a cure for sexually transmitted diseases, such as syphilis. This plant contains a number of phyto-steroids that your body converts into testosterone and estrogen. In the *Kama Sutra*, a cream including Sariva was said to be "a source of sexual attraction." Don't confuse sarsaparilla vine with the larger sasparilla and sassafras trees, the root and bark of which were once used to flavor root beer.

Datura (many different species)

Name used in the *Kama Sutra*: Datura
Part used: flowers, leaves, seeds
Habitat: worldwide
Action: intoxicant, hallucinogenic, aphrodisiac, boost energy

Vatsyayana advised that a man who applied a mixture of crushed Datura seeds and honey to his penis would be able to sexually "bewitch and subjugate his partners." (Daniélou VII-1, p. 496) But beware, because "he who takes a drink to which Datura seeds have been added becomes mad [intoxicated]." (Daniélou VII-2, p. 518) According to the *Vamana Purana* (a Hindu religious scripture interpreting the *Vedas* for the common Indian man), the Datura plant "grew out of Shiva's chest" and was considered one of Shiva's sacred plants. In India, yogis sometimes smoked a mixture of Datura and Ganja (cannabis) as a ceremonial practice in honor of lord Shiva and goddess Parvati. Datura represented the masculine-yang energy and Ganja represented the feminine-yin energy, as they merged into a single godhead.

Through smoking, the magical properties of these sacred plants were transformed into the cosmic sexual energy of the universe. The yogi's Kundalini energy would rise up from the base of his spine, through the chakras to the crown, bringing an awakened consciousness. If someone overdid it with Datura, the *Kama Sutra* advises, "by taking settled [aged] molasses, he returns to his normal state and regains consciousness." (Daniélou VII-2, p. 518)

Ashwagandha (Withania somnifera)

Name used in the *Kama Sutra*: Ashwagandha
Part used: root
Habitat: India and North America
Action: increase libido, strengthen erection, increase energy, increase endurance, elevate mood

Ashwagandha is a traditional Ayurvedic botanical also known as Indian winter cherry and Indian ginseng. It's not really ginseng, but like ginseng it is an adaptogen, helping boost energy, combat stress, and induce calmness. It also elevates your mood and stimulates sexual desire. In addition, it stimulates the production of nitric oxide, which relaxes smooth muscles and blood vessels, enabling blood to flow into the genitals of both men and women. It's often used in combination with Mucana pruriens.

Tribulus Terrestris

Name used in the *Kama Sutra*: Shvadanshtra, Gokhuru
Part used: fruit
Habitat: Eurasia, Australia, the Americas
Action: stimulate production of testosterone, strengthen erection, increase libido, increase male fertility (sperm production), increase energy, boost immune system

The *Kama Sutra* says, "Crush together Shatavari (asparagus roots), Shvadanshtra (Tribulus terrestris), and cook in four times their volume of water. Let the water evaporate. To be taken in the morning. This product assures vigor, erotic strength, and longevity. The ancient masters call it the divine elixir." (Daniélou VII-1, p. 502) Tribulus terrestris is also referred to as puncture vine, caltrop, and goathead. It's a traditional Indian Ayurvedic herb used to

increase testosterone production. It works by stimulating the pituitary gland to secrete luteinizing hormone (LH), which in turn stimulates the testicles to produce testosterone. Studies support its efficacy for increasing testosterone and libido.

Asparagus—Shatavari (Asparagus racemosus)

Name used in the *Kama Sutra*: Shatavari
Part used: roots, rhizomes, leaves
Habitat: India
Action: aphrodisiac, antispasmodic

If you've ever grown asparagus, you know that this amazing plant grows so fast you can almost see it—up to 10 inches in a day. Remind you of anything? You get the point. Shatavari is considered one of the most important Ayurvedic herbs for a woman's healthy reproductive system. It is the women's equivalent to Ashwagandha. Some refer to it as "she who possesses 100 husbands," because of the powerful effect it has on stimulating the female reproductive system and genitals. It relieves symptoms of PMS and menopause, such as vaginal dryness. By relaxing your smooth muscles it increases blood flow and intensifies orgasm.

Velvet Bean (Mucana pruriens)

Name used in the *Kama Sutra*: Kapikacchu
Part used: seeds, fruits
Habitat: India
Action: stimulate production of testosterone, inhibit prolactin, strengthen erection, increase libido

Mucana pruriens, one of the most common Ayurvedic herbs, is known to increase testosterone and human growth hormone levels. It contains the amino acid L-dopa, which is converted to the neurotransmitter dopamine. Higher levels of dopamine elevate your mood, increase sexual desire, and inhibit production of prolactin. Not enough testosterone and too much prolactin cause men to have difficulty getting and keeping erections. Velvet bean is often used in combination with Ashwagandha.

Sweet Potato—Vidari (Ipomoea digitata, Ipomoea paniculata, Ipomoea mauritiana)

Name used in the *Kama Sutra:* Vidari
Part used: root
Habitat: India
Action: aphrodisiac, boost energy, regulate menstrual cycle

"Crush Vidari roots in cow's milk, together with svayamgupta seeds (Mucana pruriens), sugar, honey, and ghee. Use it to make biscuits with wheat flour. He who eats them, as many as suits him, can enjoy an unlimited number of women, the ancient masters tell us." (Daniélou VII-1, p.501)

Long Pepper (Piper longum)

Name used in the *Kama Sutra:* Pippali
Part used: seeds
Habitat: India
Action: aphrodisiac, vasodilator (dilates arteries and veins)

"Take one part (long pepper) for two parts each morata (sugar cane) and Vidari … [it] increases virility." (Daniélou VII-1, p. 500)

Water chestnut (Trapa bispinosa)

Name used in the *Kama Sutra:* Shringataka
Part used: nuts
Habitat: India
Action: aphrodisiac

White Teak (Gmelina arborea)

Name used in the *Kama Sutra:* Kaseru
Part used: fruits
Habitat: India
Action: aphrodisiac

White Lily (Lilium polyphyllum)

Name used in the *Kama Sutra:* Kshirakakoli
Part used: bulbs
Habitat: India
Action: aphrodisiac, anti-inflammatory

The three above are Ayurvedic herbs. The *Kama Sutra* says, "Crush together Shringataka, kaseru, and wild fig, with kshirakakoli, mixed with sugar and milk. Then cook over a low fire with ghee (clarified butter) in order to make into cakes. He who eats these can sleep with innumerable women, say the ancient masters." (Daniélou VII-1, p. 500)

Mung Beans (Phaseolus radiatus)

Name used in the *Kama Sutra:* Mashaka beans
Part used: beans
Habitat: worldwide
Action: aphrodisiac

"Crumble Mashaka beans, soak in water, and heat in ghee …. Then cook in cow's milk. Eaten with honey and ghee, this product allows one to possess innumerable women, say the ancients." (Daniélou VII-1, p. 500)

Amala, Amla, Anwula, Anwla (Emblica myrabolans)

Name used in the *Kama Sutra:* Emblica myrabolans
Part used: fruit
Habitat: India
Action: aphrodisiac, cosmetic

The amla tree is considered a sacred tree in India. According to the *Kama Sutra*, you can apply this dried astringent fruit (similar to apples) directly to the penis for strengthening erection. "Anointing oneself with an ointment made of the plant Emblica myrabolans has the power of subjecting women to one's will." (VII-1) Amla is a popular Ayurvedic herb supposed to contain the highest vitamin C content of any natural substance. Amla juice has 20 times more vitamin C than orange juice.

Here are other formulas from the *Kama Sutra* with some commonly available ingredients.

"Mix garlic root with white pepper and licorice. When drunk with sugared milk, it enhances virility." (Daniélou VII-1, p. 499)

"If a man, after anointing his lingam with a mixture of the powders of the white thorn apple, the long pepper and the black pepper, and honey, engages in sexual union with a woman, he makes her subject to his will." (VII-1)

"If ghee, honey, sugar, and licorice in equal quantities, the juice of the fennel plant, and milk are mixed together, this nectar-like composition is said to be holy, and provocative of sexual vigour, a preservative of life, and sweet to the taste." (VII-1)

Other Aphrodisiacs Available Today

Here's a selection of some of the most efficient and widely used aphrodisiacs available today.

Smooth muscles and L-arginine— When NO means YES!

In the body, nitric oxide (NO) is synthesized from oxygen and L-arginine (an amino acid—one of the molecule building blocks of protein). NO is a vasodilator, and one of its most important functions inside the body is to signal smooth muscles to relax, a necessity if men are to become erect. Taking natural arginine supplements can help the body create nitric oxide and make getting erections easier. If you don't have enough NO, you won't get an erection. NO is so important that some researchers suggest it could solve up to 90 percent of impotency problems.

L-arginine also stimulates the pituitary to release human growth hormone and can help prevent and reverse atherosclerosis (blockage of arteries), hypertension (high blood pressure), and male infertility. It boosts the immune system and aids wound healing. L-arginine peaks in the blood within 1 to 2 hours after consumption. L-arginine works similarly for both men and woman, and may help women improve their orgasmic response. The pro-sexual efficacy of L-arginine is supported by research.

You can set up a biofeedback experiment using L-arginine supplements. Take 5 to 12 grams of L-arginine (depending on your body weight) approximately 1 hour before lovemaking. This should result in a noticeable difference in your ability to get and keep an erection, as well as a significant improvement in your ability to delay ejaculation. Both effects are the result of the relaxation of your internal smooth muscles. Once you experience how it feels to have your smooth muscles relaxed and

the benefits derived from that condition, you can then begin to learn the methods of sexual mastery that will enable you to keep your internal smooth muscles relaxed without L-arginine. See Chapter 13 for what to do.

Yohimbe (bark)—Yohimbine (pharmaceutical extract)

> **Part used:** bark
> **Habitat:** West Africa (Nigeria)
> **Action:** increase libido, strengthen erection

Yohimbine, the active alkaloid in yohimbe, may increase levels of testosterone and is believed to relax smooth muscles, enabling blood to flow into the penis, enhancing erection. It also excites your desire to have sex. This product is generally used by men, because it is one of the strongest pro-sexual botanicals. But it has many known side effects. You're cautioned only to use this substance for a short time and only under the supervision of your physician. Don't combine it with ephedrine, guarana, caffeine, alcohol, or most prescription drugs.

Many of the yohimbe products contain insignificant amounts of the active ingredient alkaloid yohimbine. Look for standardized extract to be sure you are getting what you pay for. If the label reads yohimbe bark, don't waste your time.

Horny Goat Weed (Epimedium sagittatum)

> **Part used:** leaves
> **Habitat:** Asia and the Mediterranean
> **Action:** increase libido in men and women, strengthen erection, alleviate menopausal discomfort, increase energy

Horny Goat Weed is a well-respected botanical in traditional Chinese medicine (TCM). In China it is called yin yang huo, which can be translated as "licentious goat plant." So this gives you some idea of how it works in humans. Tradition has it that a goat herder noticed how sexually active his goats became after eating the plant. It may take 3 or 4 days of use before you notice any effects.

Damiana (Turnera aphrodisiaca)

Part used: leaves
Habitat: Mexico, South and Central America, Southern U.S., West Indies
Action: increase libido, strengthen erection, increase female orgasmic response, boost energy

Damiana contains alkaloids that stimulate your sexual organs. It had a long history of use by the Mayan Indians as an aphrodisiac. Women drank an infusion of it a few hours before lovemaking. It can also bring about sexy dreams when you're sleeping. It may take several days of continuous use to notice any aphrodisiac effect.

Muira Puama (Olacaceae Ptychopetalum olacoides)

Part used: bark and root
Habitat: Brazilian Amazon rainforest
Action: increase libido, strengthen erection, boost memory, reduce pain

Muira puama, also called potency wood, has long been used by indigenous populations in the Amazon area for its pro-sexual benefits and as a cure for baldness. It's listed in the *British Herbal Pharmacopoeia* as a treatment for impotence. It's also used for treatment of menstrual irregularities, PMS, infertility, and depression. Studies show that Muira puama helps the body cope well with physical and mental fatigue and stress, aids memory, lowers blood pressure, and reduces pain.

Because Muira puama must be exposed to high heat in the presence of alcohol to release its active ingredients, it's not easily digestible if consumed as powdered root or bark. Take it in an alcohol-based tincture, rather than powder form.

Catuaba (Erythroxylum catuaba)

Part used: bark
Habitat: Amazon Rainforest Brazil
Action: strengthen erection, increase energy, boost memory, fight infection, lower blood pressure

Catuaba was traditionally used by Topi Indians for its aphrodisiac properties, particularly as a cure for impotence. Often used in combination with Muira puama. In Brazil, the saying goes, "until the father is 60, the child is his; after that the child is Catuaba's."

Maca (Lepidium meyenii)

Part used: root
Habitat: South America
Action: boost libido, strengthen erection, reduce symptoms of PMS and menopause, enhance strength and endurance

Botanically this herb is related to turnip and radish. It has been traditionally used as an aphrodisiac for men and women, to increase energy, vitality, stamina, and endurance in athletes, to promote mental clarity, for fertility, and for female menstrual irregularities and hormone imbalances, including PMS and menopause.

Rhodiola (Rhodiola rosea)

Part used: rhizomes and roots
Habitat: Asia, Europe, Artic
Action: boost libido, strengthen erection, overcome premature ejaculation, regulate menstrual cycle, overcome infertility, boost energy, overcome stress, anti-depressant, boost memory, boost immune system

Also referred to as golden root, arctic root, and roseroot, Rhodiola is classified as an adaptogen. Most adaptogens, for example ginseng, act by boosting the adrenal glands to produce more anti-stress hormones, but Rhodiola works by increasing the chemical neurotransmitters in the brain such as dopamine and serotonin. The efficacy of Rhodiola is well documented by clinical research. Be sure the supplement label specifies Rhodiola rosea with standardized extract of 2 percent rosavin, as there are many other varieties of this plant that do not have the same effectiveness. Not suitable for long-term use. Use intermittently.

Ginseng

Part used: root
Habitat: varieties throughout the world
Action: increase libido, strengthen erection, increase energy, increase endurance, elevate mood

All varieties of ginseng, for example Siberian ginseng and Korean red gingseng, are adaptogens, delivering energy on demand. It has a wide reputation as a sexual system enhancer, because it boosts stamina, mood, and staying power.

Pfaffia Paniculata (Amaranthaceae pfaffia paniculata)

Part used: root

Habitat: South America

Action: increase libido, strengthen erection, increase estrogen production, relieve symptoms of PMS and perimenopause, restore fertility, increase energy, lower cholesterol, induce relaxation, boost immune system, stimulate blood circulation, balance blood sugar levels, strengthen the muscular system, enhance memory, rejuvenate skin, anti-inflammatory

Also known as suma, Brazilian ginseng, and para toda (for all things), it's another adaptogen. For generations, indigenous populations throughout the Amazon rainforest have used it as a sexual tonic and aphrodisiac. It contains high concentrations of important amino acids, vitamins, and minerals, as well as plant sterols. Russian Olympic athletes have taken it for many years for muscle building and endurance, without the side effects of steroid drugs. Its efficacy is supported by considerable clinical research. Look for a high saponin content in the standardized extract.

Tantric Sex Practices: Reuniting Heaven and Earth

Just as most Westerners think of the *Kama Sutra* as only a book of exotic intercourse positions, so do they perceive Tantra as primarily a practice of ritualized sex. But Tantra is much more. It is a complex spiritual tradition that originated in the Indian sub-continent as many as 6,000 years ago.

Very simply, its central beliefs include that all creation stems from one consciousness—that all is consciousness, there is no beginning and no end. The world and all its forms are simply manifestations of divine energy. By intentionally uniting opposing elements in this world, a person can move beyond the perceived duality of life and return to a state of oneness.

Tantra, a Sanskrit word that can be translated as loom or weaving, is a spiritual path of action. Through esoteric ritual and diligent awareness, a Tantrika, a practitioner of Tantra, can access the divine energy and realize enlightenment. In some branches of Tantra, a number of the ceremonial practices are sexual. The terms Tantra and Tantra Shastra also refer to the sacred texts of this spiritual system.

Many extraordinarily diverse paths of Tantra developed in India and Tibet, China, and Japan, including within both the Hindu and Buddhist faiths. A commonality most shared was the great secrecy surrounding the sacred rites and the importance of a guru, or wise teacher, to pass on the wisdom and guide a devotee's learning.

In modern times, many of those sacred teachings, particularly those related to sexuality, have been openly conveyed to the Western world. Sacred sex practices are becoming increasingly popular, as people long to explore the connection between their spiritual and sexual selves.

The Tantric Texts

For countless years, Tantric knowledge was passed on orally from guru to disciple. The *Tantras* did not begin to appear in written form until at least 300 C.E. Many of the *Tantra Shastra* scriptures (there are a lot of them) are records of conversations between the Hindu god Shiva and his goddess Shakti, also referred to as Parvati or Devi, about the knowledge and practices that lead to enlightenment. Shiva and Shakti are considered to be masculine and feminine aspects of a single indivisible divinity. Shiva is the fundamental principle of essential, unchanging consciousness, and Shakti is the creative aspect of this consciousness, the stuff that brings life. In their lengthy dialogues, they discussed five main topics:

* Creation
* Destruction of the world
* Worshipping gods
* Attaining mastery in this world, including magical capabilities
* Meditation for uniting with the divine energy

According to some scholars, *Tantras* are not classified as included in the Hindu Vedic scriptures, but rather as existing independently alongside them. In any case, there is an unbroken line of tradition from the *Vedas* to the *Upanishads* to the *Tantras,* which spans a period of several thousand years. The central proposition carried through all these texts is the possibility that each of us can awaken to the godhead within us. The progression revealed in the *Tantras,* beyond what was in the *Vedas* and *Upanishads,* is a set of very practical techniques for individuals to apply in their spiritual quest for liberation.

The *Tantras* are at once both abstract and practical. They present an articulate conceptualization of the enlightened consciousness and also a practical approach to the personal realization of that ideal. Some *Tantras* may appear straightforward, but often the words used can be interpreted on many different levels: as literal instruction, as symbol, and as a cryptic hidden message that must be interpreted with the help of a teacher.

In their absolute state, Shiva and Shakti are one being. Their union in divine bliss is a guide, an inspiration for humanity, a promise of what we can aspire to. As the *Kulachudamani Tantra* reveals:

> *When I, desiring creation … become triple, becoming ecstatic in my wanton love play … I am the essence of creation, manifested as woman, intoxicated with sexual desire, in order to know you as guru, you with whom I am one …. I speak of the method relating to the yoga of liberation … the essence of enlightenment, free of good or evil, giver of both enjoyment and liberation ….*

Some Tantric adepts perceived such descriptions as a purely symbolic representation of joining the energies of consciousness with life force. They used it as an internal visualization during meditation—a spur to unite all aspects of their own inner being. Others took such concepts much more literally and incorporated the physical sexual act into their meditation. During ritualized lovemaking, Tantrikas would become the god and goddess, leaving their own divided selves behind.

To this day, there are strong disagreements between proponents of what is sometimes referred to as "left-handed" Tantra (vamachara) and "right-handed" Tantra (dakshinachara or samayachara). Left-handed practitioners include sacred sexuality practices as part of a spiritual discipline focused on reaching enlightenment. Those who follow the right-handed path claim that sexual practices cannot lead to illumination, that sexual energy is only a fuel for the fire of internal transformation.

Tantra and the Kama Sutra

Modern practitioners of Tantric sex are learning the knowledge and skills to enable them to become better lovers. This includes a good understanding of sexual anatomy. But, Tantrikas also want to know about giving and receiving pleasure, how to create and sustain a deep emotional and spiritual connection, and how healthy sexuality is an important part of a high-quality life. The *Kama Sutra* shares a related approach. This similarity, plus the fact that both originated in India a long time ago, is probably why many people mistakenly assume that Tantra and the *Kama Sutra* are the same thing.

Is there any connection between the *Kama Sutra* and Tantra? In his translation of the *Kama Sutra,* Sinha suggests there could be. He points out that Vatsyayana's descriptions of sexual acts (including, for example, his detailed descriptions of sexual positions, or methods for touching and kissing, the use of intoxicants during lovemaking, and so on) are "analogous to the secret ritual of the *tantras.*"

We can only surmise that since Tantra predates the *Kama Sutra,* at least in the oral tradition, Vatsyayana probably knew about it. It's entirely possible that some written Tantric texts were available during the Gupta dynasty. Vatsyayana wanted to create a comprehensive manual of instruction that included everything important, even practices he didn't agree with. He would have made an exhaustive search for existing material, so it's hard to imagine that he didn't know about Tantric sex practices.

Many of the Tantric sexual techniques and those in the *Kama Sutra* share remarkable similarities. It's their purpose that differs. For example, in Hindu, Buddhist, and Tibetan Tantra, ejaculation is resisted so that sexual energy can be directed upward to awaken the higher spiritual centers. The *Kama Sutra* also instructs men to delay ejaculation, but in order for a man to extend his own pleasure and satisfy his partner. So while Tantra and the *Kama Sutra* share some common techniques, they're in essence quite different. Although Kama was part of the path to liberation, the *Kama Sutra* is not a spiritual text, but a secular one, giving specific instruction for increasing pleasure and living the good life. The *Tantras* are clearly scriptural texts exploring how individuals can awaken to enlightenment, in some instances through meditative sexual activity. Sex becomes more than physical; it becomes spiritual.

From Sex to Spiritual Sex

What makes something spiritual? If you say spiritual sex, that's different than just saying sex, but what is that difference? We suggest that if something is spiritual, it includes two kinds of direct personal experience:

- Transcendence
- Union

Transcendence means that you go beyond your previous limits of sense of self, personality, roles, behavior, rules, and beliefs. Boundaries and self-limitations melt away. You become aware of an amazing, awesome expansion of consciousness. You'll become bigger than the room you're in, bigger than the sky, to the point where it seems as if you are everything—not part of everything, but rather that everything is what you are.

Union means that you understand, not just mentally but with your entire being, that you're connected to all; you're not a separate soul. For example, in ecstasy the boundaries between lovers disappear and they become one. It's impossible to perceive where one body ends and the other begins. There's no longer any separation between you. As you merge with your beloved you might find yourself asking, "Whose orgasm was that anyway?" You become god and goddess, you discover god within your self, not separate from you, out there somewhere. Enlightenment means "to light within," not to find the light outside yourself, in someone, or something. You awaken to a nirvana of knowing you are God, Brahman, The Creator.

Osho (Bhagwan Shree Rajneesh), a twentieth-century enlightened Tantric master, gave this beautifully poetic description of spiritual sex. It can be found in his book *Tantra: The Supreme Understanding*:

> Orgasm is a state where your body is no more felt as matter, it vibrates like energy, electricity …. And when the wife and the husband, or the lovers, or the partners, start vibrating in a rhythm, the beats of their hearts and bodies come together, it becomes a harmony—then orgasm happens, then they are two no more. That is the symbol of yin and yang, yin moving into yang, yang moving into yin, the man moving into the woman, the woman moving into the man.
>
> Now they are a circle, and they vibrate together, they pulsate together. Their hearts are no longer separate, their beats are no longer separate; they have become a melody, a harmony. It is the greatest music possible; all other musics are just faint things compared to it, shadow things compared to it."

Many lovers who choose a path of sacred sex regularly experience transcendence and union. It's possible for you, as well. You simply need to learn some new techniques and methods and, as with any disciplined practice leading to mastery, apply them consistently over a period of years. The most fundamental requirement is your commitment and intention to do so. This is an example of the spiritual aphorism that "when you knock on the door, it will open," or "seek and you shall find." The knowledge and skill set you need to create sacred sex are the same tools you use to create supercharged sex. Then, by adding your intention to go all the way to heaven, to reunite sex and spirit, you'll be propelled forward in ways that are better than you could imagine.

Tantra is a form of yoga, which means union. Remember, intention is not the same as setting a goal. There's no goal in Tantric sex (you're not trying to reach orgasm), but there is a purpose, and that purpose is union. In the *Kama Sutra* the term yoga was used to mean sexual intercourse, a very special kind of union. Your choice, your intention, is to join all the parts of yourself into one undivided whole person, to merge in union with your lover, and to allow your awareness to expand into a personal experience of god-consciousness. As you become whole within yourself, you become fit for relationship, because two whole people make one whole relationship. This is quite different from the idea that you find your missing half in another person.

It's important to note that Tantric sexual techniques can be used in a way that has nothing whatsoever to do with a spiritual path. Something is a spiritual practice, not because of what it is in and of itself, but rather because of how you engage yourself in it, how you use it, and why you are doing it. In other words, if your intention is spiritual, the act becomes spiritual.

It's also possible to awaken a mystical sexual experience without consciously planning to, simply by surrendering utterly to each other, to the connection between you. Couples often begin intentional spiritual practice after an unexpected numinous experience. That's what happened for us. We had a spontaneous mystical lovemaking encounter during our early years together. It led us to research what had occurred, to see if we could consciously participate in recreating that ecstatic expression. Happily, we learned that we could. Since then, we've made our relationship our spiritual practice and Tantric

sex is the primary form of that practice. For us, sex and spirit are reunited. It's hard now to imagine how we could ever have perceived them as separate. Now we teach and write to share with others the immense joy we've found.

For those readers interested in the spiritual aspects of Tantric sex, it's interesting to note that it's one of the few spiritual practices you can undertake together. Almost all spiritual disciplines are undertaken alone. We've seen many couples split apart when one of them goes on a spiritual quest, leaving the other behind. With or without the spiritual dimension, Tantric sex practices can help transform your relationship into one that satisfies you through and through, one in which passion remains hot, and one in which you can grow together for a lifetime.

Tantric Sex Practices

What are the sexual practices that are now commonly associated with the term Tantra in Western society? Tantric lovers tap into the great pool of sexual energy and transform it into spiritual ecstasy. They consciously move sexual energy from the lower chakra centers in the genitals and belly, up through the heart, to the higher centers in the head. They send it out to connect with their lover and with the cosmos. It's this conscious cultivating and directing of sexual energy that's at the core of Tantric sex. There are many tools you can use to help you in the process. A lot of the elements that are involved in nonsexual Tantra are part of the sexual practice as well. You'll also recognize many of the specifically sexual techniques that the *Kama Sutra* recommends.

Tantrikas employ the following in their ritualized lovemaking:

- Conscious breath
- PC muscle contraction
- Relaxation and stillness
- Visualization
- Sensate focus
- Meditation
- Mantras (sounds)

- Yantras (visual images)
- Mudras (body movements)
- Creating a sacred space
- Cleansing and purifying the body
- Eye gazing
- Dancing
- Massage and acupressure
- Spells, incantations, and sexual magic
- Food, drink, intoxicants

First, we'll explain a few of these terms that may be unfamiliar to you or that we haven't covered already in this guide. Then we'll give you a brief overview of how you can bring Tantric sex into your bedroom.

A mantra can be a phrase or special sound that you repeat over and over. The simple repetition focuses your mind and quiets the flow of thoughts. The resulting stillness may enable you to perceive in ways that are beyond the ordinary. On a deeper level, according to the *Malinivijayottara Tantra*, each word, and each letter of each word, has a special energetic significance and mystery meaning. A mantra supplied to you by a true spiritual master carries with it—in the order of the words; the sound of the words; the pitch, tone, and speed with which they are spoken—the possibility of liberating your consciousness and enabling it to soar into infinity.

Yantras (special geometric shapes) and mudras (ritualized body movements) are very similar. They are both used to focus the mind and body and establish energetic flow. Mudras can often be simple hand gestures, for instance, touching the middle finger to the thumb links your sexual energy flow to your breath. When such tools come to you from a spiritual master, they are not just shapes and movements; they are symbolic spiritual gifts, and are capable of evoking great cosmic energy.

Now let's start your Tantric spiritual playtime.

1. In order to build and circulate a high sexual charge, Tantrikas make love for extended periods. So you should set aside at least 3 or 4 hours when you will not be interrupted and can focus totally on each other.

2. Always, always keep in your awareness that this lovemaking time is a ritual of spiritual awakening through the pleasures of physical connection. Through your sacred sexuality you leave behind your regular perception of self and become the god and goddess.

3. State your intention to each other that this time of lovemaking is to be a spiritual connection. Invite your beloved on a journey of awakening with simple but heartfelt words like, "My god/goddess, I love you and want to share with you the incredible joy you bring me in all ways. Will you join with me on a splendid sensual journey to ecstasy?"

4. Create your sacred loving space, much as we discussed in Chapter 3. You may want to add ceremonies for psychic protection, to cleanse and purify the space of any negativity, so that you feel safe and free to open completely. A simple but very effective ritual is to walk in a counterclockwise circle around your room and speak out loud anything you don't want in it—fear, judgment, expectations, negative energies. Then reverse direction and invite in what you would like—passion, playfulness, being in the moment, love.

5. Bathe together to cleanse your bodies and symbolically rid yourselves of psychic dirt.

6. Engage in nonsexual ways that help bring you into your body and focus your mind. Here are some suggestions:

   - Sit quietly and breathe in harmony together.
   - Do some partner yoga.
   - Chant a mantra together—a simple "Om" is a powerful traditional mantra.
   - Dance slowly and sensually.
   - Listen to uplifting music.
   - Give each other a massage.
   - Read each other sensual, erotic poetry.

7. Men, begin to arouse your goddess with great tenderness, respect, and adoration. Bring her

to the heights of passion with kisses, caresses, and words. Use all the wonderful techniques that Vatsyayana suggested, and that we covered in Part II.

8. Now, move on to intercourse. It may be wildly intense or exquisitely gentle, depending on your mood. When you are at a peak of passion, stop actively building your charge. Go into a position of stillness—a sitting position like Milk and Water, which in Tantric practice is called YabYum, or a lying position like Sesame and Rice.

9. Stop active movement. Relax your bodies. Open your eyes and gaze at each other softly. Harmonize your breathing in slow, deep abdominal breaths.

10. Focus on moving the intense sensation, the hot sexual energy that you feel in your genitals up through your body. You can feel it as shimmering waves or an electric current, or visualize it as golden fire, or a flow of water moving from your genitals up the front, back, or center of your body to the crown of your head. Your energy goes to where you put your attention. Squeeze your PC muscles (the Mare's Trick) to help push the energy up. Run your hands up each other's bodies from genitals to head to help carry the energy—front or back works equally well. Chant together; let sound carry your love higher and higher. Let your energy merge with "*the*" energy.

11. As your passion begins to subside, or you can no longer feel the energy flow, move again into more active intercourse to build your charge again. Or, break apart from intercourse and continue with other loving activity. A woman might manually or orally pleasure her man. He might pleasure her. You might feed each other exotic treats. You might rest in stillness. You might dance, or stretch, or read, or chant.

12. Now connect again in glorious intercourse, joining your bodies in all those wondrous positions Vatsyayana suggested. When your charge builds high, particularly before the man is

ready to ejaculate, stop and in stillness focus on moving and sharing your energy.

13. Repeat this process, building to peak after peak. By the time you reach four, six, eight, or more peaks of arousal, you'll have an intense charge of hot sexual energy to work with. At first, it may seem difficult to really "feel" it if you're not accustomed to paying attention to your internal energy. With practice, you'll be able to recognize and direct it.

14. Regular lovemaking usually ends (often abruptly) when the man ejaculates, but Tantric sacred loving often ends while lovers still have desire. Tantric lovers wind down their lovemaking with slow caresses, words of endearment, and honoring each other with food and drink.

A very important point to remember is this: be respectful of your partner and yourself. Bring your focus, your love, and your playfulness to your Tantric loving experience, but leave your expectations and your goals elsewhere. Surrender in playful abandon to each moment. Know that you are perfect as you are.

Building and Moving Your Sexual Energy

There are many excellent practices for learning to work with your sexual energy—on your own, or with a partner. The Sexual Fire Breath is one of our favorites. It's an active breath and body technique that helps you begin to move your sexual energy from your genitals, up to your crown, and out into the cosmos. Try it to the rhythm of a sexy, strong beat like Enigma's *Principles of Lust*. Or, if you want some verbal instruction you can get the full version of this meditation on Pala's *Apertio: Tantra Energy Meditations* CD. See Appendix F for details.

Experiment with the Sexual Fire Breath in these situations:

- As a meditation on your own, without sexual stimulation
- During self-pleasuring

❋ When you want to get charged-up quickly for lovemaking

❋ As your lover is pleasuring you manually or orally

❋ During intercourse—but exercise caution here if you're in horizontal positions. The excitement can build too rapidly and send many a novice explorer over the edge into ejaculation. You'd be better off adapting it to an upright posture such as the YabYum.

The Sexual Fire Breath

You can adapt the Sexual Fire Breath to many situations and a number of positions: sitting, standing, lying sideways. But to begin with it's easiest to learn lying on the floor on a mat.

❋ Lie on your back with your knees bent, legs shoulder width apart, and your feet flat on the floor.

❋ Close your eyes. Rest your hands at your sides, with the palms up.

❋ Start to take deep, slow breaths. Fill your lungs, from the bottom up.

❋ When you've gotten into a comfortable breathing rhythm, focus your attention on your genitals, your root chakra. Picture the air coming into your body through your genitals as you breathe.

❋ Start to rock your pelvis gently. Leave your back on the floor, but tilt your pelvis up, then drop it back. Help your rocking rhythm by pushing a little with your feet. Endeavor to keep your belly relaxed.

❋ Now, match your breathing to your rocking rhythm. Exhale as you tilt your pelvis up. Inhale as you rock back. If your body wants to do it the opposite way, let it.

❋ After a few moments, begin to add sound. As you exhale, send out a deep "Aaaaahhhh!" If making sound is hard for you to do, remember it will help carry your sexual energy up with it, so push your envelope a little and make even a small sound.

❋ The next step is to add PC squeezes and match them to your rocking, breathing pattern. For instance, tighten your PC muscles as you inhale and rock back. Relax them as you exhale and rock forward. Again, if your body wants to match these up differently, go right ahead. The important point is to include all the elements.

❋ Add visualization to your mixture. Picture your sexual energy as a golden fire in your genitals. Start sending it up through the center of your body as you squeeze, rock, and breathe. Visualize it going to each of your energy centers: from your genitals, to your belly, to your solar plexus, to the center of your chest, to your throat, to your forehead, to the top of your head.

❋ Use your hands to help direct the energy, by running them up the front of your body, either touching or above you.

❋ When the energy reaches your crown chakra, at the top of your head, send it out to join with the energy of the cosmos, or if you're making love with a partner direct it to your lover through eyes, breath, lips, or tongue. Do not build it up in your head—you'll get a headache.

❋ Let yourself go into the energy flow. Move faster if you feel the urge—allow the energy to pulsate through you.

❋ When you reach a high energy charge, you can prolong this sublime orgasmic state by stopping your movement, relaxing your body, and slowing your breath.

❋ When you're finished practicing, lie still and feel the energy coursing through you, enlivening and charging every bit of your being.

❋ If you do feel any pressure in your head, press firmly on the top of your head with your fingertips for a couple of minutes. Then brush your hands down your body and curl and relax your toes against the floor. This will help ground the excess energy.

The Ananga Ranga

Written sometime in the sixteenth century, the *Ananga Ranga* is often considered India's second-most prominent book of love. Like its great predecessor the *Kama Sutra*, the *Ananga Ranga*, or *Stage of the Bodiless One*, is a compilation of the works of sages, poets, and men wise in the arts of love. The author, Kalyana Malla, who modestly described himself as a "great princely sage and arch-poet," condensed and recorded what he considered the essence of these great men's knowledge. Like many Indian texts that taught of spiritual and practical matters, its language often bore a double meaning, so that the work as a whole could be interpreted on two levels, "either mystical or amatory."

Thanks to Sir Burton

During his years in India, Sir Richard Francis Burton was introduced to the *Ananga Ranga* and, stirred by the power of the fulfilling lovemaking it suggested, felt it would be an invaluable aid to the suppressed sex lives of the British. With the aid of Indian scholars, he translated the work into English, adding some of his personal opinions about men, women, sex, and marriage along the way. He first attempted to publish an English language version in 1873, with the title *Kama-Shastra, or The Hindoo Art of Love (Ars Amoris Indica)*. But the printers were alarmed about the erotic nature of the work and, fearing prosecution due to the strict censorship of Victorian England, stopped publication after half a dozen copies were printed.

This experience, among others, led Burton and his partner F.F. Arbuthnot to found the Kama Shastra Society, at least partly as a publication vehicle for erotic Eastern works. The *Ananga Ranga* was published by the society in 1885, as a book for private circulation to subscribers. It wasn't until 1960, after a court battle, that both it and the *Kama Sutra* were allowed general publication in England.

The Essence of the Ananga Ranga

Kalyana Malla's focus is much narrower than the broad scope of life and relationship that Vatsysyana offered readers. While the *Kama Sutra* is a comprehensive and general guide for men and women pursuing the third aim of life, the *Ananga Ranga* is more about the right kind of mate and how to have fulfilling sexual encounters. Of course, this was also part of the way to spiritual liberation. Much of what's found in the *Ananga Ranga* is a simple reworking of particular sections of the *Kama Sutra*.

Composed for his sovereign, Lada Khan Rajah of the Lodi family, the *Ananga Ranga* is a presentation of how a man can best understand woman in all her forms, keep his wife (wives) sexually satisfied, and thereby have a happy marriage. Men were enjoined to become knowledgeable about the ways of the *Kama Shastra* and to pay attention to the complexities of both a woman's individual nature and the female sex as a whole. Dedicated to men who wanted to study the art, the mystery, and the science of love, "man's highest enjoyment," it exhaustively categorized types of women, what they respond to, how they respond, and when they respond.

The purpose of the *Ananga Ranga* was to help men and women learn how to sustain a successful marriage by avoiding the common pitfalls that so frequently lead marriages to fail. In Malla's view, the most divisive effect on married life came from boredom in the bedroom. He believed that "if husband and wife live together in close agreement, as one soul in a single body, they shall be happy in this world, and in that to come." (Chapter IX) But monotony in bed disrupted that harmony and led husbands and wives alike to seek new sexual experiences with other people. "Malicious feelings" and "every manner of vice" were the result.

Malla believed that if men and women knew the right sexual techniques, they could create enough variety in their lovemaking to sustain their interest without going elsewhere for satisfaction. He warned readers that if they did not learn and follow the teachings of the *Ananga Ranga,* "neither sex will be thoroughly satisfied; indeed, both will be disposed to lust after strange embraces, and thus they will be led by adultery into quarrels, murders, and other deadly sins …." (Chapter II)

The Ananga Ranga at a Glance

The *Ananga Ranga* is comprised of an introduction, nine chapters, and two appendixes. Its introduction is a flowery invocation to the gods, a heaping of praise on Lada Khan, and a vehement declaration of the importance of the art and pleasure of love.

Chapter I, which has no title, is divided into four sections:

- Of the Four Orders of Women
- Personal Peculiarities of the Four Classes
- The days of greatest enjoyment for the Four Classes
- Of the hours which give the highest enjoyment

Section I names the four basic categories that women can be divided into: Padmini or Lotus-woman, Chitrini or Art-woman, Shankhini or Conch-woman, and Hastini or Elephant-woman. It also states that these classifications of women also symbolize the four stages of Moksha—liberation from reincarnation.

Section II gives a brief overview of the mental, physical, emotional, and sexual qualities of these categorizations. If a woman showed most, or all, of those particular qualities, you could classify her as that type, and thereby have a pretty good idea of what she liked in life and what she liked in bed. For instance, the Padmini woman (the most desirable, by the way) was bright-eyed, fair-skinned, firm-busted, straight-nosed, softly fleshed, of melodious voice and small appetite, graceful, reputable, religious, smart, and well-mannered. She liked the finer things in life, and "her Yoni resembles the open lotus-bud, and her Love-seed (Kama-salila, the water of life) is perfumed like the lily which has newly burst."

The idea of classifying people this way—Malla did it with men, too, later in his book—can seem very odd to us today. But in reality it's still common; we just don't use the same criteria for creating categories. In footnotes to his translation, Burton noted that the *Ananga Ranga* divisions were roughly similar to the way people were characterized during his day. Then, there were four European temperaments: nervous, sanguine, bilious, and lymphatic. Modern methods of people pigeonholing include the Jungian Myers-Briggs system, which also has four groups: Extraversion—Introversion; Sensing—Intuition; Thinking—Feeling; Judging—Perceiving.

In Section III, the poet presents a table showing the exact days of the month when each of the four classes of women can be sexually satisfied. He suggested that lovemaking during other times would not be successful, no matter how much sex you have.

Section IV becomes even more specific. He identified the exact hours, "according to the state of the moon and the hour of the day or night" during which lovemaking will yield the best results for each of the four types of women.

In Chapter II, "Of the Various Seats of Passion in Women," Malla presented instructions about which class of women enjoy which body parts the most and at what time, because passion moves from place to place throughout a woman's body according to the cycle of the moon. He provided detailed correlations between the four classes of women, the various body parts, the type of stimulation that is appropriate to that body part, and the day of the month when such stimulation would produce the desired result of arousal and orgasm. "Thus he will know that the paroxysm has taken place, and the beloved one is thoroughly satisfied."

Chapter III: "Of The Different Kinds of Men and Women" also has four sections:

* Men
* Women
* Of Congress
* Of Other Minor Distinctions in Congress

Section I identifies three types of men, according to the size of their lingams. In Section II, the four classes of women are divided into three groups depending upon the depth of their yonis. This classification of men and women according to genital size is equivalent to the classification in the *Kama Sutra* (see Chapter 2).

In Section III, just as Vatsyayana did in the *Kama Sutra*, Malla proposed that the best combination for lovemaking is when the lingam and yoni are matched in size: "a Linga of small dimensions fails to satisfy. On the other hand, excess of length offends the delicacy of the parts, and produces pain rather than pleasure. But the proportion of enjoyment arises from the exact adaptation of the Linga."

Section IV, presents information about sexual temperament of the lovers. Like Vatsyayana, Malla

considered their intensity of libido, and the length of time it takes for them to achieve satisfaction, and what effect that would have on their lovemaking experience.

Mixing and matching the types of lovers, shapes of their genitals, force of desire, and length of time for satisfaction, led to a multiplicity of possible love combinations. "Altogether we have 27 kinds of congress, which, by multiplying the 9 species and the 3 periods, give a grand total of 243."

Chapter IV "Description of the General Qualities, Characteristics, Temperaments, etc., of Women," presents the four stages of a female's life according to her sexual development and availability for lovemaking:

* Childhood—Birth to age 8
* Adolescence—Age 8 to 11, at which point she's ready to consummate a marriage
* Young womanhood—Age 11 to 55
* Old womanhood—Over 55

It wasn't appropriate to make love with a woman under the age of 11 or over the age of 55.

To make things even more complicated for those wishing to understand their partners, Malla added two more considerations:

* The three temperaments of women: Kapha, Pitta, Vata, which are the three dynamic forces and governing principles of all life according to Ayurveda.
* The Satva, one's temperament carried over from a previous lifetime, which affects a person's nature in this life.

Malla also presented:

* Fifteen signs by which a man would know if a woman was interested in sex, such as "She rubs and repeatedly smoothes her hair."
* Eight signs that show her indifference, for instance, not looking her husband in the eyes.

- The six conditions that lead women astray (into the arms of other men or lots of other men)—number three is "the prolonged absence of her husband."

- Fifteen reasons why women become unhappy, such as poverty, rough language, physical abuse, and an impotent husband.

- Twelve circumstances under which women are most desirous of sex and most easily satisfied, for instance, during thunder, lightning, and rain, and just before and after menstruation.

- Four types of love connection between a man and woman, such as one born of friendship, or lust.

In this chapter, the *Ananga Ranga* extols the virtues of a man capable of repeated acts of sexual intercourse, because such a man thoroughly pleases his woman. According to Malla, women desire sex as much as men, but because of social custom they may conceal their lust. Sound familiar?

Chapter IV also presents a description of four types of yoni, as well as clearly identifying the existence of what is now commonly called the G-spot. In this and many other chapters, the *Ananga Ranga* mentions the Kama-salila, or juice of love, referring to various lubricants in the yoni, but, primarily, female ejaculate when referring to women, and male ejaculate when referring to men.

Chapter V, "Characteristics of the Women of Various Lands," describes the sexual responsiveness characteristics of women depending upon which country or which part of India they live in. For example: "The woman of Kamarupa-desha (Western Assam) has a soft body and sweet voice; her affections are warm, and she is well skilled in all the arts of love. During congress she abounds in the Kama-salila."

A man was advised to study and experience women of many regions, so that he'd know the proper times and ways to please them and "thus endear himself to womankind."

Chapter VI, "Treating of Vashikarana," presents recipes concocted of bodily substances like menstrual blood and male or female ejaculate mixed with various herbs and plant materials. Such mixtures, applied to various parts of your body or to the object of your affection, acted as charms to attract their sexual favors or to subdue them to your will. There are also instructions for aphrodisiac potions and ointments.

Burton seemed rather astonished by the practices of using bodily secretions, "the fouler the better," as he said, to cast a spell on another. "The European reader will hardly believe how extensively this practice is carried out all over the East." But, in the Eastern view, bodily fluids had great power, particularly those excreted during lovemaking, which were considered to carry the best elements of the body within them. Tantric practitioners particularly valued and utilized such fluids as part of the transformatory power of sex. Exchanging male and female essences helped to balance masculine and feminine energies. As well, skill in magic and casting charms was one of the 64 arts from long before the *Kama Sutra* was written.

Feeling charming? Here are two simple spells for winning the undying devotion of your lover. You could put them to the test easily enough. Men, try this: "The man who, after enjoying his wife, catches some of his own Kama-salila in his left hand, and applies it to her left foot, will find her entirely submissive to his whim." Women, try this: "The woman who before congress will touch with her left foot the Linga of her husband, and will make a practice of this, undoubtedly subdues him, and makes him her slave for life."

Chapter VII, "Of Different Signs in Men and Women," is a long, rambling chapter presenting many topics connected with happiness in marriage and success in life. It includes the following:

- The characteristics of a woman who'd make a good wife, from temperament, to family ties, to physical appearance.

- The characteristics of a woman to avoid marrying.

- The qualities of an excellent man, one a reader would want as a son-in-law.

- The qualities of a man you'd want to keep your daughter away from.

- The study of palmistry and other bodily marks and signs that would affect future happiness; for instance, a very long lingam foretold poverty, while a thin, lean one meant luck.
- Warnings about negative affects of having sex with another man's wife.
- Times when it's allowed for people to have sex with someone other than their spouse—basically, if you were so lovesick that you'd die if you didn't.
- A list of women you could never have a sexual relationship with, no matter what.
- How you can tell if a woman wants you or not.
- Women who are easy to score with and those who aren't.
- Where and when you can and can't have sex.

Chapter VIII, "Treating of External Enjoyments" presents information about foreplay, the activities of lovers before the start of sexual intercourse. Like the *Kama Sutra*, the *Ananga Ranga* insists on the importance of adequate foreplay. "These embraces, kisses, and sundry manipulations must always be practiced according to the taste of husband and wife, and if persisted in as the Shastra directs, they will excessively excite the passions of the woman, and will soften and loosen her Yoni so as to be ready for carnal connection." See the section below for some examples.

Chapter IX, "Treating of Internal Enjoyments in its Various Forms," presents instructions for sexual intercourse. Malla assumed that the length and manner of foreplay would have adequately prepared a woman, fully arousing her sexual desire, so that she would be ready and eager for intercourse. See below for some *Ananga Ranga* love postures.

Appendix I, "Astrology in Connection with Marriage," explores the use of astrology to help determine if a proposed marriage is a good match, boding well for future prosperity and happiness, or a pending disaster. Along with considerations regarding caste, creed, and financial and social status of the family, natal charts gave important guidance for the prospects of marriage partners, and are still utilized in arranging many marriages today.

Appendix II offers six recipes intended as a "preparation of metals for medicinal purposes." With regard to these two segments of the book, according to Burton it is "more than doubtful if they belong to the original work." He therefore added them as appendixes.

Foreplay from the Ananga Ranga

Almost all of the foreplay practices—embraces, kissing, scratching, biting, and love blows—are duplicates of those presented in the *Kama Sutra*. There are two minor but interesting variations. One is a technique of caressing a woman's hair during lovemaking. The other is a separation of love blows into men's and women's.

Hair can be a luxuriantly erotic element of a woman's or a man's personal appearance and a source of tactile delight, both for the head that bears it and the hands or other body parts that play with it. Malla combined specific ways of hair handling with certain kisses or embraces.

"One of the best ways of kindling hot desire in a woman is, at the time of rising, softly to hold and handle the hair." We think men like to have their hair played with, too, especially if it's long, and women love to tangle their fingers in it. Remember that when this was written, both men and women had lengthy locks, so you may have to make a few adaptations to accommodate today's shorter styles. The four ways of caressing hair are:

- Holding the Hair with Both Hands, *Samahastakakeshagrahana*, takes place with the Throbbing Kiss of the lower lip. This is a gentle hair touch, just as the kiss is tentative, a beginning of the build-up. With your two hands behind your lover's head, softly enclose your lover's hair between your palms.

* Kissing the Hair in Sinuous Fashion, *Taranga rangakeshagrahana*, turns the temperature up a little. With one hand, grasp the hair at the back of your lover's head and draw her close for a kiss. Try this one with the Bent Kiss or the Kiss of the Upper Lip.

* As your arousal escalates, employ The Dragon's Turn, *Bhujangavallika*. Standing close together, your legs intertwined, amorously seize the back of your beloved's hair. "It is one of the most exciting of all toyings."

* Holding the Crest Hair of Love, *Kamavatansakeshagrahana*, takes place during intercourse, when you both seize the hair just above each other's ears. At the same time, kiss each other passionately on the mouth. A forceful Straight Kiss and Fighting of the Tongue are excellent selections. You can also use this hair grasp during oral sex, as long as it's agreeable with your partner and not too controlling.

The *Ananga Ranga* listed the same four love taps as the *Kama Sutra*, but suggested those are to be employed by men on women, while women should use the following variations on their lovers. All occur during intercourse to increase excitement.

* *Santanika*, using a closed fist to gently pat his chest, "so as to increase his pleasure."

* *Pataka*, a light, open-handed slap on various parts of his body—back, thighs, buttocks, sides.

* *Bindumala*, playing upon his body with thumbs only.

* *Kundala*, striking him with your thumb and forefinger.

Love Postures from the Ananga Ranga

The *Ananga Ranga* lists 32 intercourse positions, separated into 6 categories that are similar to the divisions we gave you for the *Kama Sutra* poses. Malla suggested that by cleverly exploring all these postures, a couple would find great diversity and satisfaction, and thereby bring harmony and devotion to their married life. In fact, a man could experience living with one wife, as if she were "thirty-two different women, ever varying the enjoyment of her, and rendering satiety impossible." (Chapter IX)

The intercourse poses Malla presented are sorted as follows:

* The woman lying supine (upon her back), *Uttana-bandha*, what we call "Man on Top"—eleven variations.

* Lying on her side (right or left), *Tiryak*, "Sideways"—three variations.

* Sitting in various ways, *Upavishta*, "Sitting"—10 variations.

* Standing, *Utthita*, "Standing"—three variations.

* Lying prone (upon breast and stomach), *Vyanta-bandha*, "Rear Entry"—two variations.

* Woman on Top (the man is lying supine, on his back), *Purushayitabandha*, "Woman on Top"—three variations.

A number of the *Ananga Ranga* poses are quite similar to those of the *Kama Sutra*, especially the man-on-top versions. But there are definitely some interesting differences, most notably with the introduction of 10 sitting variations. As with the *Kama Sutra*, the descriptions of the positions in the text are very brief. We've selected nine positions to present in more detail. Some are basic and comfortable for lovers of all ages and physical capacities. Others will offer a challenge for even the most adventuresome among you.

In many of the man-on-top poses, the man doesn't actually lie on top of his partner but is squatting "upon his hams" as she lies on her back. And 1,200 years later, Malla still described woman-on-top poses the way Vatsysyana did, as "the reverse of what men usually practice."

Man-on-Top Poses

Feet in the Air (*Vyomapada*)   Feet in the Air is a position that requires quite a bit of female flexibility. Lying on your back, you grab your feet and pull them over your head. The farther back you can lift them, the more exposed your vulva will be. Your lover can sit with his legs stretched straight out in front alongside your body, or he can kneel in front of you, or he can squat. He fondles your breasts. The more impassioned you both are, the harder he'll squeeze. Now may be a good time for those exotic nail presses, Peacock's Foot and Jump of a Hare.

Experiment with raising and lowering your legs to alter the angle of penetration. Thrusting techniques that will work well include Moving Forward, Churning, and Giving a Blow. For this last thrust, if he's sitting, he needs to be very flexible in his lower back and hips to pull far back before the deep strike.

Kama's Wheel (*Smaracharka*)   Love's Wheel gets its name from the positions of your limbs and for the turning action of your body. Apparently it was very popular with extremely passionate and flexible lovers. You lie on your back and open your legs wide. He squats between your thighs. In a squat his feet are flat on the floor, his knees are bent, and his butt's down at his heels—quite a challenge for most adult Westerners.

With his hands, he spreads your thighs as far apart as you can comfortably manage. Holding onto your legs, he moves and turns your body about on his lingam. The more relaxed you are, the better. You'll get very interesting thrusting sensations without either of you actually moving your hips. It's an unusual Blow of the Boar effect. His hands are occupied, but yours are free to caress him or play with your clitoris. You'll be a whirling dervish of delight.

The Bow (*Jrimbhita*)   Your body shape gives this pose its name. With pillows under your head and

your hips, your body is arched like a bow. He kneels on a little cushion in front of you. When you're both set, he takes aim and shoots you with his love arrow. This "admirable form of congress is greatly enjoyed by both." If you try it you'll understand why. It's comfortable for both of you; with your head raised, you can see a lot of the exciting in-and-out action; and if he's got a slightly supple back, he can lean in close to kiss you passionately, whisper in your ear, or nibble your nipple. All four hands are free to make magic on each other's skin. Start with Moving Forward thrusts, then Pressing, then some Rubbing for G-spot strokes, then Pressing, and then finish with a rousing round of Sporting of a Sparrow.

Sitting Positions

The Tortoise (*Kaurmak*)   You sit upright, with your ladylove facing you on your lap, and match your bodies part for part. Mouth meets mouth, arms rest along arms, chest presses to chest, thigh curls along thigh. She's pulled in tight to you—your lingam nestled deep inside her yoni. You rock back and forth together on love's endless wave. It's an elegantly simple pose that's wonderful for emotional connection and sharing of your male and female energies.

Turning (*Paravarita*)   Turning is a more complex version of the Tortoise. All your bits still mirror your lover's, but now you raise her legs out to the sides and hold them up with your elbows under her knees. It's best to start in the Tortoise and move one of her legs at a time. If you reach around behind her back and clasp your hands together, it'll help you support her legs.

She doesn't have much room to maneuver but her hands are available to make scratches on your back. With her legs raised this way she'll be well and fully impaled on your jade stalk. To maintain your erection in this relatively still pose, it's a good idea for you both to be doing PC squeezes.

Roaring (*Vinarditasana*)   Another challenging posture, Roaring is suited for a strong man and a lightweight woman. It was probably created for those young brides who were married as children and then shipped off to their husbands at puberty.

Likely not fully grown, they'd be much easier to lift than a mature woman of today. If you're into bodybuilding, this will be a great addition to your workout.

You sit with your lover in your lap facing you. As she settles down on your lingam, she lifts her thighs high. Passing your arms under her thighs, you raise her in the air. With pressure from your elbows, you move her from side to side until the "supreme moment" arrives. For regular-size women who don't have weightlifter mates, you might be able to manage it if she leans back on her arms to support some of her weight.

Monkey (*Markatasana*)   The Monkey is a variation of Roaring, but instead of side-to-side movements, you move her backward and forward "in a straight line away from [your] face." She can help by clasping you around the neck or shoulders and pulling herself close as you glide her toward you along your lingam. Each time you pull her in, she passionately kisses your lips with the hungry Clasping Kiss. Again, you can try an easier version with your lover leaning back on her arms. Your legs are stretched straight out and she's between them. Instead of holding her up in the air, you can slide her back and forth along the bed. Penetration in both these positions is nicely deep.

Standing Positions

Knee and Elbow (*Janu-Kuru*)   Knee and Elbow is a standing pose for those who like extreme sex. Again, you've got to be strong, and it's helpful if she's petite, because you support her in the air with your arms under her knees. Her weight rests on your inner elbows as you hold her up. Clasping your hands together behind her back can give you some assistance.

She wraps her arms around your neck and gazes at you with absolute admiration. She feels so secure to be supported this way. You sway together in the rush of strength and power. Pressing's about the best and only thrusting you'll probably be able to do, unless she's so light that she can bounce up and down a little on your arms. You might like to start this position with her sitting on a table or countertop. Kneel down and thrill her with some oral caresses; then stand up and slide her off the table and onto your waiting lingam.

Woman-on-Top Positions

Elevated (*Utthita*)   You lie him on his back, with his legs stretched straight out, and lower yourself onto his lingam, facing toward his head. Once he's gripped tight inside you—the Mare's Trick comes in handy here—you cross your legs over his belly.

You can both take turns directing the action. He can grab hold of your hips and waist and move you side to side, back and forth, or in a circle. Each movement will create unique and intriguing sensations for both of you. He can reach up to twirl one nipple and also titillate your clitoris, as you gyrate against his hand and lingam. Or, he can surrender all control, lying back to watch and absorb the pleasure, as you wriggle up and down, "advancing and retiring," while teasing your clitoris with your fingertips. The *Ananga Ranga*'s certain you "will derive great comfort from this process."

The Perfumed Garden

When modern lovers look to the ancient East for inspiration, they consult the *Kama Sutra*, of course, but they often turn their attention to another intriguing guide as well: the Arabian classic, *The Perfumed Garden*. Written sometime between the end of the fourteenth century and the middle of the sixteenth century C.E., *The Perfumed Garden* has much in common with its Indian predecessor, but it also shows entertaining stylistic and social differences.

A Kama Sutra Soulmate?

Originally entitled *The Scented Garden for the Soul's Recreation* (*Er Roud el Âater p'nezaha el Khater*), the manuscript was composed for the Bey (the governor of Tunisia, in North Africa) by the physician and scholar Sheikh Umar Ibn Muhammad el Nafzawí. Like the *Kama Sutra*, it shares an attitude of appreciation for all things sexual. The sheikh considered lovemaking a healthy, joyous, natural activity, a gift from the creator to be studied thoroughly and reverently. As he wrote in his preamble: "I swear before God, certainly! the knowledge of this book is necessary. It will be only the shamefully ignorant, the enemy of all science, who does not read it, or who turns it into ridicule."

As with Vatsyayana's version, *The Perfumed Garden* is not simply a sex manual. It's a guide for promoting a long and happy married life based on an understanding of the intricacies of sexuality. Like the *Ananga Ranga*'s Malla, Nafzawí felt that the surest route to marital bliss was harmony in the bedroom. He aimed to enlighten his readers about the serious matter of sexual, erotic, and romantic relations between men and women, and the achievement of sexual fulfillment, because he saw it as a basic, universal need. "In every country, large or small, both the rich and poor have a taste for this sort of book, which may be compared to the stone of philosophy transforming common metals into gold." (IX) He was particularly hopeful that his book would benefit those who had difficulty with their sexual lives and help them to "recover their former vigor." (IX)

Due to centuries of trade between the regions and from Arabian conquest of parts of India, Nafzawí was certainly aware of the *Kama Sutra*. And as you'll see, especially when we discuss intercourse positions, he was strongly influenced by it. Yet while certain aspects of content are quite similar, the styles of the two works differ greatly. Whereas Vatsyayana composed short verses that were to be passed on orally and expanded on by a knowledgeable teacher, Nafzawí's work was a document to be slowly read and savored. His guidance wasn't just in the form of concise sexual do's and don'ts; he lavishly illustrated his points with bawdy stories and erotic poems.

The *Arabian Nights*–type stories he included reveal much about sexuality in medieval Arab Islamic society, and despite what may now seem to be historic and religious peculiarities, at least some of the information has a timeless, universal application for erotic relationships between men and women. They reveal how powerful a force sexual desire is for men and women alike. Besides that, they're often funny and sexually arousing—as Nafzawí intended them to be.

Whereas both men and women were encouraged to study the message of the *Kama Sutra*, *The Perfumed Garden* was directed to men only. Women, as in most places of the world then, and, sadly, in some places now, were denied access to formal education. Men were to learn the secrets of love and use them to full advantage for arousing women and having their way with them. "God, the magnificent, has said: 'Women are your field. Go upon your field as you like.'" (VI) For a real man, having his way also meant that the woman he made love to would thoroughly enjoy it. He was supposed to "observe the proper movements," so that she would "experience a pleasure which will satisfy all her desires." (V)

Sir Burton Again

In 1886, when Sir Francis Burton was serving as Her Majesty's British Consul in Trieste, he received a copy of the sheikh's book in the form of a French translation. In the late 1840s, a French Foreign Legion officer, Monsieur le Baron R, had found a copy of the Arabian manuscript and translated it as *Le Jardin Parfumé*. A revised edition was published in 1886 and it was from this that Burton in turn translated the work into English. His fluency with French and his extensive knowledge of Arab culture made him the perfect person for the task.

That same year, through his Kama Shastra Society, Burton published a limited edition of "*The Perfumed Garden of the Cheikh Nefzaoui: A Manual of Arabian*

Erotology." At least one chapter of the sheikh's original work was excluded from the French translation—sections on homosexuality, for example—so Burton set about to create an enlarged version from Arabic manuscripts. He had just completed it when he died in 1890. Due to extreme social prejudice against homosexuality at that time—it was actually a criminal act—Burton's widow Isabel burned the manuscript to protect his reputation. Only his 1886 rendition survived and since his death, as with the *Kama Sutra*, many versions containing forewords by a variety of authors have been published.

A Stroll Through the Perfumed Garden

Burton's translation contains an introduction and 21 chapters, each devoted to a separate sex and relationship topic.

From his very first lines the sheikh revealed both the essence of his treatise and his enthusiasm for it. "Praise be to God, who has placed man's greatest pleasure in the natural parts of woman, and has destined the natural parts of man to afford the greatest enjoyment to woman."

Nafzawí also recorded how he came to write the book, his intentions for it, and how it's laid out.

In Chapter I, "Concerning Praiseworthy Men," through prose and poetry, the sheikh outlined the attributes of a "meritorious" man—virile, strong, eager for lovemaking and very, very skilled at it, with a penis no shorter than the breadth of six fingers and no longer than the breadth of twelve. It didn't hurt to be rich, either.

Two stories provide further insight. The first explains the importance of scents and perfumes in sexual conquest. The second illustrates the battle of the sexes, the matching of wits, the sexual rivalry between a man and woman, in a playful, delightful, and humorous way. It emphasizes making love multiple times and the beauty of a man's erection.

Chapter II, "Concerning Women Who Deserve to be Praised," provides physical and behavorial descriptions of the day's perfect woman. You'll see that she's somewhat different than the current Western "ideal." First of all, she's quite voluptuous, "plump and lusty," with large black eyes, perfectly oval cheeks, deep red lips, and pleasant body aromas. "Her bust and her belly [are] large … she must have the thighs and buttocks hard, the hips large and full, a waist of fine shape, hands and feet of striking elegance, plump arms, and well–developed shoulders."

She was expected to conduct herself with great humility, existing primarily in service to her husband. Speaking and laughing rarely, she was to stay at home, shunning neighbors, denying friends, relying solely on her husband, supporting him in all his business and personal activities, ready and willing to make love whenever he liked. "She does not surrender herself to anybody but her husband, even if abstinence would kill her." A tale of lust, infidelity, and greed illustrates the complex double standard toward fidelity for men and women.

Chapter III, "About Men Who Are to be Held in Contempt," contends that women disdain men who aren't physically attractive or capable of satisfying them sexually. It contains a short story about a man with a small penis and unhappy wife, who goes to a wise man, gets a special recipe to make his member larger and more skilful, and proceeds to make his wife very happy indeed. Because she's so thoroughly satisfied, she gives him all of her considerable fortune.

As you might expect, Chapter IV, "About Women Who Are to be Held in Contempt," describes women who are essentially the opposite of those in Chapter II. They're unattractive, loud, thoughtless, like to party and flirt, and don't pay much attention to their husband's desires, physical or otherwise.

In Chapter V, "Relating to the Act of Generation," the sheikh advised that lovemaking will only be "wholesome and good" if you engage in it with "your stomach not loaded with food and drink." More importantly, he stressed the necessity of attentive foreplay and afterplay to make sure a woman is sexually and romantically happy.

"O you men, one and all, who are soliciting the love of woman and her affection, and who wish that sentiment in her heart to be of an enduring nature, toy with her previous to coition; prepare her for enjoyment, and neglect nothing to attain that end. Explore her with the greater assiduity, and, entirely occupied with her, let nothing else engage your thoughts."

Chapter VI, "Concerning Everything that is Favorable to the Act of Coition" lists numerous lovemaking positions and thrusting techniques, some of which you'll find later in this appendix. Like Vatsyayana, Nafzawí believed that it was easiest to make fabulous love if you were healthy, fit, and matched in every way. But while Vatsysyana only suggested positions for lovers who were mismatched in genital sizes, Nafzawí took it a few steps further and recommended poses for couples who differed in other ways. He made suggestions for lovers who were very fat, extremely tall, exceptionally short, pregnant, humpbacked, or paralyzed. He also encouraged couples to be imaginative, because "sometimes most enjoyable coition takes place between lovers, who, not quite perfect in their proportions, find their own means for their mutual gratification."

In Chapter VII, "Of Matters Which Are Injurious in the Act of Generation," the sheikh warned men of the dangers of excess copulation. "All sages and physicians agree in saying that the ills which afflict man originate with the abuse of coition." Many of his suppositions are quaint oddities:

- Sideways sex predisposes you to gout.
- You'll get back pain and weak eyesight if you have sex with a woman who's fasting or getting ready to cook.
- Sex while bathing, or just afterward, is dangerous, because "water penetrating into the sexual parts of man or woman may lead to grave consequences."

We do agree, however, with one point, that ejaculating too frequently can be draining for men. Too bad he wasn't aware of the ejaculation mastery practices we presented in Chapter 13. For women, according to the Sheikh, there are no such dangers. "Women are more favored than men in indulging their passion for coition. It is in fact their specialty; and for them it is all pleasure."

Chapter VIII, "The Sundry Names Given to the Sexual Parts of Man," presents a list of 39 evocative names for a man's lingam. Unlike Vatsyayana who only classified penises according to size, Nafzawi described them according to size, temperament, and character. Among the colorful collection are the following:

* The Extinguisher of Passion (*Mochefi el Relil*)— a big, strong, masterful organ that excited and satisfied women better than any other.

* The Impudent One (*El Besiss*)—the lingam with a mind of its own, who "lifts impudently the clothing of its master by raising its head fiercely and makes him ashamed, while itself feels no shame."

* The Weeper (*El bekkaï*)—who, easily excited, drips pre–cum prodigiously "as soon as it gets an erection, it weeps; when it sees a pretty face, it weeps; handling a woman, it weeps. It goes even so far as to weep tears sacred to memory."

In a self–confessed rambling aside, the Sheikh also presented interpretations of sexual symbols in dreams. For example, "The man who dreams that his member has been cut off is certain not to live long after that dream."

Chapter IX, "Sundry Names Given to the Sexual Organs of Women," presents 43 names for the yoni. They're as delightfully vivid as their male counterparts.

* The Duellist (*El molki*)—a vagina that engages in love's battle with glee and strategy, as both partners urge each other toward climax while holding themselves back from the edge. The one who comes first loses. "The one who is slowest is the victor; and, assuredly, it is a fine fight! I should like thus to fight without stopping to the day of my death," professed the sheikh.

* The Crusher (El deukkak)—so thoroughly adept at the Mare's Trick that she can move the lingam every which way inside her "and would, if it could, absorb also the two testicles."

* The Beautiful (El Hacene)—firm, plump, white, and shaped like a dome. "To look at it changes a feeble erection into a strong one."

More sexy dream interpretations are stated with great confidence: "The correctness of these prognostications is not subject to any doubt." As well, the story presented in this chapter is one of the most erotic in the book.

Chapter X, "Concerning the Organs of Generation of Animals," assigns names to penises of various animals in four classifications and gives special attention to the mating habits of lions.

Chapter XI, "On the Deceits and Treacheries of Women," warns readers of the many ways women can defeat men in the battle of the sexes. Seven stories describe cunning, treacherous methods women use to get the sex they want. Each tale ends with an ominous warning: "Appreciate, after this, the deceitfulness of women, and what they are capable of."

The sheikh seemed both dismayed and in awe of women's capabilities, for "the stratagems of women are numerous and ingenious. Their tricks will deceive Satan himself." The *Perfumed Garden*'s view of women as delightful creatures who are nevertheless shameless, deceitful hussies desperately needing to be kept in their place, is by no means limited to medieval Arabia and the Islamic religion. You'll find the same bias in Christianity, as far back as the story of Adam and Eve. Our earliest attitudes toward sexuality, and women's role in sexuality, have been strongly influenced by this legend. As Kate Millett noted in *Sexual Politics*, "This mythic version of the female as the cause of human suffering, knowledge, and sin is still the foundation of sexual attitudes, for it represents the most crucial argument of the patriarchal tradition in the West."

Chapter XII, "Concerning Sundry Observations Useful to Know for Men and Women," like the *Kama Sutra* and the *Ananga Ranga*, attempts to give men insight into the complex characters of women—their attitudes, peculiarities, likes, and dislikes, particularly in relation to sex. The sheikh, too, categorized both men and women in terms of temperament.

In Chapter XIII, "Concerning the Causes of Enjoyment in the Act of Generation," the sheikh identified six conditions he believed lead a man to passionate desire for sexual intercourse, five vaginal qualities that give the most pleasure, and eight ways to strengthen ejaculation. He also provided 10 aphrodisiac recipes for increasing libido and strengthening erections. They're fascinating, but are unlikely to be effective, except perhaps psychologically, like this one: "Melt down fat from the hump of a camel, and rub [your] member with it just before the act; it will then perform wonders."

Chapter XIV, "Description of the Uterus of Sterile Women, and Treatment of the Same," is a short chapter that identifies some common causes of sterility in women, and offers several folk herbal remedies to reverse this condition. If you read *The Perfumed Garden* and are amazed and amused at some of the medical assumptions and suggestions in this and the following chapters, remember that although there've been considerable advances since the sheikh's time, modern science is still a long way from understanding the full complexities of the human body.

Chapter XV, "Concerning Medicines which Provoke Abortion" offers the sheikh's special recommendations for preventing or terminating pregnancy and expelling a fetus.

Chapter XVI, "Concerning the Causes of Impotence in Men," briefly considers the problems of premature ejaculation and impotence in men. The sheikh presented herbal medicines to overcome such difficulties.

Chapter XVII, "Undoing of Aiguillettes (Impotence for a Time)," discusses physical causes of impotence in men and, like the *Kama Sutra*, offers herbal remedies to correct the situation. The sheikh astutely presented several psychological reasons for temporary sexual dysfunction as well.

Chapter XVIII, "Prescriptions for Increasing the Dimensions of Small Members and for Making Them Splendid," tells men how to get a bigger one.

And according to the Sheikh, that's definitely what both men and women want. "For the men, because from a good–sized and vigorous member there springs the affection and love of women; for the women, because it is by such members that their amorous passions are appeased, and the greatest pleasure is procured for them." Just like Vatsyayana, the sheikh suggested some rather unusual methods for penis enlargement, such as rubbing the penis with oil made from bruised leeches. But who's to say these treatments were any less effective than the penis-enlargement creams offered today?

Chapter IX, "Of Things That Take Away the Bad Smell from the Armpits and Sexual Parts," cleverly points out that "bad exhalations from the vulva and from the armpits are … the greatest of evils"—not from a moral point of view but from an amatory one. He'd already discussed the importance of exotic scent for stimulating sexual appetite. Here he provided means for combating unwanted body odors using various herbs and chemicals—medieval versions of modern deodorants and cleansers.

Chapter XX, "Instructions with Regard to Pregnancy," presents indications that the lady is pregnant, including that her period has stopped. It also offers clues to help parents know the sex of their unborn child.

It's a boy!

- If she does not become freckled during the pregnancy
- If her nipples turn red
- If she bleeds from her right nostril

It's a girl!

- If she has frequent nightmares
- If she gets lots of freckles
- If she bleeds from her left nostril

Chapter XXI, "Forming the Conclusion of This Work," offers additional aphrodisiac recipes for strengthening erection and prolonging sexual intercourse. Eggs are featured heavily, along with asparagus, onions, honey, and camel's milk. None of these things are likely to harm you. Some may even help.

There's also a story with amazing details of mythic virility, potency, and mastery of ejaculation.

The sheikh concludes his masterpiece with this heartfelt request.

> O God! award no punishment for this on judgment day!
> And thou, oh reader, hear me conjure thee to say:
> So be it!

Playing in the Garden Before and After

Although Sheikh Nafzawí was adamant that satisfying lovemaking wasn't complete without lots of foreplay, he didn't go into much detail about specific pre-intercourse practices. There's none of the *Kama Sutra*'s exhaustive enumeration of embraces, kisses, bites, and slaps. However, throughout his text the Sheikh exhorted men to play with their women by bestowing all manner of caresses over every bit of their bodies.

"You will excite her by kissing her cheeks, sucking her lips, and nibbling at her breasts. Lavish kisses on her navel and thighs, and titillate the lower parts. Bite her arms, and neglect no part of her body; cling close to her chest, and show your love and submission." (V)

Like Vatsyayana, the Sheikh stressed the power of kisses—before, during, and after penetration. Kissing is deemed so vital, that "no kind of position or movement procures the full pleasure" (VI) without it. He particularly favored kisses that are long, wet, lip sucking, and tongue nibbling. With them, a woman's free–flowing saliva becomes "more intoxicating than wine drunk to excess." (VI) Dismissed as providing no pleasure, worthy only for children and hands, are kisses given just on the lips, especially if they're accompanied by a smacking sound

"comparable to the one by which you call your cat." (VI)

Much as he enjoyed kissing, and all sorts of touching, nibbling, and stroking, the Sheikh didn't see much value in partaking of such activities for their own sake. They are only gratifying as preludes to and parts of intercourse. "Therefore abstain from them, if you do not want action; they only fan a fire to no purpose." (VI) For the sheikh and his readers, lovemaking was ultimately all about copulation and climax. The crowning achievement of love's battle was to reach her X-spot (see Chapter 11) at the "mouth of her womb" with your mighty member, for then you'd both "imbibe an endless pleasure." (VI)

No matter how perfect the preliminaries, it didn't allow a man to get up and run as soon as he and his paramour had climbed to their passionate apex. Nafzawí shared Vatsyayana's contempt for the inconsiderate lover who left right after he'd gotten what he came for. He advised a man to stay a while, withdrawing his lingam cautiously as he lay close to his ladylove. Not only would she find it pleasant, so would he.

Positions for Love

Like Vatsyayana, Sheikh Nafzawí carefully documented positions for intercourse. Although he wrote that "the ways of doing it to women are numerous and variable," (VI) his research revealed only 11 "usual" positions favored by his countrymen. Nafzawí therefore added 29 positions adapted from Indian texts, like the *Kama Sutra*, because "the inhabitants of those parts have multiplied the different ways to enjoy women, and they have advanced further than we in knowledge and investigation of the coitus." (VI) Despite their different names, some poses are exact duplications of *Kama Sutra* positions. Others show intriguing variations.

The Perfumed Garden considered woman-on-top positions not only unnatural but also dangerous to a man's health. As Nafzawí counseled, "If you do it with the woman bestriding you, your dorsal cord will suffer and your heart will be affected; and if in that position the smallest drop of the secretions of the vagina enters your urethral canal, a stricture may result." (VII) Consequently, all 11 Arabian positions are either man-on-top or sideways, with both face–to–face and rear–entry versions.

To stimulate your own experimentation, here are 12 examples from Nafzawi's list of 40 positions. Because they range from fairly simple to acrobatically complex, proceed slowly, with humor feeding your lustiness.

Manner the Seventh

Manner the Seventh, one of the sheikh's group of 11, is an athletic sideways adaptation. As she lies on her side, you squat between her thighs. One of her legs is below you, between your thighs. The other you raise up and rest against your shoulder. Use your hands to move her body toward and away from you as you thrust. Make lots of eye contact and let her know how much you appreciate this decidedly different angle of penetration. If you can't squat, you can kneel, but be careful about resting too much weight on her leg beneath you. This position might be easier for her if she only half turns, rather than lying completely sideways.

Frog Fashion (Second Manner—*El Modefedâ*)

In this flat–footed, slightly constricted version of the *Kama Sutra* Yawning pose, she lies on her back with her knees bent. Her feet are flat on the bed, with her heels tucked in as close to her butt as possible. If you're quite limber, you'll follow the sheikh's instructions and squat in front of her—your weight balanced on your feet, your butt hovering above the bed. With your legs bent and her knees tucked up into your armpits, you grasp her by the upper arms and use them for support as you thrust in and away. The more flexible she is, the closer you can bring her upper body, and as your passion mounts "you draw her toward you at the crisis." (VI)

If, like many Westerners, squatting isn't comfortable for you, you can still mate like a frog by kneeling in front of her. Spreading your knees wide will bring you in close to her delightful yoni. Grasping her by

the hips will be easier on her than holding her by the upper arms. Because Frog Fashion offers the possibility for lots of eye contact and tight compacting of your bodies, very slow thrusting can make this pose deeply emotional and exquisitely tender.

Piercing with the Lance (Seventh Manner—*Er Zedjadja*)

Many modern sex guides consider Piercing with the Lance too difficult and exclude it from their descriptions because it involves suspending the woman "from the ceiling by means of four cords attached to her hands and feet; the middle of her body is supported by a fifth cord, arranged so as not to hurt her back." (VI) Although it's unlikely you'd have an apparatus exactly like the sheikh suggested, the wide variety of love swings available today can make this pose easy and comfortable for both lovers. With a little investigation, you'll find love swings to suit your living space and your budget. There are models that hang from the ceiling, insert in a doorway, or come with self–supporting frames. Very simple but not-as-maneuverable versions sling over your shoulders.

Whatever form of swing you choose, during lovemaking you arrange it so that your lovely lady's vulva is at the precisely perfect level for your penis, swinging her forward and back you impale her again and again on your magnificent member. It's a great opportunity for experimenting with the whole range of thrusting patterns and rhythms. Some tantalizing Churning followed by deliberate, delicate, and inch-by-inch Moving Forward—with lots of eye contact, of course—will melt her heart as you heat her body. As its name suggests, Piercing with the Lance lends itself most eagerly to powerful Giving a Blow thrusts. Just remember to make your aim sure and true as you withdraw completely and re–enter, so that your lance finds its target without harm to either of you from a misplaced strike.

The Somersault (Ninth Manner—*El Kelouci*)

Playful seduction leads up to this acrobatic pose. Dressed only in loose-fitting pants (harem-girl-style pantaloons were the sheikh's choice), you stand with your back to your lover and slowly, tantalizingly wriggle them down past your hips to your calves. Coyly, you bend over, presenting your beautiful backside to his lustful gaze. When you've bent double and peek challengingly at him between your legs, he seizes you and—carefully—flips you over in a somersault. You end up on your back with your feet extended and trapped behind your head. Your head and neck are supported by the waistband of your pants. Your vulva is wide open for penetration. He kneels before you and slips deep inside, careful not to rest too much of his weight on your body.

A gentler version of the Somersault involves dropping your pants just to your knees. When he tips you over, your legs are still imprisoned by the cloth, but they'll rest only against your chest. You can hold onto your ankles or calves to aid in your stretch. Your bend won't be nearly so intense, nor will your vulva be so fully exposed.

If practiced regularly, the yoga Plough asana will stretch your back so well that you might become one of those limber ladies whom the sheikh said, "can place their feet under the head without the help of pantaloons or of their hands." (VI)

Tail of the Ostrich (Tenth Manner—*Hachou en Nekanok*)

Tail of the Ostrich, which offers you ultra–deep penetration, is an extreme variation of the Kama Sutra's Widely Opened. She lies on her back. You kneel in front of her and lift her legs high in the air. Only her head and shoulders remain on the bed. She twines her legs lovingly around your neck. Grasping her buttocks or hips, you move her about on your happy penis—Churning, Blow of a Bull, and Blow of a Boar are especially thrilling strokes for this pose. Once again, she'll need a strong, supple back to be

at all comfortable. Take care as you swivel her hips. By raising and lowering her buttocks, she'll change the angle of penetration and provide even more subtle sensations.

Fitting on of the Sock (Eleventh Manner—*Lebeuss el Djoureb*)

A gentle and sensual position, Fitting on of the Sock spreads warm love from lingam to yoni and back again. Ideal for getting her juices flowing early in your lovemaking, it's also a great pose for easy lovin' between more frisky romps. You sit upright with your legs stretched out in front, your thighs spread wide enough for her to lie between them. With her buttocks flat on the bed, she rests her legs over yours and pushes her vulva in close to you.

Tenderly, you slide the head of your lingam into her yoni and, using your thumb and forefinger, close her vaginal lips around it. Your other hand is free to brush her breasts or captivate her clitoris. With shallow strokes you give her a "lively rubbing." If she arches her back, she can angle her G-spot to receive many pleasurable pulses. When she's really, really ready, "prepared for the enjoyment by the alternate coming and going of your weapon in her scabbard, put it into her full length." (VI)

Reciprocal Sight of the Posteriors (Twelfth Manner—*Kerhef el Astine*)

When you're feeling adventurous and raunchy, Reciprocal Sight of the Posteriors provides a titillating take on the *Kama Sutra*'s Mare's Position. He lies on his back with his knees bent. With your back to him, you lower yourself onto his penis, so that you're sitting on his lower belly, between his legs. Your knees are bent, your feet flat on the bed, as you lean forward. He tightens his legs against the sides of your body, holding you snug.

Supporting your weight on your arms, bend forward as far as you can and open your thighs a little. As you duck your head down you can see his bottom and his lingam—your yoni enveloping and releasing it with each bob of your butt in full Sporting of the Sparrow thrusts. He has a similar view of you from the other end. Remember, such sights and strokes, so animalistically alluring, can be supremely arousing for your man. Keep an eye on more than his beautiful behind, unless you want him to plunge over the precipice.

Pounding on the Spot (Fifteenth Manner—*Dok el Arz*)

Although the sheikh encouraged couples to try many positions so they'd know which satisfied them most, he was quite certain that Pounding on the Spot was a universal favorite. He found that women especially have "a predilection for the Dok el Arz, as, in the application of the same, belly is pressed to belly, mouth glued to mouth, and the action of the womb is rarely absent." (VI)

You'll both derive great pleasure from this comfortable sitting posture. As the sheikh noted, women particularly enjoy the tender intimacy of so much skin contact, the ease of kissing, the depth of penetration, and the fact that they're primarily in control of thrusting. Men get really turned on by their lady's ecstatic delight. Plus, a man can usually last longer while he's remaining relatively motionless.

He sits up straight and stretches his legs out in front. You sit on his lap, his lingam nested deep inside you, your arms wrapped around his neck, your legs crossed behind his back. He embraces you, and with his strong arms helps you "rise and descend upon his verge." Because he's basically just sitting still—which ordinarily could lead to a fading erection—you might find you can move as fast as you like for as long as you like and he'll be able to stay right there with you.

Did the sheikh not notice that sitting postures are essentially woman-on-top poses? Because, despite his repeated warnings about difficulties that could arise from a woman bestride her man, he sure waxed enthusiastic about Pounding on the Spot.

Perhaps it made a difference that the lovers' bodies are upright rather than lying down, with the man entirely beneath his lady.

Belly to Belly (Seventeenth Manner—*El Keurchi*)

The sheikh's Belly-to-Belly position provides a subtle alternative to Vatsyayana's standing poses. Both of you keep your feet on the floor for this perpendicular prance. She stands facing you with her legs spread, welcoming you to wriggle your way between her thighs. You move in close, one foot slightly in front of the other, and direct your penis into her waiting vagina.

Arms lovingly cradling each other's hips, you sway together in a thrusting move called the Bucket in the Well (First Movement—*Neza' el Dela*.) You push your hips toward her, and then pull back a little. You wait as she mimics your movements with her own—advancing and withdrawing. Now it's your turn again. Find a flowing rhythm together—slow and soulful or fast and fiery, depending on your mood and the location of your lovemaking. If there's a considerable difference in height, try Belly to Belly on a staircase (cautiously) or with the help of a sturdy footstool.

Race of the Member (Twenty-fifth Manner—*Rekeud el Air*)

Another strenuous woman-on-top position, Race of the Member is as spicy as its name suggests. Pillows under his head and shoulders, he lies on his back and, bending his legs, draws his knees up as close to his face as possible. With your feet flat on the bed on either side of his hips, you lower yourself onto him and guide his lingam deep inside you. Your upper body stays erect as you sit astride him, "as if on horseback, the saddle being represented by the knees and stomach of the man." (VI) Use the strength of your thighs to glide up and down along his length. With the Mare's Trick as your able accessory, you'll give him the ride of his life.

He can take a more active part and intensify proceedings if you vary the pose by placing your knees on the bed. Place your left hand on his right shoulder for support—your other hand can tickle his nipples or anus or wave gleefully in the air with a robust "Yee-ha!" He helps raise and lower you with the rhythm of his thighs.

The Fitter–In (Twenty–sixth Manner—*El Modakehli*)

An active but easy sitting pose, the Fitter–In can be frivolous or frenzied according to your libido's urgings. You'll probably have more fun with this one if you go at it on the floor rather than the bed. A firmer surface will give you more traction for your action.

Sit facing each other, your weight resting primarily on the tip of your tailbone. Your knees are bent, your feet on the floor. Scoot in tight to each other. She places her right thigh over your left thigh. You oblige with your right over her left. With your penis snugly insider her, clasp each other's upper arms and rock together, back and forth, as if you were on a see–saw. Lean back slightly and push with your heels to give you more leverage as you sway. You'll most definitely "fit in."

The One That Stops at Home (Twenty–seventh Manner—*El Khouariki*)

You'll need good upper-body strength and a fine sense of rhythm to enjoy the intricacies of the One That Stops at Home. A soft bed also helps with this refined man-on-top pose. She lies down on her back with her knees bent and her feet flat on the bed. Place some firm pillows along both sides of her upper body. You'll use them to give you added distance above her. Slip your lingam inside her and lie between her legs, but do not put any weight on her body at all—support yourself entirely with your arms.

As with Widely Opened, she pushes her feet against the bed and lifts her buttocks as high as she can.

You rise up with her, with your groin pressed firmly to hers. Now she lowers herself back to the bed and bounces her pelvis lightly up and down. You "stick like glue to her" (VI) as she repeats her upward lift followed by rapid bounces. She'll love setting the rhythm. You'll gladly surrender to follow her lead in this rollicking dance of love.

Thrusting Techniques

Unlike the *Kama Sutra*, which described thrusting techniques as essentially all–male action, *The Perfumed Garden* included movements by both partners. In addition to the Bucket in the Well, the sheikh detailed the following rhythms of love:

* The Mutual Shock (Second Movement—*En Netahi*) Both lovers simultaneously push their groins together, and then pull slightly apart, without the lingam leaving the yoni completely. It's a standard sort of thrust that satisfies in just about any position.

* The Approach (Third Movement—*El Motadani*) Lovers take turns thrusting, mimicking each other's rhythms, one after the other. Nafzawí didn't describe the particulars of movment; he simply instructed you to move "as usual." Thrill each other with your own creative and unique patterns.

* Love's Tailor (Fourth Movement—*Khiate el Heub*) The sheikh described this pattern from the man–only point of view, but women, especially when they're on top, can be equally adept at it. With your lingam just an inch or two inside her yoni, you deliver a series of short, fast thrusts, and then plunge deeply. Your entire length fills her with your power and passion. "This is the movement of the needle in the hands of the tailor" and you're advised to keep sewing as long as you can.

Because of the rapid speed suggested for this version, the Nafzawí warned that it "only suits such men and women who can, at will, retard the crisis." (VI) However, if you were to slow the whole process way down, you'd transform it into the Taoist Shallow–Deep thrusting technique. It gives her maximum pleasure while helping you last longer.

 The Toothpick in the Vulva (Fifth Movement—*Souak et Feurdj*) You'll need a lot of skill and stamina—in the sheikh's words, "a very vigorous member"—to perform the Toothpick well. It's similar to Blow of a Bull in that you're attempting to pleasure every inch of her sacred cave. While inside your ladylove, you drive your lingam up and down, and then right to left.

 The Boxing Up of Love (Sixth Movement—*Tachik el Heub*) Like Vatsyayana's Pressing thrust, Boxing Up of Love finds you as deep inside her as you can possibly get. You're pressed so tightly together that your "hairs are completely mixed up with the woman's." (VI) But unlike Pressing, where you stay quite still, this method requires you to "move forcibly, without withdrawing [your] tool in the least." (VI)

Nafzawí considered this to be the best of all thrusts because, according to him, it gives women utmost satisfaction, appeasing "their lust most completely." (VI) He particularly recommended it in conjunction with his revered pose Pounding on the Spot.

Recommended Reading & Resources

Books

Alain Daniélou, trans. *The Complete Kama Sutra*, by Vatsyayana. Park Street Press. 1994. ISBN: 0965717828

Daniélou's translation is unabridged and includes the original numbering for all verses. Also included are two commentaries inserted with their relevant verses from the *Kama Sutra* and quite distinct from them. The best English language version for academic research.

Cynthia Mervis Watson. *Love Potions*. Jeremy P. Tarcher/Perigee. 1993. ISBN: 0874777240

Watson, a medical doctor, turns her expertise to the topic of aphrodisiacs, and offers detailed information about many of the best sex-enhancing substances available, including both foods and supplements. She even offers recipes for creating your own aphrodisiac tinctures.

Daniel Odier. *Yoga Spandakarika: The Sacred Texts at the Origins of Tantra*. Inner Traditions. 2004. ISBN: 1594770514

This book presents translations of early Tantras (sacred Tantric texts), with detailed commentary and explanation.

Edward Rice. *Captain Sir Richard Francis Burton*. Harper Perennial. 1991. ISBN: 0060973943

Find out all about the extraordinary man who brought the *Kama Sutra*, *Ananga Ranga*, *1001 Arabian Nights*, and *The Perfumed Garden* to the Western world.

Diana Richardson. *Tantric Orgasm for Women*. Destiny Books. 2004. ISBN: 0892811331

The best discussion we have seen of the experience of valley orgasm. She explains how to relax into a whole-body orgasm rather than striving toward it as a goal.

Indra Sinha, trans. *The Love Teachings of Kama Sutra: With Extracts from Koka Shastra, Ananga Ranga, and Other Famous Indian Works on Love*. Marlowe and Company. 1997. ISBN: 156924779X

A wonderfully poetic translation, it's illustrated with color photos of Indian art and sculpture.

Johanna Wikoff and Deborah S. Romaine, *The Complete Idiot's Guide to the Kama Sutra*. Alpha, Second Edition. 2004. ISBN: 1592571840

A clear and comprehensive guide to the *Kama Sutra*, revealing its relevance to modern lovers. The authors explain in detail how you can use the guidance of the *Kama Sutra* to unite the physical, emotional, and spiritual aspects of lovemaking and create an astounding and long-lasting relationship.

Judith Kuriansky. *The Complete Idiot's Guide to Tantric Sex*. Alpha, Second Edition. 2004. ISBN: 1592572960

Lots of helpful information to get beginners to actually start introducing Tantric practices into their busy lives. Kuriansky, a clinical psychologist and sex therapist, is also a certified Ipsalu Tantra teacher.

Julie Henderson. *The Lover Within: Opening to Energy in Sexual Practice*. Barrytown Limited. 1999. ISBN: 1581770170

This book is an excellent how-to manual for working with your sexual energy. It provides exercises to do alone or with a partner, and offers instruction on how to move, collect, heighten, and share energy.

Linda Johnsen, *The Complete Idiot's Guide to Hinduism*. Alpha. 2001. ISBN: 0028642279

A loving, wise, and humorous look at the spiritual beliefs and life practices that informed the *Kama Sutra*.

Martha Hopkins and Randall Lockridge. *Intercourses: An Aphrodisiac Cookbook*. Terrace Publishing. 1997. ISBN: 0965327507

This book is a feast for the eyes. The authors show how to combine food items commonly available at every supermarket and joyful sex, for creating unforgettable moments of passionate intimacy.

Michael Reed Gach. *Acupressure for Lovers: Secrets of Touch for Increasing Intimacy*. Bantam Books. 1997. ISBN: 055337401X

An excellent manual teaching the art of acupressure, specifically for lovers. Touching the right spots, in the right way, at the right time, can enhance your lovemaking dramatically.

Nicole Bailey. *Pure Kama Sutra*. Duncan Baird Publishers. 2005. ISBN: 184483154X

In this excellent illustrated version of *Kama Sutra* love techniques, Bailey divides positions into four categories: slow and soulful, fast and passionate, deep and erotic, and adventurous. She adds extra positions from the *Ananga Ranga* and the *Perfumed Garden*, and a chapter on Tantric sex.

Nik Douglas and Penny Slinger. *Sexual Secrets: 20th Anniversary Edition: The Alchemy of Ecstasy*. Destiny Books. 1999. ISBN: 0892818050

First published in 1979, this popular book (over 1 million copies sold) presents a concise and articulate overview of the history and philosophy of sacred sex, particularly in India and China. Practical exercises and meditations are interspersed throughout. It overflows with wonderful erotic drawings by Penny Slinger.

Nitya Lacroic. *Kama Sutra : A Modern Guide to the Ancient Art of Sex*. Hylas Publishing. 2003. ISBN: 1592580386

Lacroix has over 40 books on better sex, massage, Tantra, and the *Kama Sutra*. The sexual intercourse positions are particularly well presented and described. She explains how each position benefits men and women differently.

Pala Copeland and Al Link. *Soul Sex: Tantra for Two*. New Page Books. 2003. ISBN: 1564146642

Our first book exploring relationship as spiritual practice using Tantric and Taoist approaches to sacred sexuality. We help you learn how to create love for a lifetime together.

Reay Tannahill, *Sex in History*. Scarborough. 1980. ISBN: 0812861159

An extraordinarily comprehensive look at sex and its role in social, political, and religious life from humanity's earliest days to the later decades of the twentieth century.

Richard Francis Burton and F. F. Arbuthnot, trans. *The Kama Sutra of Vatsyayana*, by Vatsyayana. Kama Shastra Society. 1883.

Burton's translation continues to be a top seller with hundreds of editions being published over the past century.

Richard Francis Burton and F.F. Arbuthnot, trans. *Ananga Ranga; (Stage of the Bodiless One) or, The Hindu Art of Love. (Ars Amoris Indica)*. Kama Shastra Society. 1885.

Richard Francis Burton, trans. *The Perfumed Garden of the Cheikh Nefzaoui, A Manual of Arabian Erotology (XVI. Century)*. Kama Shastra society. 1886.

Richard Francis Burton, trans. *The Perfumed Garden of the Cheikh Nefzaoui, A Manual of Arabian Erotology (XVI. Cantury)*. Kama Shastra Society. 1886. Free downloadable version of the classic text. Adobe Reader Format. Available from their website: www.tantra-sex.com/perfumedgarden.html.

Ron Louis and David Copeland. *The Pocket Idiot's Guide to the Kama Sutra*. Alpha. 2005. ISBN: 1592573312

Authors Louis and Copeland have turned their knowledge of dating, seduction, and relationships to creating a concise rendering of the *Kama Sutra*. With photographs of some love poses, it's definitely a handy reference to carry with you for those all-important loving moments.

Theresa L. Crenshaw. *The Alchemy of Love and Lust*. Pocket. 1997. ISBN: 0671004441

All sorts of snazzy insight into how hormones affect male/female relationships.

Electronic Books

Al Link and Pala Copeland. *100 Ways to Keep Your Lover*. 4 Freedoms Relationship Tantra eBooks. 2003. Adobe Reader and Microsoft Reader Format. Order from their website: www.tantra-sex.com/100Ways.html

We've distilled the essence of nurturing relationship, keeping monogamy hot, and sustaining passionate romance into 100 sexy activities you can implement immediately.

Al Link and Pala Copeland. *Tantra and Kama Sutra Sex Positions*. 4 Freedoms Relationship Tantra eBooks. 2003. Adobe Reader and Microsoft Reader Format. Order from their website: www.tantra-sex.com/KamaSutraPositions.html

Expand your lovemaking repertoire and increase your pleasure with this photo manual of Tantra and Kama Sutra sex positions. In this modern interpretation of classic love postures, each of the color photos appears in large format on a single page. We also include useful information about sacred sex practices.

Al Link and Pala Copeland. *Voluntary Ejaculation and Male Multiple Orgasms* eBook. 4 Freedoms Relationship Tantra eBooks. 2004. Adobe Reader and Microsoft Reader Format. Order from their website: www.tantra-sex.com/EjaculationMastery.html

Learn simple techniques to master your ejaculation response, making it completely voluntary. Ejaculate when and if you want to. Take your lovemaking to unimaginable heights with the easy-to-learn techniques.

Johanna Wikoff and Deborah S. Romaine, *The Complete Idiot's Guide to the Kama Sutra*. Alpha, Adobe Reader Format. The comprehensive guide to the *Kama Sutra* in digital format.

Pala Copeland and Al Link. *Awakening Women's Orgasm*. 4 Freedoms Relationship Tantra eBooks. 2004. Adobe Reader and Microsoft Reader Format. Order from their website: www.tantra-sex.com/womenorgasm.html

You'll learn about the many different types of orgasm a woman's body is waiting to give her. Exercises for mind, heart, spirit, and body help women open up to their sexual selves, on their own and with their partners.

Richard Francis Burton and F. F. Arbuthnot, trans. *The Kama Sutra of Vatsyayana*, by Vatsyayana. Kama Shastra Society. 1883. Free downloadable version of the classic text. Adobe Reader Format. Available from their website: http://www.tantra-sex.com/kamasutra.html

Richard Francis Burton and F.F. Arbuthnot, trans. *Ananga Ranga; (Stage of the Bodiless One) or, The Hindu Art of Love. (Ars Amoris Indica)*. Kama Shastra Society. 1885. Free downloadable version of the classic text. Adobe Reader Format. Available from their website: www.tantra-sex.com/anangaranga.html

Audio-Visual

Anal Sex and Prostate Massage DVDs. Order from their website: www.tantra-sex.com/v-anal.html

Three excellent video productions from Joseph Kramer and the EROSpirit Research Institute that teach techniques and provide information about anatomy, hygiene, healing, and giving pleasure. Highly informative for heterosexuals as well as gays.

Gay Sex Wisdom Vol 9: Rosebud Massage

Gay Sex Wisdom Vol 10: Exploring the Land Down Under

Uranus: Self Anal Massage for Men

Ancient Secrets of Sexual Ecstasy DVD. 1997. Tantra. com. Order from their website: www.tantra-sex.com/v-tantra.html

The best video available on the topic of sacred sexuality for modern lovers. We suggest the X-rated version in which the explicit sexuality sequences are erotic, informative, and artfully presented. Packed full of useful techniques.

Apertio: Tantra Energy Meditations CD. Pala Copeland (meditations) and Jeff Davies (music). 2000. ASIN: B000054490. Order from their website: www.tantra-sex.com/cd-order.html

Pala Copeland guides you through energy meditations set to the mystical music of Jeff Davies. Learn to feel your energy body—calm it, balance it, play with it—join it with your beloved.

4 Freedoms Tantra Audiobooks. Al and Pala bring their Tantra weekend into your home with audio books in mp3 format. Listen on your iPod or your home or car stereo. This is as close as you can get to taking a workshop from Al and Pala without actually being there. Order from their website: www.tantra-sex.com/audiobooks.html.

Female Ejaculation Instructional DVDs. Deborah Sundahl. Order from their website: www.tantra-sex.com/v-female.html

Titles include "How To Female Ejaculate," "Tantric Journey to Female Orgasm," and "Ejaculation Female Ejaculation for Couples."

Kama Sutra Sexual Positions DVDs. Order from their website: www.tantra-sex.com/v-kama.html

A selection of videos guiding couples in their exploration of the many sexual intercourse positions mentioned in the *Kama Sutra*, *Ananga Ranga,* and *Perfumed Garden.*

Internet

4 Freedoms Relationship Tantra

www.tantra-sex.com

Contact by e-mail: 4freedoms@tantraloving.com

Sacred sexuality weekends held monthly near Ottawa, Canada, facilitated by Al Link and Pala Copeland. Large selection of pro-sexual learning resources including books, music, videos, and sensual products. Lots of links to free articles and other sexuality websites.

4 Freedoms Guide to Aphrodisiacs

www.tantra-sex.com/aphrodisiacs.html

This is our online guide to aphrodisiacs for men and women. It includes detailed reviews of a large number of aphrodisiac products and formulas with hotlinks to Internet suppliers.

4 Freedoms Guide to Pheromones

www.tantra-sex.com/ep6.html#lure

If you want to experiment with pheromones, here's our online guide to some of the best available on the Internet, with hotlinks to suppliers.

4 Freedoms Guide to Sex Toys

www.tantra-sex.com/sextoyprimer.html

Our online guide to sex toys with hotlinks to suppliers on the Internet.

4 Freedoms Guide to Music for Lovers

www.tantra-sex.com/erotic-music.html

Our online music store with hotlinks to some of the CDs we find to be sexy and romantic.

Internet Sacred Text Archive

www.sacred-texts.com/index.htm

Searchable database of sacred, spiritual, and religious texts from around the world and for all faiths. Many of the works are presented in full online text versions, because they're now in the public domain.

Kama Sutra Oils of Love

Order from their website: www.tantra-sex.com/ep6.html#lotions

A fine selection of sensual massage oils.

Liberator Shapes—Bedroom Adventure Gear

Order from their website: www.tantra-sex.com/liberatorshapes.html

Liberator Shapes can help you experiment with all of the sexual intercourse positions from the *Kama Sutra*, and do so in comfort and style. The foam cores covered in washable fabrics are stackable for creative combinations to enhance your lovemaking.

MinkgLove.com—Handmade Fur Massage Gloves

Order from their website: www.tantra-sex.com/minkglove.html

Handmade rabbit, fox, chinchilla, and mink fur gloves for the erotic massage of your life.

Tantra.com

www.tantra.com

Tantra.com maintains a database of sacred sexuality teachers and workshops around the planet, but only including those websites that pay for a listing. Tantra.com produced the excellent sacred sexuality instruction DVD *Ancient Secrets of Sexual Ecstasy*.

About Al and Pala's Publications and Workshops

"Al and Pala are first-rate talk show guests. They are smart, articulate, accessible, and down to earth. They offer an extraordinary life-transforming weekend ...," Bob Berkowitz, host of "Love Bytes" on eYada.com, and author of *His Secret Life: Male Sexual Fantasies*, and *What Men Won't Tell You but Women Need to Know*.

About Al and Pala's book *Soul Sex: Tantra for Two*

"Copeland and Link ... represent the new generation of spiritual sexuality work that will give realistic support to sincere, dedicated couples." Mantak Chia, author of *The Multi-Orgasmic Man* and *The Multi-Orgasmic Couple*

"A book that focuses on the process and pleasure of sexual interactions, not on the goal of orgasm, with which I wholeheartedly agree ... I am very impressed by the exercises and the depth presented in *Soul Sex: Tantra for Two*." Beverly Whipple Ph.D., Professor Emeritus, Rutgers University, past president Society for the Scientific Study of Sexuality

"Canada's Tantric sex super-duo, Pala Copeland and Al Link ... help couples create a deeper, more spiritual, and hotter connection." Josey Vogels, sex and relationship columnist; creator of "My Messy Bedroom"

Advance praise for Al and Pala's book Sensual Love Secrets for Couples: The Four Freedoms of Body, Heart, Mind & Soul

"Body pleasure, relationships, and the integration of body, mind, heart, and soul are the central organizing themes of this journey to find happiness and love .... We need miracles and *Sensual Love Secrets* provides a path to the discovery of those miracles." James W. Prescott, neuropsychologist and director, Institute of Humanistic Science

Sensual Love Secrets: "... just reading it together and talking about it would promote emotional and sexual intimacy." Pepper Schwartz, professor of sociology, Univ. of Washington, author *Everything You Know About Love and Sex is Wrong*

"*Sensual Love Secrets* ... is a welcome contribution to the literature of sexual enrichment for loving couples ... I particularly like the many concrete exercises you propose." John Ince, lawyer and author *The Politics of Lust*

About Al and Pala's Workshops

"A wonderful weekend! Delightful, educational, erotic ... This is what sex education should be, but isn't .... These workshops reveal the true mystery of sex and how to explore its nature .... Pala and Al convey all that is good about intimate relationships from celebrating difference to the ecstasy of the energetic sexual connection." Patricia Rockman, M.D.

"Al and Pala have given us a glimpse into bliss and ecstasy available to all. They have connected the divine and sexuality in their living ... Theirs is a quest for spiritual enlightenment through sexuality that promotes wholesome, healthy, and divine living." Reverend Gary A. Williams

"Pala and Al provide a totally nourishing and healing experience. They are knowledgeable, humorous, articulate, and authentic. A weekend of exploration and education with them opens your heart and mind and leaves you yearning for more." Mary Jane, Corporate Wellness Consultant